WITHDRAWN

THE NEW MIDDLE AGES

BONNIE WHEELER, *Series Editor*

The New Middle Ages is a series dedicated to pluridisciplinary studies of medieval cultures, with particular emphasis on recuperating women's history and on feminist and gender analyses. This peer-reviewed series includes both scholarly monographs and essay collections.

PUBLISHED BY PALGRAVE:

Women in the Medieval Islamic World: Power, Patronage, and Piety
  edited by Gavin R. G. Hambly

The Ethics of Nature in the Middle Ages: On Boccaccio's Poetaphysics
  by Gregory B. Stone

Presence and Presentation: Women in the Chinese Literati Tradition
  edited by Sherry J. Mou

The Lost Love Letters of Heloise and Abelard: Perceptions of Dialogue in Twelfth-Century France
  by Constant J. Mews

Understanding Scholastic Thought with Foucault
  by Philipp W. Rosemann

For Her Good Estate: The Life of Elizabeth de Burgh
  by Frances A. Underhill

Constructions of Widowhood and Virginity in the Middle Ages
  edited by Cindy L. Carlson and Angela Jane Weisl

Motherhood and Mothering in Anglo-Saxon England
  by Mary Dockray-Miller

Listening to Heloise: The Voice of a Twelfth-Century Woman
  edited by Bonnie Wheeler

The Postcolonial Middle Ages
  edited by Jeffrey Jerome Cohen

Chaucer's Pardoner *and Gender Theory: Bodies of Discourse*
  by Robert S. Sturges

Crossing the Bridge: Comparative Essays on Medieval European and Heian Japanese Women Writers
  edited by Barbara Stevenson and Cynthia Ho

Engaging Words: The Culture of Reading in the Later Middle Ages
  by Laurel Amtower

Robes and Honor: The Medieval World of Investiture
  edited by Stewart Gordon

Representing Rape in Medieval and Early Modern Literature
  edited by Elizabeth Robertson and Christine M. Rose

Same Sex Love and Desire Among Women in the Middle Ages
  edited by Francesca Canadé Sautman and Pamela Sheingorn

Sight and Embodiment in the Middle Ages: Ocular Desires
  by Suzannah Biernoff

Listen, Daughter: The Speculum Virginum *and the Formation of Religious Women in the Middle Ages*
  edited by Constant J. Mews

Science, the Singular, and the Question of Theology
  by Richard A. Lee, Jr.

Gender in Debate from the Early Middle Ages to the Renaissance
  edited by Thelma S. Fenster and Clare A. Lees

Malory's Morte D'Arthur: *Remaking Arthurian Tradition*
  by Catherine Batt

The Vernacular Spirit: Essays on Medieval Religious Literature
    edited by Renate Blumenfeld-Kosinski, Duncan Robertson, and Nancy Warren

Popular Piety and Art in the Late Middle Ages: Image Worship and Idolatry in England 1350–1500
    by Kathleen Kamerick

Absent Narratives, Manuscript Textuality, and Literary Structure in Late Medieval England
    by Elizabeth Scala

Creating Community with Food and Drink in Merovingian Gaul
    by Bonnie Effros

Representations of Early Byzantine Empresses: Image and Empire
    by Anne McClanan

Encountering Medieval Textiles and Dress: Objects, Texts, Images
    edited by Désirée G. Koslin and Janet Snyder

Eleanor of Aquitaine: Lord and Lady
    edited by Bonnie Wheeler and John Carmi Parsons

Isabel La Católica, Queen of Castile: Critical Essays
    edited by David A. Boruchoff

Homoeroticism and Chivalry: Discourses of Male Same-Sex Desire in the Fourteenth Century
    by Richard E. Zeikowitz

Portraits of Medieval Women: Family, Marriage, and Politics in England 1225–1350
    by Linda E. Mitchell

Eloquent Virgins: From Thecla to Joan of Arc
    by Maud Burnett McInerney

The Persistence of Medievalism: Narrative Adventures in Contemporary Culture
    by Angela Jane Weisl

Capetian Women
    edited by Kathleen D. Nolan

Joan of Arc and Spirituality
    edited by Ann W. Astell and Bonnie Wheeler

The Texture of Society: Medieval Women in the Southern Low Countries
    edited by Ellen E. Kittell and Mary A. Suydam

Charlemagne's Mustache: And Other Cultural Clusters of a Dark Age
    by Paul Edward Dutton

Troubled Vision: Gender, Sexuality, and Sight in Medieval Text and Image
    edited by Emma Campbell and Robert Mills

Queering Medieval Genres
    by Tison Pugh

Sacred Place in Early Medieval Neoplatonism
    by L. Michael Harrington

The Middle Ages at Work
    edited by Kellie Robertson and Michael Uebel

Chaucer's Jobs
    by David R. Carlson

Medievalism and Orientalism: Three Essays on Literature, Architecture and Cultural Identity
    by John M. Ganim

Queer Love in the Middle Ages
    by Anna Klosowska

Performing Women in the Middle Ages: Sex, Gender, and the Iberian Lyric
    by Denise K. Filios

Necessary Conjunctions: The Social Self in Medieval England
    by David Gary Shaw

Visual Culture and the German Middle Ages
    edited by Kathryn Starkey and Horst Wenzel

Medieval Paradigms: Essays in Honor of Jeremy duQuesnay Adams, Volumes 1 and 2
    edited by Stephanie Hayes-Healy

False Fables and Exemplary Truth in Later Middle English Literature
    by Elizabeth Allen

Ecstatic Transformation: On the Uses of Alterity in the Middle Ages
   by Michael Uebel

Sacred and Secular in Medieval and Early Modern Cultures: New Essays
   edited by Lawrence Besserman

Tolkien's Modern Middle Ages
   edited by Jane Chance and Alfred K. Siewers

Representing Righteous Heathens in Late Medieval England
   by Frank Grady

Byzantine Dress: Representations of Secular Dress in Eighth- to Twelfth-Century Painting
   by Jennifer L. Ball

The Laborer's Two Bodies: Labor and the "Work" of the Text in Medieval Britain, 1350–1500
   by Kellie Robertson

The Dogaressa of Venice, 1250–1500: Wife and Icon
   by Holly S. Hurlburt

Logic, Theology, and Poetry in Boethius, Abelard, and Alan of Lille: Words in the Absence of Things
   by Eileen C. Sweeney

The Theology of Work: Peter Damian and the Medieval Religious Renewal Movement
   by Patricia Ranft

On the Purification of Women: Churching in Northern France, 1100–1500
   by Paula M. Rieder

Writers of the Reign of Henry II: Twelve Essays
   edited by Ruth Kennedy and Simon Meecham-Jones

Lonesome Words: The Vocal Poetics of the Old English Lament and the African-American Blues Song
   by M. G. McGeachy

Performing Piety: Musical Culture in Medieval English Nunneries
   by Anne Bagnell Yardley

The Flight from Desire: Augustine and Ovid to Chaucer
   by Robert R. Edwards

Mindful Spirit in Late Medieval Literature: Essays in Honor of Elizabeth D. Kirk
   edited by Bonnie Wheeler

Medieval Fabrications: Dress, Textiles, Clothwork, and Other Cultural Imaginings
   edited by E. Jane Burns

Was the Bayeux Tapestry Made in France?: The Case for St. Florent of Saumur
   by George Beech

Women, Power, and Religious Patronage in the Middle Ages
   by Erin L. Jordan

Hybridity, Identity, and Monstrosity in Medieval Britain: On Difficult Middles
   by Jeffrey Jerome Cohen

Medieval Go-betweens and Chaucer's Pandarus
   by Gretchen Mieszkowski

The Surgeon in Medieval English Literature
   by Jeremy J. Citrome

Temporal Circumstances: Form and History in the Canterbury Tales
   by Lee Patterson

Erotic Discourse and Early English Religious Writing
   by Lara Farina

Odd Bodies and Visible Ends in Medieval Literature
   by Sachi Shimomura

On Farting: Language and Laughter in the Middle Ages
   by Valerie Allen

Women and Medieval Epic: Gender, Genre, and the Limits of Epic Masculinity
   edited by Sara S. Poor and Jana K. Schulman

Race, Class, and Gender in "Medieval" Cinema
   edited by Lynn T. Ramey and Tison Pugh

Allegory and Sexual Ethics in the High Middle Ages
   by Noah D. Guynn

England and Iberia in the Middle Ages, 12th–15th Century: Cultural, Literary, and Political Exchanges
  edited by María Bullón-Fernández

The Medieval Chastity Belt: A Myth-Making Process
  by Albrecht Classen

Claustrophilia: The Erotics of Enclosure in Medieval Literature
  by Cary Howie

Cannibalism in High Medieval English Literature
  by Heather Blurton

The Drama of Masculinity and Medieval English Guild Culture
  by Christina M. Fitzgerald

Chaucer's Visions of Manhood
  by Holly A. Crocker

The Literary Subversions of Medieval Women
  by Jane Chance

Manmade Marvels in Medieval Culture and Literature
  by Scott Lightsey

American Chaucers
  by Candace Barrington

Representing Others in Medieval Iberian Literature
  by Michelle M. Hamilton

Paradigms and Methods in Early Medieval Studies
  edited by Celia Chazelle and Felice Lifshitz

The King and the Whore: King Roderick and La Cava
  by Elizabeth Drayson

Langland's Early Modern Identities
  by Sarah A. Kelen

Cultural Studies of the Modern Middle Ages
  edited by Eileen A. Joy, Myra J. Seaman, Kimberly K. Bell, and Mary K. Ramsey

Hildegard of Bingen's Unknown Language: An Edition, Translation, and Discussion
  by Sarah L. Higley

Medieval Romance and the Construction of Heterosexuality
  by Louise M. Sylvester

Communal Discord, Child Abduction, and Rape in the Later Middle Ages
  by Jeremy Goldberg

Lydgate Matters: Poetry and Material Culture in the Fifteenth Century
  edited by Lisa H. Cooper and Andrea Denny-Brown

Sexuality and Its Queer Discontents in Middle English Literature
  by Tison Pugh

Sex, Scandal, and Sermon in Fourteenth-Century Spain: Juan Ruiz's Libro de Buen Amor
  by Louise M. Haywood

The Erotics of Consolation: Desire and Distance in the Late Middle Ages
  edited by Catherine E. Léglu and Stephen J. Milner

Battlefronts Real and Imagined: War, Border, and Identity in the Chinese Middle Period
  edited by Don J. Wyatt

Wisdom and Her Lovers in Medieval and Early Modern Hispanic Literature
  by Emily C. Francomano

Power, Piety, and Patronage in Late Medieval Queenship: Maria de Luna
  by Nuria Silleras-Fernandez

In the Light of Medieval Spain: Islam, the West, and the Relevance of the Past
  edited by Simon R. Doubleday and David Coleman, foreword by Giles Tremlett

Chaucerian Aesthetics
  by Peggy A. Knapp

Memory, Images, and the English Corpus Christi Drama
  by Theodore K. Lerud

Cultural Diversity in the British Middle Ages: Archipelago, Island, England
  edited by Jeffrey Jerome Cohen

Excrement in the Late Middle Ages: Sacred Filth and Chaucer's Fecopoetics
  by Susan Signe Morrison

Authority and Subjugation in Writing of Medieval Wales
  edited by Ruth Kennedy and Simon Meecham-Jones

The Medieval Poetics of the Reliquary: Enshrinement, Inscription, Performance
  by Seeta Chaganti

The Legend of Charlemagne in the Middle Ages: Power, Faith, and Crusade
  edited by Matthew Gabriele and Jace Stuckey

The Poems of Oswald von Wolkenstein: An English Translation of the Complete Works (1376/77–1445)
  by Albrecht Classen

Women and Experience in Later Medieval Writing: Reading the Book of Life
  edited by Anneke B. Mulder-Bakker and Liz Herbert McAvoy

Ethics and Eventfulness in Middle English Literature: Singular Fortunes
  by J. Allan Mitchell

Maintenance, Meed, and Marriage in Medieval English Literature
  by Kathleen E. Kennedy

The Post-Historical Middle Ages
  edited by Elizabeth Scala and Sylvia Federico

Constructing Chaucer: Author and Autofiction in the Critical Tradition
  by Geoffrey W. Gust

Queens in Stone and Silver: The Creation of a Visual Imagery of Queenship in Capetian France
  by Kathleen Nolan

Finding Saint Francis in Literature and Art
  edited by Cynthia Ho, Beth A. Mulvaney, and John K. Downey

Strange Beauty: Ecocritical Approaches to Early Medieval Landscape
  by Alfred K. Siewers

Berenguela of Castile (1180–1246) and Political Women in the High Middle Ages
  by Miriam Shadis

Julian of Norwich's Legacy: Medieval Mysticism and Post-Medieval Reception
  edited by Sarah Salih and Denise N. Baker

Medievalism, Multilingualism, and Chaucer
  by Mary Catherine Davidson

The Letters of Heloise and Abelard: A Translation of Their Complete Correspondence and Related Writings
  translated and edited by Mary Martin McLaughlin with Bonnie Wheeler

Women and Wealth in Late Medieval Europe
  edited by Theresa Earenfight

Visual Power and Fame in René d'Anjou, Geoffrey Chaucer, and the Black Prince
  by SunHee Kim Gertz

Geoffrey Chaucer Hath a Blog: Medieval Studies and New Media
  by Brantley L. Bryant

Margaret Paston's Piety
  by Joel T. Rosenthal

Gender and Power in Medieval Exegesis
  by Theresa Tinkle

Antimercantilism in Late Medieval English Literature
  by Roger A. Ladd

Magnificence and the Sublime in Medieval Aesthetics: Art, Architecture, Literature, Music
  edited by C. Stephen Jaeger

Medieval and Early Modern Devotional Objects in Global Perspective: Translations of the Sacred
  edited by Elizabeth Robertson and Jennifer Jahner

Late Medieval Jewish Identities: Iberia and Beyond
  edited by Carmen Caballero-Navas and Esperanza Alfonso

Outlawry in Medieval Literature
  by Timothy S. Jones

Women and Disability in Medieval Literature
  by Tory Vandeventer Pearman

The Lesbian Premodern
  edited by Noreen Giffney, Michelle M. Sauer, and Diane Watt

Crafting Jewishness in Medieval England: Legally Absent, Virtually Present
  by Miriamne Ara Krummel

Street Scenes: Late Medieval Acting and Performance
  by Sharon Aronson-Lehavi

Women and Economic Activities in Late Medieval Ghent
  by Shennan Hutton

Palimpsests and the Literary Imagination of Medieval England: Collected Essays
  edited by Leo Carruthers, Raeleen Chai-Elsholz, and Tatjana Silec

Divine Ventriloquism in Medieval English Literature: Power, Anxiety, Subversion
  by Mary Hayes

Vernacular and Latin Literary Discourses of the Muslim Other in Medieval Germany
  by Jerold C. Frakes

Fairies in Medieval Romance
  by James Wade

Reason and Imagination in Chaucer, the Perle-*poet, and the* Cloud-*author: Seeing from the Center*
  by Linda Tarte Holley

The Inner Life of Women in Medieval Romance Literature: Grief, Guilt, and Hypocrisy
  edited by Jeff Rider and Jamie Friedman

Language as the Site of Revolt in Medieval and Early Modern England: Speaking as a Woman
  by M. C. Bodden

Ecofeminist Subjectivities: Chaucer's Talking Birds
  by Lesley Kordecki

Contextualizing the Muslim Other in Medieval Christian Discourse
  edited by Jerold C. Frakes

Ekphrastic Medieval Visions: A New Discussion in Interarts Theory
  by Claire Barbetti

The [European] Other in Medieval Arabic Literature and Culture: Ninth-Twelfth Century AD
  by Nizar F. Hermes

Reading Memory and Identity in the Texts of Medieval European Holy Women
  edited by Margaret Cotter-Lynch and Brad Herzog

Market Power: Lordship, Society, and Economy in Medieval Catalonia (1276–1313)
  by Gregory B. Milton

Marriage, Property, and Women's Narratives
  by Sally A. Livingston

The Medieval Python: The Purposive and Provocative Work of Terry Jones
  edited by R. F. Yeager and Toshiyuki Takamiya

Boccaccio's Decameron *and the Ciceronian Renaissance*
  by Michaela Paasche Grudin and Robert Grudin

Studies in the Medieval Atlantic
  edited by Benjamin Hudson

Chaucer's Feminine Subjects: Figures of Desire in The Canterbury Tales
  by John A. Pitcher

Writing Medieval Women's Lives
  edited by Charlotte Newman Goldy and Amy Livingstone

The Mediterranean World of Alfonso II and Peter II of Aragon (1162–1213)
  by Ernest E. Jenkins

Women in the Military Orders of the Crusades
  by Myra Miranda Bom

Icons of Irishness from the Middle Ages to the Modern World
  by Maggie M. Williams

The Anglo-Scottish Border and the Shaping of Identity, 1300–1600
  edited by Mark P. Bruce and Katherine H. Terrell

Shame and Guilt in Chaucer
  by Anne McTaggart

Word and Image in Medieval Kabbalah: The Texts, Commentaries, and Diagrams of the Sefer Yetsirah
   by Marla Segol

Rethinking Chaucerian Beasts
   edited by Carolynn Van Dyke

The Genre of Medieval Patience Literature: Development, Duplication, and Gender
   by Robin Waugh

Heloise and the Paraclete: A Twelfth-Century Quest (forthcoming)
   by Mary Martin McLaughlin

THE GENRE OF MEDIEVAL PATIENCE LITERATURE

DEVELOPMENT, DUPLICATION, AND GENDER

Robin Waugh

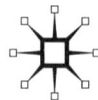

THE GENRE OF MEDIEVAL PATIENCE LITERATURE
Copyright © Robin Waugh, 2012.

All rights reserved.

First published in 2012 by
PALGRAVE MACMILLAN®
in the United States—a division of St. Martin's Press LLC,
175 Fifth Avenue, New York, NY 10010.

Where this book is distributed in the UK, Europe and the rest of the world, this is by Palgrave Macmillan, a division of Macmillan Publishers Limited, registered in England, company number 785998, of Houndmills, Basingstoke, Hampshire RG21 6XS.

Palgrave Macmillan is the global academic imprint of the above companies and has companies and representatives throughout the world.

Palgrave® and Macmillan® are registered trademarks in the United States, the United Kingdom, Europe and other countries.

ISBN: 978–0–230–39186–4

Library of Congress Cataloging-in-Publication Data is available from the Library of Congress.

A catalogue record of the book is available from the British Library.

Design by Newgen Imaging Systems (P) Ltd., Chennai, India.

First edition: November 2012

10 9 8 7 6 5 4 3 2 1

CONTENTS

List of Illustrations	xiii
Preface and Acknowledgments	xv
Abbreviations	xvii
Introduction: *clarissimum in feminis*	1
1. The Female Patience Figure as Speaker	37
2. The Female Patience Figure as Frozen Speaker	75
3. The Female Patience Figure as Counterfeit	113
4. The Female Patience Figure as Frozen Empress	121
5. The Female Patience Figure at an Extreme	131
6. The Female Patience Figure as Shrine	157
Notes	175
Index	215

ILLUSTRATIONS

2.1	Lot's Wife. Public Domain	83
2.2	BL Claudius B.iv, 33r. © The British Library Board	85
2.3	BL Claudius B.iv, 33r. © The British Library Board	86
2.4	BL Claudius B.iv, 32v and 33r. © The British Library Board	88, 89
2.5	The Hague KB 78 D 38 I, 23r. National Library of the Netherlands	90
2.6	The Hague MMW 10 B 34, folio 32r. Museum Meermanno	90
2.7	Lot's Wife Canterbury Cathedral. © Sonia Halliday Photographs	91
2.8	The Hague MMW A 11 (Book 4, 1), folio 178r. Museum Meermanno	94
6.1	Mosaic of saints in Santa Prassede, Rome. © Holly Hayes/Art History Images	161
6.2	Mosaic of saints in Santa Cecilia in Trastevere, Rome. © Holly Hayes/Art History Images	161

PREFACE AND ACKNOWLEDGMENTS

I would like to acknowledge the Social Sciences and Humanities Research Council of Canada, which generously provided a Standard Research Grant in support of the research for this book. The Research Office, the Faculty of Arts, and the Department of English and Film Studies, all at Wilfrid Laurier University, each provided help in a variety of ways, including funding for research trips, funding for travel to academic conferences in order to present research results, and funding for preparation of the index. I also acknowledge the helpful comments of anonymous reviewers, though I am of course responsible for any errors that remain in this volume. My gratitude goes out to the graduate students in Wilfrid Laurier University's Masters Program in English Literature and in the University's PhD Program in English and Film Studies. I have found that being part of a graduate program that specializes in issues of gender and genre has had many positive effects on the paths of inquiry for my research, while discussions with graduate students both within and outside my classes have nearly always been both gratifying and inspiring.

I had valuable help from several research assistants. Dr. Ronald A. Ross performed computer analyses of the various words denoting "fame" and "women" in the *Patrologia Latina*. This groundbreaking work drew my attention to several texts, passages, and approaches that proved to be essential to my arguments. Ms. Susan Henry and Ms. Tina Garbas researched images of Lot's wife and the locations of important shrines to female saints in Southern Europe. Ms. Natalie Boon prepared the index. The Oral Studies Research Site at Wilfrid Laurier University provided the use of computer equipment essential to the completion of this project. I am deeply indebted to colleagues in the Faculty of Arts at Wilfrid Laurier University who were generous with their time and help: Dr. Anne Russell, Dr. Chris Nighman, Dr. Eleanor Ty, Dr. Maria DiCenzo, Dr. Viviana Comensoli, Dr. Jonathan Finn, and Dr. Andrea Austin. The editorial team at Palgrave Macmillan has been wonderfully easy to work with: supportive, genuinely helpful, and sympathetic.

Research results for this project were orally presented at the International Congress on Medieval Studies at Kalamazoo, the Biennial Conference of the Rhetoric Society of America, the Annual Meeting of the Rocky Mountain Medieval and Renaissance Association, the Canadian Society of Medievalists Conference, and various local colloquia at Wilfrid Laurier University and the University of Guelph. Parts of chapters 5 and 6 first appeared as "A Woman in the Mind's Eye (and not): Narrators and Gazes in Chaucer's *Clerk's Tale* and in Two Analogues," *Philological Quarterly* 79 (2000): 1–18. The editors of *Philological Quarterly* have kindly agreed to allow material from the article to appear in this book.

I dedicate this book to the memory of my father, Dr. Frederick P. Waugh, who constantly inspired me through being fascinated by all kinds of cultural material, and who died while the volume was receiving its final touches.

ABBREVIATIONS

BL	British Library, London (in citations of manuscripts)
CCSL	Corpus Christianorum Series Latina
CSEL	Corpus Scriptorum Ecclesiasticorum Latinorum
FC	Fathers of the Church (series)
LA	*Legenda Aurea*
PG	*Patrologia Graeca*. Ed. J. P. Migne et al. Paris, 1857–67, cited by volume and column.
PL	*Patrologia Latina*. Ed. J. P. Migne et al. Paris, 1857–91, cited by volume and column.
SC	Sources Chrétiennes

INTRODUCTION: *CLARISSIMUM IN FEMINIS*

> *The critical task is ... to locate strategies of subversive repetition enabled by ... constructions [of identity], to affirm the local possibilities of intervention through participating in precisely those practices of repetition that constitute identity and, therefore, present the immanent possibility of contesting them.*
>
> —Judith Butler, *Gender Trouble: Feminism and the Subversion of Identity* (New York: Routledge, 1990), p. 147

> *In your patience you shall possess your souls.*
>
> —Luke 21:19

The main argument of this book is that, in certain medieval compositions, women become famous for patience in the way that men are famous for the traditional heroic virtues, such as physical strength and courage, and that this new kind of fame leads to a recognizable and specific genre of medieval composition: patience literature. Although scholars have long acknowledged that many and varying kinds of works emerged from the popularity of martyrs and from early accounts of these figures, many gaps remain in the account of how these emergent works then developed into stable and recognizable forms, with conventions and traditions all their own. The genre of patience literature, thus, demands a sustained attempt to record its literary history. It also demands a critical assessment that would trace its development from passions in the early martyrologies or passionals through to the works of writers such as Margery Kempe, Geoffrey Chaucer, and Christine de Pizan (to name but three possible subjects for the moment) because, for instance, the trials that Margery describes in her *Book* become more comprehensible if one treats them as self-conscious attributes of the patience genre, Grisilde's outrageous passivity in Chaucer's *Clerk's Tale* is less alienating if one recognizes the tale as a sophisticated reductio ad absurdum of the patience genre, and Christine's moral fundamentalism is less paradoxical if one interprets her version of the Griselda story as a precise satire of male-centered interpretations of patience literature and of knightly romances. Yet no-one to my knowledge has defined the genre of patience literature before, or described its history. Previous researchers have examined the patience of martyrs in a general fashion, but, surprisingly, no-one has attempted to define hagiography as a kind of literature of patience, despite many patristic writings that suggest this strong connection, and despite the fact that such a definition would (ideally) contribute to the increased recognition of specific roles for women in medieval literature, to further reassessment of the traditional canon, and to further (re)discovery of neglected works.

My idea for the genre of patience literature came from examining passages such as this one from Geoffrey Chaucer's *Clerk's Tale* (written c. 1390, and appearing in Fragment IV of *The Canterbury Tales*):

> Men speke of Job, and moost for his humblesse,
> As clerkes, whan hem list, konne wel endite,
> Namely of men, but as in soothfastnesse,
> Though clerkes preise wommen but a lite,
> Ther kan no man in humblesse hym acquite
> As womman kan, ne kan been half so trewe
> As wommen been, but it be falle of newe.[1]

A reader is likely to interpret this passage as merely a contributor to the development of an important theme in this tale: the heroine Grisilde's fame for patience. When the passage compares women's fame for being "true" and "humble" with men's reputations for (presumably) traditional heroic deeds, it assumes a competition among reputations and implies also a competition between men and women for the rewards of reputation, as the lines that immediately follow the passage indicate: "Fro Boloigne is this Erl of Panyk come, / Of which the fame up sprang to moore and lesse" (939–40). The poem's switch to the earl is unexpected. His role in the story is tiny, and most readers would consider his fame irrelevant. So, Chaucer seems to mention the earl's reputation specifically in order to point up the contrast between fame for men versus women, while the extreme events and attitudes that *The Clerk's Tale* exhibits suggest a revision of the prevailing masculinist ideas concerning fame into a kind of heroism of patience. Not surprisingly, then, many critics deem Chaucer's Grisilde to be "heroic."[2] However, none of them takes the next logical step and proposes that Grisilde's heroism of patience builds on the conventions of a significant genre of medieval literature; nor do they recognize, even when they acknowledge and refer to the many sources and analogues for *The Clerk's Tale*, that the story of patient Griselda, which appears in several languages and in a variety of versions, is a remarkably popular and resilient example of this genre.[3]

The critics who find Grisilde heroic simply follow the lead of the *Tale's* narrator, who observes "Ther kan no man in humblesse hym acquite / As womman kan" (936–37). But, often for these critics, Grisilde's heroism really means that they consider the depiction of her to be unrealistic, and relatively few of them judge her in a positive way. Many of them have condemned both Walter and Grisilde as monstrous characters, particularly when the latter "no chiere maade of hevynesse" as her children are taken from her, presumably to be murdered (678); when her eyes remain dry as she walks through a weeping multitude after Walter casts her out of his castle in favor of a younger bride (899); when, after this series of horrifying mental tortures (and more), Chaucer's Clerk seems to praise her for being "ful of pacient benyngnytee, ... to hire housbonde evere meke and stable" (929–31).[4] She is too abstract for many readers. "Ay sad and constant as a wal," Grisilde is an inanimate object as opposed to a convincing human being (1047).

On the other hand, certain critics conclude that the major characters in *The Clerk's Tale* are not supposed to be convincing or realistic. These critics usually reach this conclusion by placing the *Tale* (and often similar works as well) in the genre of secular hagiography. In *The Dialogic Imagination*, M. M. Bakhtin (unwittingly perhaps) defines secular hagiography during his attempt to inventory the identifying attributes of the heroes of early Greek romances. While his connections between medieval romances and saints' lives undoubtedly help to define the romance genre, which he calls "an adventure *novel of ordeal*" and a "*test of the heroes' integrity, their selfhood*," his phrases, particularly the emphasized ones, describe secular hagiography (and even more so, I would argue, patience literature) better than they describe the romance genre.[5] Yet, Bakhtin is one of the very few major early twentieth-century critics to even mention the early martyrologies, let alone describe the specialized heroism of the saint-figure, and secular hagiography remained a very neglected genre until further identifications of it appeared in the works of critics such as Laurel Braswell, Valerie Edden, Kathryn McKinley, Diana T. Childress, Margaret Hurley, Jocelyn Wogan-Browne, Saul Nathaniel Brody and others.[6] Chaucer's martyrs of love in *The Legend of Good Women* have provided the subject-matter for much of this secular hagiographical criticism.[7]

Within the bounds of secular hagiography, then, Grisilde acts in a conventional fashion for the genre in which she appears. She is a pseudo-saint, so her actions transcend any behaviors that might occur in the real world. She is an allegorical representation of an abstract virtue: patience (proverbially, even), so she cannot be expected to act and speak as a more typical literary character would, and, if one tests her, one tests only the "durability of an already finished product."[8] Moreover, the nature of the virtue that she represents makes her difficult to understand even if one resigns oneself to treating her allegorically. As many scholars of intellectual history have observed, the virtue of patience is nearly impossible to identify as a force unto itself because it has no immediate presence of its own, while any attempt to examine Grisilde's patience as an allegorical concept only parallels the journey into interpretive quicksands that so many critics of *The Clerk's Tale* have taken.[9]

Pacientes vincunt: The Virtue of Patience in Medieval Tradition

Exhibiting patience amounts to a repression of emotions such as anger and frustration rather than a (perhaps cathartic) expression of them.[10] Without adversities and the typical, instinctive human responses to them patience would not exist.[11] So, unlike many other human attributes, this virtue is always negatively established.[12] Medieval and classical writers are certainly aware of patience's elusive nature. They tend to define it through its presumed opposites, such as anger and extreme sadness, and often find it difficult if not impossible to separate psychic states of patience from the many qualities that it relates to, or seems to stem from, such as strength and temperance.[13] Augustine, for instance, identifies patience (rather unhelpfully) as an offshoot of *caritas*.[14] Generally, the intellectual history of patience in early Christian documents only demonstrates how it merely lands among other items on an ever-growing list of desirable virtues, "without allowing itself to be [really] added in or totalized," according to Derrida's reading of intellectual history. Such a virtue must remain "quasi-transcendental." No wonder, then, that Grisilde comes over as such an unsympathetic figure. Not only does her "character" amount to nothing but an abstract virtue, but this virtue also, by its very nature, must always be classified as adjunct, "*secondary*," and "*provisional*."[15]

Even the existence of patience is very hard to prove. For instance, martyrs under torture might decide to suppress their cries and therefore exhibit patience, but how can a spectator be sure of the cause of this quietness? Several of the early passios describe martyrs in trancelike states of silence that may indicate only that these torture victims physically cannot speak: "After being tossed a good deal by [a bull, Blandina, a Christian martyr] no longer perceived what was happening because of the hope and possession of all she believed in and because of her intimacy with Christ."[16] Only an onlooker who is familiar with the character of a person undergoing trials would even be able to suspect whether or not that victim were exhibiting patience by refusing to show "normal" emotions or behaviors that the onlooker had previously witnessed. One can only conclude that a decision to be patient is best described as an act of the will, and it is difficult, often impossible, to gain access to another person's will. Certainly any general judgment that an individual is acting in a way that seems to flout typical human instincts must remain interpretive—often an attempt at mind-reading—rather than definitive.

Chaucer's writings indicate that he is aware of the difficulties in defining patience. The first few lines of his *Tale of Melibee* (Fragment VII in *The Canterbury Tales*) describe the beating of the hero's wife, Dame Prudence, and the wounding of Sophie, the couple's daughter, by enemies who enter Melibee's house while he is away (970–75). Much of the rest of this lengthy prose tale then depicts Prudence's efforts to prevent Melibee from taking revenge. Her arguments are logical, exceptionally learned, full of citation, and persuasive on almost every level. Melibee nearly always expresses willingness to accept her premises and follow her advice (1517, 1539). Nothing in the tone of his replies indicates that he has lost control of his emotions. But (to typical readers' frustration) he is still unable to let go of his desire for vengeance even as the tale nears its end and despite all of his wife's efforts (1680–86). He seems obsessively stubborn, stupid, and childish. As is typical of Chaucer's writings (and as the dryness of Prudence's discourse intimates), the hero's reactions are nevertheless quite convincing psychologically. He is a more "realistic" character than his wife, who is saddled with the more allegorical name. Yet, this tale betrays, through Prudence's constant references to scripture and to the idea of imitating Christ, the author's almost certain knowledge that there is but one way to define patience in positive terms. This way suits the genre of secular hagiography, suits Grisilde's allegorical potential in *The Clerk's Tale*, and is supported by theologians from all ages, including the early Christian apologists and later medieval writers: patience is part of God's perfection, and comes only and always from Him (Psalms 70:5, 61:6). For instance, the fathers often describe acts of patience as imitations of Christ's behavior on the cross. Such deeds show obedience to His commands to forgive, to love one's enemies, and to turn the other cheek (Matthew 5:3–12, 39–45).[17] Obeying these rules can lead to a demonstration of, occasionally, just how miraculous the virtue of patience can be. A widely cited exemplum of the virtue tells the story of a demon who declares that he is *In sola patientia victus*, "conquered by patience alone."[18] So, learned as he is, Chaucer in *The Tale of Melibee* seems to recognize that the apologists and hagiographers never really concern themselves with defining patience per se. Instead, they—together with Dame Prudence—assert "righteous" patience, as Julianus Pomerius (c. 480) calls it, which the early Christian writers often distinguish from the patience that their classical predecessors profess.[19]

The idea of righteous patience certainly fits with Grisilde's character. *The Clerk's Tale* describes her as a "flour of wyfly pacience" (919), and the narrator, at least for most of the length of the *Tale*, presents her temperament and actions in an utterly straightforward fashion, as if readers were to take them at face value. She is ideally humble, good, discreet, modest, honorable (926–30), constant (1008), guileless, innocent, steadfast (1045–50), "mooste servysable of alle" (979), "oon in herte and in visage" (711), and genuinely in love with her husband. She thus fits with the many early Christian discussions of patience that view it simply as miraculous.[20] One of the reasons, then, that her story, and Chaucer's version of it particularly, come over as an example of secular hagiography is that Grisilde's patience descends from that of the proverbial patience figure, Job, who enjoys an unusually direct relationship with God (932–38). Melibee's patience is also miraculous. He decides to forego revenge ultimately because of pure faith and blind trust in his wife's advice. His patience amounts to an act of the will—clearly against his own instincts (1870–75; cf. 1278–80)—that reads like a conversion story.

But the miraculous patience idea means that these kinds of readings would consign *The Clerk's Tale* and *The Tale of Melibee* to the genre of hagiography rather than to that of secular hagiography, or at least mess up the distinctions between these two genres. A definition of patience as God-originating and miraculous relies on faith as opposed to reason, as the treatises concerning this virtue written by the church fathers such as Basil and Cyprian confirm when they again and again presuppose the existence of patience, a concept that they sanctify at length but usually decline to specifically define or redefine in a way that is both comprehensible and recognizably Christian.[21] However, in this world and in the world of Chaucer's *Clerk's Tale*, even for the faithful, trying to define patience means dealing in terms that "admit into their games ... contradiction."[22] For instance, the miraculous definition of patience would render any testing of Grisilde so baseless, pointless, and sadistic that any right-thinking person would condemn it (714). Certainly the Clerk condemns it (723, 734). Then how can one justify the reconciliation of Walter and Grisilde near the end of the *Tale*? How can one even entertain the idea of Walter as a God-figure when he is childish, capricious, irresponsible, and sadistic? The miraculous definition of patience also makes any direct emulation of the life of a perfectly patient person impossible, as the Clerk concludes near the end of his narrative (1139–44, 1164–68), as Melibee announces (*Tale of Melibee* 1517–18), and as the life of Jesus proves. Divine power is necessary in order to accomplish perfect patience. A mere human cannot imitate the divine creation and redemption of the world or encompass all of creation with an idea in the way that

God, according to the theologians, embraces all of the world with His patience.[23] In the existing criticism of secular hagiography, then, scholars of *The Clerk's Tale*, while they make the useful connection between Grisilde and saints, while they rightly and carefully narrow their definitions of secular hagiography, and while they provide important background for the *Tale* by outlining patience as a theme or virtue in medieval literature, tend nevertheless to take the genres of hagiography and secular hagiography very much for granted. For example, they seem content to leave the patience figure as an abstract idea that conveys only a cryptic and unpalatable message.

They also ignore a number of important questions. For instance, how did secular hagiography arise and start to gain popularity? How did the genre develop from the early passios, as most critics presume that it did, into the depictions of the saintly characters that one sees in Chaucer's works, such as Grisilde and Custance in *The Man of Law's Tale* (Fragment II), whose deeds, temperaments, and attitudes are very different from those of the early martyrs in most respects? In fact, the early saints frequently exhibit emotions that would seem to be inimical to characters such as Grisilde, as when Vettius Epagathus, one of the martyrs from Lyons and Vienne, "became highly indignant" at the judgment of Roman authorities against the Christians (65).[24] And, since the critical history of genres has for the most part employed male-oriented attributes such as heroic attributes, what are the relationships between secular hagiography and female protagonists, and why do such associations exist?—two questions that are probably the most important for scholars who are interested in feminist approaches.

Patience Literature

As part of the process of trying to answer these questions, I would define patience literature as a genre that features and praises, explicitly or implicitly, the "ability to endure," to keep on being the same person despite oppressive suffering, that Brent D. Shaw notices as a developing aspect of self-definition in characters from various Hellenic, Jewish, and Latin works, starting about 200 years before Christ.[25] It is not surprising that a representative literary genre should establish itself alongside "a new self-understanding of the human subject in the early Roman Empire, a new 'subjectivity'—the self as sufferer," as Judith Perkins puts it (see Shaw, "Body," 300).[26] During this period, the various clashes of tribes, ethnicities, economies, and religious ideas, which must take place when Roman imperial initiatives meet up with both long-settled and nomadic cultures, give rise to increasing self-consciousness concerning language, and particularly with regard to the never-ending debate between the authority of oral language as opposed to written language.[27] Indeed the miracle of Pentecost and phrases like "The Word was made flesh" demonstrate (Acts 2:1–21; John 1:14), among other things, that a crisis in spiritual thinking generally and the rise of an individual religious cult more particularly would cause a reoccurrence of oral modes of thought, if only because any new religion needs time to create, recognize, and establish its core traditions, which tend to eventually become texts. When oral modes of thought dominate, it is more difficult to hide the fact that the body and, therefore, desire are involved in the very substance of language—in its very grammar, as Derrida would have it.[28] And, if the Word is made flesh, then the crucifixion and, therefore, suffering more generally conceived can become involved in the very substance of language—in one's very identity, as Perkins would have it.[29] During the early Roman Empire, then, I would argue that prevailing attitudes concerning the body and suffering become radically rearticulated, reflect a movement toward defining the self in terms of the suffering of that self, and express themselves in examples of patience literature.

Both sacred and secular examples of this genre start appearing in large numbers in the second century AD, with the period of the persecution under Diocletian and his immediate successors "account[ing] for well nigh half of all recorded and memorialized martyrdoms" and thus representing a particularly prolific period for patience narratives.[30] Then, according to Shaw, "The ideology [of endurance] became increasingly formalized in the mid-third century" ("Body," 298). Examples of the patience genre are still being created, but its greatest influence probably occurs during the most widespread composition of hagiographical works in Europe during the Middle Ages, with Jacobus de Voragine's *Legenda Aurea* (c. 1260) a superlative candidate for representing the cult of patience literature at its height.[31] That said, I do not think of patience literature as dominating literature and culture in a monolithic kind of way. Instead, I think of the genre as functioning in the Middle Ages much like courtly love: a loosely conceived and constantly evolving body of conventions that are continually both promoted and undercut in the existing literature; a body of conventions that deals in ideas that are always subject to controversy, not only in the medieval age but also in the contemporary one.[32]

Patience Literature Becomes Gendered

One major shift in the content of patience literature has been well-documented. As Christianity became tolerated by the Roman Empire and then became the state religion, incidents of Christian martyrdom declined, and other "proofs," such as asceticism, of Christian belief gained prominence.³³ Gregory the Great sought to generalize the Christian concept of heroic endurance so that it might apply to aspects of Christian life beyond blood martyrdom. He argues that a Christian could aspire to patience, which he defines as *aliena mala aequanimiter perpeti* [to endure external evils with equanimity], through exhibiting this equanimity and indifference to wealth and social status.³⁴ Gregory gleans these principles from the Bible and discussions of ethics in the works of classical authors.³⁵ His campaign is extensive, as Ralph Hanna III notes, with subsequent reformers repeating and instituting Gregorian policies from the fifth through the seventh century, a period that "witnessed a massive increase in the number of Christian miraculous texts, saints' lives, relics, shrines, and images."³⁶

But a more striking shift happens earlier, from late antiquity on. This shift is not so well-documented, and its consequences continue to manifest themselves right to the later Middle Ages. In examples of patience literature, the occurrence of male and female protagonists is similar to that of comparable genres, at first. Once the body is generally reinterpreted due to the new way of identifying oneself through suffering however, female protagonists of patience works (of which Grisilde is a very late example) become much more common than male: a major generic transition from patience literature to gendered patience literature. Chaucer offers famous evidence for this change when the Clerk proclaims "Ther kan no man in humblesse hym acquite / As womman kan" (*The Clerk's Tale* 936–37), and when Criseyde jokingly notes that "holy seyntes lyves" are the proper reading for a widow (*Troilus and Criseyde* 2.118).³⁷ I do not mean to suggest that all or even most examples of patience literature after the shift have female protagonists. I am also not going to pretend that I am the first to notice connections between hagiography and examples of secular literature that feature patience. But I think that this shift has been largely ignored because critics have tended to take associations between women, passivity, and suffering for granted: passivity becomes a "choice" for men, according to Shaw, in the early Roman Empire, whereas "for women it remained, as it had always been, a constant role" ("Body" 295, and nn. 85 and 86). I find that the shift is more profound than Shaw implies, and that the incidence of women in patience literature from both before and after the shift is highly significant.

Female Protagonists in the Passions of the Early Martyrs

The unusually high participation of women in the first examples of patience literature, such as the earliest trials of Christian martyrs, is almost certainly an accident of history. Early Christianity, anxious for converts, tried to appeal as directly as possible to as many people as possible. Therefore, its rhetoric becomes remarkably egalitarian—revolutionary, really—for its day. Clement of Rome, for instance, writing around AD 100, outlines the martyrdoms of the apostles and of others, and then adds: "women were persecuted, who as Danaids and Dircae suffered terrible and impious indignities and thereby safely completed the race of faith and, thought weak in body, received a noble reward of honor."[38] According to the early church father Tertullian (c. AD 205), members of *tot uiris ac feminis, omnis sexus, omnis aetatis, omnis dignitatis* [both sexes—men and women—of every age, of every station] were ready for martyrdom. This egalitarian rhetoric may even mask the very real possibility that "many more females than males were converting to Christianity in its first centuries."[39] More generally, as one sees in the late second-century dialogue called *Octavius*, where the Christian apologist Minucius Felix dismisses the traditional worldly and Roman values of riches, honor, and power and concludes that *Omnes tamen pari sorte nascimur, sola virtute distinguimur* [we (Christians) are all born equal and moral goodness alone gives us a mark of distinction], the egalitarian ideas of the early Christians are baldly stated, unequivocal, and uncompromising.[40] Moreover, as Shaw and many other critics point out, these ideas are an "implicit condemnation of the whole [political] system" of late antiquity, and therefore of the Roman Empire more generally ("Body," 302). Roman authorities would almost certainly look upon the implications of equal status for women that appear in so many of these early apologetic works as just one more reason to treat Christians as politically dangerous.[41] One of the typical authority-figures in *The Acts of Martyrs*, for instance, calls the martyr Crispina *dura es et contemptrix* (Musurillo, ed., 302) [a stubborn and insolent woman (303)]. More generally, Christianity's collapse-of-classes ideals create an ideological gap between this faith and the society that it needs to inhabit in order for the movement to succeed.

 The earliest state-sponsored persecutions of Christians begin in the second century, and accounts of these events by the Roman authorities support the egalitarian assertions of the early Christian writers—and from outside the apologists' biased point of view. In about the year AD 112, Pliny the Younger, Governor of Bithynia, writes to the emperor Trajan that *Multi enim omnis aetatis, omnis ordinis, utriusque sexus etiam uocantur in periculum et uocabuntur. Neque ciuitates tantum, sed uicos etiam atque agros superstitionis istius contagio peruagata est* [many persons of all ages and classes and of both sexes are being put in peril by accusation, and this will go on. The contagion of this superstition has spread not only in the cities, but in the villages and rural districts as well].[42] The rhetoric of the popular earliest *passios* records similar egalitarian ideas. For instance, the second-century martyr Sanctus tries to obliterate any distinguishing information about himself such as "his own name, his race, or the city he was from, [or] whether he was a slave or a freedman" by answering all of the persecutors' questions on these points with "I am a Christian" (Musurillo, ed., 69). Of course, such insistence upon one sole point of identification has the effect of leveling any other distinguishing aspects.

In addition, the similarities of the martyrs' tortures and executions throughout their passions (Musurillo, ed., 51, 57, 69, 97, etc.) suggest that suffering and death, which define these works as examples of patience literature, were meted out with an astonishingly even hand.[43] The various types of protagonists appear so randomly in the passios that the martyrs would seem to be as likely to come from any social class and from any Mediterranean state; as likely to be "Jew [as] Greek ... bond [as] free ... male [as] female" (Galatians 3:28), "circumcision [as] uncircumcision ... Barbarian [as] Scythian" (Colossians 3:11), military as civilian, clerical as lay, rich as poor. Perhaps, through chance alone, the two earliest passios of all have female protagonists. The earliest example is from AD 57. A woman named Pomponia Graecina is *nupta ac superstitionis externae rea, mariti iudicio permissa* [accused of foreign superstition and handed over to her husband for trial]. according to Tacitus's *Annals*. If the "foreign superstition" is Christianity, the existence of this story would mean that probably the earliest of all references to a possible Christian in a Roman chronicle is to a woman.[44] In the next earliest example, the only Christians that Pliny the Younger puts to torture, according to his letter, are two "maidservants" who are also referred to in the text as *ministrae*. They are clearly church officials of some sort: *ministrae* is usually translated "deaconesses."[45]

On the other hand, the incidence of women's martyrdoms in the passios, once these works start to appear in large numbers, fails to live up to the promise of early Christian rhetoric. Of the 146 martyrs recorded in Eusebius of Caesarea's *Historia Ecclesia* (c. 310) about 20 seem to be women, although he also records whole villages being wiped out, and presumably about half of these populations would be female.[46] According to Shaw, a wider reckoning of the accounts of martyrs reveals that "males were celebrated four times (or more) as frequently as females," a gender imbalance, probably due to sexism, that continues into later hagiography.[47] Still, the fact that women appear in such propaganda at all is the significant point, regardless of the numbers.

Blandina

Exactly how revolutionary this martyrological rhetoric was in the second century AD becomes clear in the story of Blandina. She appears in the text of an anonymous letter from the church of Southern Gaul to a church in Asia and Phrygia. This document is preserved only in Eusebius's *Historia Ecclesia* (written in Greek) and is usually called "The Martyrs of Lyon and Vienne." The events occur about AD 177.[48] Blandina is introduced as the last of a group of four martyrs who are singled out by the crowd, "the prefect, and the soldiers" as targets for "all" of their "wrath." The other three martyrs are men, described in conventional terms for the early passios. But Blandina's participation in the soon-to-be-related events marks a break with convention, according to the narrator: "through [her] Christ proved that the things that men think cheap, ugly, and contemptuous are deemed worthy of glory before God, by reason of her love for him which was not merely vaunted in appearance but demonstrated in achievement" (Musurillo, ed., 67). The narrative omits any reason why men might be inclined to hold such negative opinions of Blandina. At first, readers are likely to conclude that the disparagement is triggered by her sex because she is the only woman in the group and there seems to be no alternative reason, while Clement of Rome mentions the supposed weakness of the female body in his account of the early martyrs, as if such sexist attitudes might be commonplace.[49] But one soon realizes that "cheap" and "ugly" are not typically sex-specific terms and the very next passage in "The Martyrs of Lyon and Vienne" allows questioning of this purely sexist attitude. The text identifies Blandina, seemingly in passing, as a slave. "Cheap" even hints at the price that a slave might fetch. Shaw declares that here "the irony is that her body is doubly weak: that of a woman and that of a slave" ("Body," 308), but I think that the mentioning of Blandina's slave status in the text means that *any* reason that readers might prejudge her becomes ambiguous.[50] Certainly this text declines to equate the status of a woman with that of a slave. The presence of Blandina's mistress (not prejudged as "cheap" or as anything else) in the larger group of persecuted Christians who appear at the arena with Blandina belies such a simple formula. Slave status and gender are supposed to bleed into one another in this text, where they can suggest to the reader the impossibility of dealing with gender issues exclusive of class issues, where they can suggest a profound repudiation of the Roman social and political system, where they can foreground the principle of even-handedness in itself to the ideal reader (see Galatians 3:28); where, in other words, they can become an important example of hybridity as Susan Stanford Friedman describes it.[51] Overt subversion of social hierarchy certainly occurs in "The Martyrs of Lyon and Vienne," with Blandina herself becoming a "symbol of social reversal."[52] Her mistress remains anonymous throughout the narrative, and ensuing events further emphasize the revolutionary aspects of the presence of a slave in the same, typically male-dominated, venue as a free woman, male spectators, and male authorities. Blandina's mistress is "in agony lest because of her [Blandina's] bodily weakness she would not be able to make a bold confession of her faith" (Musurillo, ed., 67). Yet this slave-woman defeats these expectations and eclipses the other woman's fame. The latter is mentioned briefly only once in the story, in reference to her expectations for her servant. The narrative ignores Blandina's mistress thereafter. On the other hand, the slave's trials, in three successive episodes, receive detailed descriptions and Blandina's final appearance marks the climax of the narrative. She appears and dies last in her group of martyrs, in a spectacle that the persecutors seem to design for a female victim. She outlasts the male adolescent that is tortured alongside her and supplants the male martyr who seemed to be the central figure of this passio at the outset, Vettius Epagathus (65). She receives much praise throughout the narrative. In the middle of her trials, the narrator describes her as "filled with ... power," the only martyr of this group to achieve such acclaim (67). Blandina's martyrdom ends with "the pagans themselves admitted that no woman had ever suffered so much in their experience" (81). This extreme language asserts that she supersedes all other martyrs as "the ultimate virtuoso of torture."[53] The very earliest patience literature, then, like "the Greek romance, reveals its strong ties with a *folklore that predates class distinctions*," as Bakhtin says—and gender distinctions, apparently. Indeed the depiction of a female slave as martyr renders "The Martyrs of Lyon and Vienne" a "queerly open text," according to Virginia Burrus.[54]

Heroic Rhetoric in the Passios

As critics have often noted, early hagiography also reveals strong ties with heroic works. The acts of the martyrs are often described as skirmishes in an ongoing war with the devil (Musurillo, ed., 25, 63, 75, 287; Shaw, "Body," 289–90). Their deeds are compared to "heroic" ones explicitly (Musurillo, ed., 63, 103, 131) and, more generally, to participation in military (205, 215, 217, 237, 251, 277) and athletic contests: "like a noble athlete he [the martyr Papylus] received the angry onslaught of his adversary" (27; see 75, 117, 125, 127, 161, 197, 235).[55] The martyrs, like traditional heroes, are praised for "nobility" (27; see 67, 75, 83, 133, 241), "strength" (67; see 69, 75, 227), and "courage" (11; see 69, 99, 127, 199, 213, 245, 323, 351). They undergo "training" for their deeds (63; see 65, 75, 237), and achieve "victories" (125; see 193, 201, 213, 235, 356; and "crowns" (75; see 227, 245) just like ancient athletes would (73, 217).[56] Even early accounts of the martyrs go beyond this basic athletic allegory in order to describe them as defenders of, or even parts of, the church as an ideal structure or as the new city of Jerusalem ("sturdy pillars," for example [63, 67]), represented as a kind of fortress under attack from the forces of evil. Eusebius, the most important early historian of the Christian church, and Tertullian, the most important apologist for the martyrs and therefore of early patience literature, also habitually exalt them and other persecuted Christians by using heroic terms. Moreover, Tertullian lends credence to the connection between believers and heroes by comparing the acts of Christian martyrs to accounts of famous self-sacrificing figures from classical literature, while his work clearly demonstrates that patience treatises were just as important and influential as patience narratives even from the earliest examples of patience literature.[57] Shaw rightly points to the summations of heroic values in 4 Maccabees as the most explicit articulation in a patience treatise of how martyrs gain power and become new heroes: "All people, even their torturers, marveled at [these Jewish martyrs'] courage and endurance, and they became the cause of the downfall of tyranny over their nation. By their endurance they conquered the tyrant, and thus their native land was purified through them" (4 Maccabees 1:11; Shaw, "Body," 278–80). This kind of extreme admiration, emerging even from unexpected sources, together with the way in which the early martyrs' actions galvanize and transform an entire "nation" clearly recalls the achievements of such heroes as Aeneas.[58]

In early patience literature this heroic, athletic, military, and competitive terminology applies equally to both men and women. Blandina, for example, demonstrates a near equality between male and female heroism when her exposure to wild animals causes her no harm in the arena. This unexpected result is hailed as a "victory," and, through her "conflict," she wins "the crown of immortality" (Musurillo, ed., 75). Blandina's torturers end up "exhausted" and "beaten" as if she overmatches them physically (Musurillo, ed., 67; Shaw, "Body," 309), and her final trial is to be thrown to a bull, an obvious representation of hypermasculinity and the kind of beast that the hypermasculine heroes, such as Heracles, typically fight.[59] She is compared to "a noble athlete," just like a male martyr in the same narrative (67). This gender equity is rare and significant. According to Shaw, "the involvement of female 'criminals' in this sort of public punishment ... signalled something unusual" because punishment through being exposed to beasts was usually reserved for young male criminals.[60]

The story's concern with her reputation is also in the heroic tradition. Blandina announces "we [Christians] do nothing to be ashamed of" (Musurillo, ed., 67). She ponders the crowd's evaluation of her and promotes her own view of right and wrong. A "private and isolated" figure in so many ways, Blandina thus demonstrates that a female martyr "quite often behaves ... precisely like the public man of the rhetorical and historical genres," to use Bakhtin's words.[61] And, when her pagan adversaries admit that "no woman had ever suffered so much" (Musurillo, ed., 81) and when an account of another early female martyr introduces its main character as "the famous Potamiaena" (133), any reader or listener would surely recognize that these works are assessing their female protagonists with the typically competitive language of masculine reputations, as when Aeneas says *sum pius Aeneas ... fama super aethera notus* [I am the good Aeneas ... my fame has reached to above the heavens].[62] Even Tacitus's account of the very early Pomponia Graecina, who believes in a "foreign superstition," describes her as *insignis* [distinguished].[63] In sum, regardless of the actual numbers of women being martyred for early Christianity, *The Acts of Martyrs* present them in the same situations as men and describe them in the same heroic terms. These are exceedingly rare developments in literary history taken as a whole.

At the same time, the narrator of "The Martyrs of Lyon and Vienne" recognizes that a reader needs to think of the typical heroic traditions in an entirely new way when they are applied to martyrs, and particularly to female martyrs. For instance, this narrator notes that Blandina's victory occurs despite the fact that she is "tiny, weak, and insignificant" (Musurillo, ed., 75), while, more generally, when the apologists and hagiographers apply their unrevised heroic terms to the saints and even more so when they apply them to female saints, this heroic rhetoric comes over as slightly forced—a little "raw."[64] Also, while the heroic traditions are important to the passios, they do not dominate the discourse all of the time; there is even some undercutting of heroic patience. One cannot help but notice, for instance, that the early saints' lives, unlike the later ones, include examples of Christians who find the patience challenge too oppressive to bear (65), while many early works concerning patience acknowledge its difficulty. There are also many instances in early hagiography that demonstrate that many of even the most patient of martyrs cannot completely suppress their emotions, a point that later theologians concede.[65] Some writers conclude that a saint's emotions might even be amplified by the kind of suffering that is bound to occur during a martyrdom. In fact, it is important to stress the possibility for failure that is mixed in with the heroic imagery of these early passios because this possibility means that the early martyrs, when they declare their confidence, are not then merely "postur[ing] heroically when [they] are in fact perfectly safe" in the embrace of God's omnipotence and benevolence.[66] And, on occasion, heroic imagery during the persecutions gives way to different kinds of imagery. For instance, the martyrs' trials are occasionally compared to those "of a woman in childbirth," and hence openly feminized (Shaw, "Body," 290). This kind of comparison occurs commonly in Christian propaganda, where conversions and other spiritual processes are often represented as new births.[67] That said, heroic imagery remains easily the most prominent kind in early saints' lives, and connection between this heroic rhetoric and endurance under torture persists into examples of patience literature from the late Middle Ages, with women frequently as protagonists.

Patience as Passive Suffering

Shaw believes that the typical heroic and militaristic terms that the descriptions of the early martyrs revel in, together with the "feminized rhetoric" of these works and others, point to a general shift in many works, both spiritual and secular, from the praise of more aggressive values, traditionally associated with men, to praise of the "ability to endure, ... [ὑπομονή] *hypomonê*" in Greek ("Body," 279; 278). This abstract noun "first commonly appears" in "Graeco-Judaic texts of the Hellenistic period, mainly in the so-called pseudoepigrapha," and, "reduced to its constituent elements, the bare word means 'to remain underneath something' or 'to lie beneath something'" ("Body," 287).[68] It certainly suits the central actions of the typical patience works. When Eleazar, a Jewish martyr, for instance, "[falls] to the ground because his body could not endure the agonies" from his torture (4 Maccabees 6:7), the event is an absolute antithesis to the typical heroic deed. Shaw further defines the change that he observes: "Praise ... of active and aggressive values entailed in manliness [shifts to] elevation to prominence of the passive value of merely being able to endure: ... voice, activity, aggression, closure, penetration, and the ability to inflict pain and suffering [versus] silence, passivity, submissiveness, openness, suffering" ("Body," 279). For example, Ignatius of Antioch (c. 108) finds himself able to say, "I desire (or 'love') to suffer," a phrase almost inconceivable in works written just a few years before, and "Nobility through patience" becomes possible and desirable, as Blandina's story attests ("Body," 289, and note 65; 309).[69]

In the course of their arguments concerning *hypomonê* in Graeco-Judaic texts of the Hellenistic period, Shaw and Perkins examine texts from several genres, including hagiography, secular romances, and philosophical works, in order to make their cases. With the emergent quality of endurance appearing in compositions from several distinct genres, a larger generic classification, patience literature, gains in plausibility, whereas the epithet "secular hagiography" falls short of classifying in any concrete way the works that feature endurance, as Bakhtin suggested above, and as Perkins and Shaw make abundantly clear. The epithet implies that hagiography predated the other examples of patience literature. Instead, the stories of Judeo-Christian martyrs appear at almost exactly the same time as many Greek romances that feature the sufferings and patience of their (sometimes female) protagonists. The genres of hagiography and romance are therefore almost certainly related to one another. Significant examples of both start to appear in the second century AD, and they express similar attitudes. In the popular Greek romance *The Adventures of Leucippe and Clitophon* by Achilles Tatius, from the late second century or so, the heroine utters words that could just as readily appear in a contemporary passio: "Here is my body, burn it. Bring also the sword; here is my neck, pierce it. Feast your eyes with a new sight; one woman contends against all manner of tortures, and overcomes all her trials."[70]

Such events and attitudes on view in the early passios, then, and in the other works that Shaw and Perkins include in their arguments, would seem to justify Perkins's proposal of a new subjectivity.[71] And these same events and attitudes would further seem to justify Shaw's proposal for a connection of the self as sufferer to "a civil body under trial and test in a civic regime of power" ("Body," 311). Perkins, in her turn, takes the next logical step. She identifies Shaw's idea of a civil body as "a corporate body, the Christian community," which is defined and strengthened by these events and attitudes.[72]

Patience as Feminine Suffering

Obviously the interpretation of the term *hypomonê* as "to lie beneath something" has "strong implications for a gendered discourse," as Shaw notes ("Body," 288, and n. 58). He interprets the rise of this term as a "feminization" of the rhetoric surrounding acts of endurance in literary works. Until *hypomonê* appears in its new guise, the mind, soul, and body, according to classical thought, inevitably contained "weaker," less desirable, feminine parts "with which the man had to contend." Endurance, for instance, was "as necessary for his survival as the 'higher' male virtues" ("Body," 285). Shaw then notes that popular attitudes in the early age of Imperial Rome, just before the Christian martyrdoms began, confirm the division between male and female virtues, yet also demonstrate a growing interest in the feminine capacity for endurance, as one may see in the writings of Musonius Rufus and Seneca.[73] But Shaw relies on an interpretation of Michel Foucault's ideas concerning sexuality for his argument, and Foucault's ideas can be oversimplified and taken out of context if one uses the observations in *The Use of Pleasure* to set up a dichotomy between "early" and "late" Foucault and dominant men and passive women. In the first volume of his *History of Sexuality*, Foucault takes pains to specify that no such "system of Law-and-Sovereign," of "duality extending from the top down" can define power. Therefore, "we must immerse the expanding production of discourses on sex in the field of multiple and mobile power relations"; or, as Derrida puts it, "Force itself is never present; it is only a play of differences and quantities."[74]

Certainly the remarkably precocious creation and development of a cult of martyrs—regardless of whether or not they actually existed—together with the remarkably swift grafting of these figures onto the Christian historical traditions represent a distinct status for them as compared to the literary characters of Greek romances. Perkins often admits that the martyrs are more than mere demonstrators of a characteristic and increasingly important virtue.[75] Their appearance between the emergence of *hypomonê* and the writing of more derivative passios such as the one in Jerome's *Epistola 1* has important consequences for the development of the attitudes toward this passive virtue, and particularly for the understanding of the roles of women who are described as possessing it.[76] Women are revolutionary in early Christianity precisely because they are treated with the same *commonplace* phrases, situations, and attitudes that men are.

The Mother of 2 and 4 Maccabees Compared to Blandina

Likely the dominance of other female figures over Blandina in Shaw's argument occurs because they fit his argument better, and, according to him, the crucial change to "sheer *endurance* [being] lauded both as a behavioral practice and as a high moral ideal" occurs most clearly in the description of the Jewish martyrs of 4 Maccabees, which is, in his view, the literary work most responsible for the growth of the suffering self as an ideal (Shaw, "Body," 278). Nevertheless, Shaw declines to distinguish between the two kinds of feminized rhetoric that these late classical patience works (to his mind) reveal. For instance, he attributes the focus on Blandina's suffering in the passio of the martyrs of Vienne and Gaul to the subsequent development of sheer endurance as an identifying value, and suggests that this growth stems from figures such as the mother in 2 Maccabees. But this mother and Blandina represent feminist rhetoric in entirely different ways. The motherhood of the former—apparently, not an independent figure in the way that Blandina seems to be—is all important. The mother's familial relationship to the seven men is the sole aspect that sets her at odds with the Roman authorities. In 4 Maccabees, the brothers are introduced as being "handsome, modest, noble, and accomplished in every way." The Jewish mother's only attribute at her introduction is that she is "aged" (4 Maccabees 8:3).

Her role is limited to encouraging her children in "the language of their fathers" (an inheritance from men) to hold fast to their beliefs and to one another, even though Antiochus, the Roman authority figure, has threatened them with torture if they do not eat pork, an act that would break their religious laws (2 Maccabees 7:21–22). The mother is singled out as "especially admirable and worthy of honorable memory. Though she saw her seven sons perish within a single day, she bore it with good courage because of her hope in the lord" (2 Maccabees 7:20). But her courage is not bravery in the face of threats or action directed against herself, as courage (particularly physical courage) is usually defined. The account goes on to imply that courage is a masculine virtue, which she only takes on by observing male examples of it: "she fired her woman's reasoning with a man's courage" (7:21).

While the narrative undoubtedly singles the mother out as heroic, there are many junctures of 2 Maccabees that slight her status, when no such slighting occurs in Blandina's passio. Blandina certainly receives apparent criticism as well as praise, but it is easy to argue in her case that any negative phrases appear precisely so that her ultimate achievement may come over as even greater than it normally would. To label her as "tiny, weak, and insignificant" (Musurillo, ed., 75), for instance, is a rhetorical stratagem that is meant to defeat readers' expectations at her triumph and thus intensify the impact of these events. The undercutting of the mother has a different effect. She, for instance, rather unexpectedly, denies any real role in the creation of her sons and attributes their creation to (the male) God. She says to them "'I do not know how you came into being in my womb. It was not I who gave you life and breath'" (2 Maccabees 7:22).[77] The most obvious slighting occurs when one compares the episode of the mother and her sons to the one just previous in 2 Maccabees, an account of the torture and death of Eleazar, a scribe. He is "forced to open his mouth to eat swine's flesh." He spits the meat out and goes "to the rack of his own accord" (6:18–20). Then, invited by sympathetic authorities to eat meat that looks like pork but is not, so that Eleazar could satisfy the demands of the higher authorities through a pretense of compliance, he refuses, declaring that others would be led astray by his example (6:24–28). The persecutors ask the Jewish mother, in parallel fashion, to try to persuade her youngest and last remaining son to give in to their demands. The king will reward him handsomely. She seems to accede to Antiochus's wishes when she begins speaking to the boy in Hebrew. Of course, she takes the opportunity to disparage the king and to remind her son that she carried him in her womb and reared him: a forceful repudiation of the persecutor's requests and promises. However, through the very act of speaking to the boy privately, she consents to pretend in a way that Eleazar refused to do. Any Hebrew speaker would be able to detect her ruse, but Antiochus and many of the other witnesses presumably think that she is performing as he asks. Moreover, the boy cuts off her speech—silencing her and implying that her words do not matter to him—in order to make his own declarations to Antiochus (7:25–29). His interruption again implies that she is doing what the persecutor wants because witnesses might assume, if they cannot hear or understand what she says, that the son interrupts the mother out of impatience with arguments that run contrary to his belief. In any case, the contradictory evaluations of Blandina and the mother help to prove that the primary texts of patience literature reflect the inevitable confusion and contradictions concerning the establishment of any virtue, particularly one of a more abstract nature such as patience.

The most significant difference between the accounts of Blandina and the mother of the seven brothers is that, although the latter is executed after her sons, she is left untortured, as if her body were of different status from those of her boys or of the later female martyrs. Perhaps, it is sacrosanct after a fashion (4 Maccabees 17:1). Her suffering, then, cannot be equal to the men's. The narrative describes it as the watching of her children being tortured—undeniably a horrifying mental trial, but not a physical one (2 Maccabees 7:30–38, 41). In contrast, torments that are similar to those inflicted upon the male martyrs are visited upon Blandina's body: "the scourges, the animals, and the hot griddle" (Musurillo, ed., 79). Such physical equality between the genders is absent from 2 and 4 Maccabees. So, if one follows Shaw in interpreting 4 Maccabees as "accept[ing] the torture of the human body as *the* paradigm of the problem of suffering and the definition of the self," with the body playing a crucial part in this observation, then women are left out of his definition, because no woman is tortured physically in either account of these Jewish martyrs ("Body," 288, 299–306). One could then see the stories of Blandina and the mother of the seven brothers as parallel but divergent. Where one could interpret the mother as *only* a mother in her narrative, so that her role is gradually reduced by the death of each son until, with the death of the last, she amounts to nothing and therefore might as well die, Blandina's role and power, despite the fact that she is a mere slave, grow with each successive torment until she becomes a metaphorical mother to her fellow Christians and therefore can be compared to the mother of 2 Maccabees. The narrative hints at this comparison when Blandina is paired with a "boy of fifteen named Ponticus" at her last appearance in the arena. The crowd has "little pity for the child's age and no respect for the woman" (Musurillo, ed., 79), as if childhood and being female were comparable, though this connection is soon belied by the events. Then the comparison is made explicit: "like a noble mother encouraging her children, [Blandina] sent [fellow martyrs] before her in triumph to the King, and then, after duplicating in her own body all her children's sufferings, she hastened to rejoin them" (79). She absorbs the tradition of the mother. Furthermore, the equal sharing of her fate with male martyrs means that she is included in a history that is otherwise dominated by men. The mother is not included in the same way. The rhetorical unanimity of the seven sons is rendered clearly when they speak in chorus (2 Maccabees 8:29). Their mother does not join this chorus. And, in this account, the physicality of the rhetoric comes over as even more explicitly masculine than that of 2 Maccabees, for one of the brothers calls upon the sympathy of the king, asking him to identify with other men: "As a man, were you not ashamed, you most savage beast, to cut out the tongues of men who have feelings like yours and are made of the same elements as you?" (4 Maccabees 12:13). The mention of these "elements" heightens the connection between tongue-severing and castration. The mother, with her female body, cannot identify with a man and must be excluded from such a discussion. 4 Maccabees even hints at a moral imperative that her body be treated differently from any male one: "Some of the guards said that when she also was about to be seized and put to death she threw herself into the flames so that no one might touch her body" (17:1).

The Lioness

This exclusion of the mother from "bodily rhetoric" in 2 and 4 Maccabees is remarkable because there is an analogous text that pointedly includes a woman in just such a discussion. In Pausanias's *Arcadia* and Pliny the Elder's *Naturalis historia*, Tertullian finds the story of an "Athenian courtesan," who is tortured so that she might reveal the whereabouts of the hiding place of two male "conspirators."[78] Tertullian finds her behavior under duress so admirable that he singles her out in his *Apologeticum* as one of the famous precursors of the Christian martyrs: *carnifice iam fatigato postremo linguam suam comesam in faciem tyranni saeuientis exspuit, ut expelleret et uocem, ne coniuratos confiteri posset, etiam si uicta uoluisset* [when her executioner was at length weary, (she) bit off her own tongue and spit it into the face of the raging tyrant, that she might thereby spit out her voice, too, and not be able to confess the names of the conspirators, even if she should want to].[79] Pliny also admires her, calling her the most renowned of women: *clarissimum in feminis* (see Shaw, "Body," 276, n. 19),[80] and her story is later appropriated into several martyrdoms, for instance, Christina's, where the saint retains the ability to speak though she spits out her tongue and blinds her persecutor (*LA*, 420).[81]

On the one hand, this woman, named Leaena in Tertullian's sources, seems conventionalized by male attitudes. In the story as a whole, she would be a peripheral character compared to the male conspirators who partake in the principal events. She is a prostitute, and her torment is thus an overt and physical articulation of her image, profession, and livelihood.[82] All of these are forced upon her by her male-centered society and by men in general, who now attack her body directly as if she were a slave. By spitting "out her voice" Leaena silences herself, so the torture and her self-mutilation amount to in some ways a continuation of the male language and actions that are being organized against her. In fact, this torture and her own participation in it connect with ideas from Foucault and Roland Barthes that spell out the dominant, sadistic, masculinist values of her society: by biting out her tongue, she merely confirms her status. "The slave is one who has his tongue cut off," as Barthes says.[83] She also seems to lack the essential heroic attribute that Shaw attributes to the martyrs in general: "having ... control over one's own body enables the tortured to be silent, to speak through their bodies, and thus *not* to speak the required words" ("Body," 278), because Leaena bites out her tongue due to fear that she might not be able to withstand her trials—at least, Tertullian implies this motive with his phrase "even if she should want to."[84] More generally, her cause is personal loyalty, so her patience is that of the body only: *patientia corporis* (see Shaw, "Body," 276, n. 19) as opposed to the more intellectualized virtue of patience that Cicero and Tertullian, in their very different ways, describe and declare as more valuable than physical patience.[85] And, perhaps most significantly, she performs her deeds in order to try to save the lives of two men, as if her life and body were less important than theirs. Tertullian does not even name her, a paradoxical omission when she is supposedly famous.

On the other hand, Leaena's eulogizers praise her actions for their bravery. Pausanias notes that her name means "lioness" and that a bronze statue of a lioness was erected in her memory.[86] Tertullian acclaims the severing of her tongue as a courageous deed. Significantly, it is absent from the catalog of typical heroic deeds of daring, perhaps because it suggests self-castration. The seven brothers of 2 and 4 Maccabees do not bite off their tongues, which are severed by torturers. Leaena's act then comes across as individually heroic, yet also intrinsically female. She uses part of her body as both a kind of speech and as a kind of last-ditch physical assault, which not only provides a subversive commentary on typically male ideas of speech as battle and vice versa, but also fits in very well with Hélène Cixous's call to women to write with their bodies.[87] Though Leaena's speech-act is by definition her final speech, it represents political power in that it denies the men what they want to hear, while it is also certainly a kind of heroic statement—in some ways a statement par excellence. For instance, it takes place at the climax of the narrative and it is both oral and literate: the spitting is, besides a new kind of speech, also an attempt to use blood from the tongue to "write" an account of herself upon her torturers' clothes and bodies in apposition to the "text" of her own mutilated body (see also Shaw, "Body," 306). So, Leaena's story could represent a brief and concentrated attempt for a woman's language to emerge outside of male structures and attitudes, whereas the treatment of the mother in 2 and 4 Maccabees, despite its focus on suffering, merely reiterates in the end how these male structures and attitudes assert and reassert themselves. Leaena's treatment also remains distinct from that of Blandina in her martyrology, and, despite the latter's apotheosis as a new version of the mother of seven sons, the placing of Blandina and the mother in the same literary tradition is so jarring that one wishes that Shaw had described the transition (if it exists) between texts such as 4 Maccabees and Blandina's story much more fully.

Women as the Inheritors of Job's Patience

In the Greek pseudoepigraphic text *The Testament of Job*, women are depicted as quintessential patience figures in a particularly authoritative way.[88] Job's daughters inherit from him three girdles that are emblematic of the patience that he has exhibited during his severe testing (46–47).[89] All three daughters, Hemera, Cassia, and Amaltheias-Keras, then demonstrate that they are conversant with God and his messengers, just as their father was. Upon donning their girdles, the women speak in their own highly individual languages (48–50), and become parties to a vision of their father's soul being transported to heaven, while their brothers are apparently excluded from these conversations and this vision (52). *The Testament of Job* does not appear to have been very influential, but the basic idea of women as inheritors of Job's patience occurs in the canonical Old Testament Book of Job when it names the daughters, praises them, and identifies them as inheritors alongside their (nameless) brothers: very unusual treatment of women for a biblical work. Many later patience works in turn connect the patience of a female figure to that of Job, as Chaucer's *Clerk's Tale* does (932–35; cf. *Wife of Bath's Tale*, lines 434–37).

Women as Heroes of Patience

In short, the first important observation concerning the history of patience literature is that when the earliest persecutions of Christians take place a virtually unprecedented mode of expression arises that unites endurance under torture with rhetoric from the traditions of heroism. The second is that, in a rare event for literature, women participate on an equal level with men in both the modes of expression and in the heroic rhetoric of these patience works. The subsequent developments in this proposed sequence are more difficult to construe, though they are discernible. Accounts like Eusebius's go on to make the fame of female figures from the early passios such as Blandina more or less immortal. Patience treatises, such as Tertullian's *de patientia* and *Apologeticum*, Augustine's *de patientia*, Basil's *Homilia in Psalmum LXI*, Cyprian's *de bono patientiae*, Gregory's *Regulae Pastoralis* and *Dialogia*, and other patristic works further contribute to the martyrs' cults, and to the growing celebrity of a particularly female kind of reputation.[90] At the height of the heroic history of gendered patience literature one may see in saints' lives women who attack and change traditional civic, moral, and intellectual authorities (*LA*, 32, 172, 173, 421, 444, 634), who debate with men concerning philosophical issues and win (420, 776, 790–92), and who revolt against traditional attitudes toward families, parental authority, marriage, and sexual practice (114, 136–37, 343, 771–72). Thus, medieval literature records a brief acknowledgment of women's power and expression in early martyrologies, particularly through fame for pseudoheroic deeds. As the patience genre develops and moves farther away from the martyrs' trials, other early saints' lives, and the Greek romances however, the attitudes toward the fame of women and toward supposedly feminine virtues (such as patience) evolve. A focus on suffering per se emerges at the expense of other motifs, separating female heroes of patience works from male ones. The accomplishments of women become more artificial, more static, and their earthly rewards dwindle. Patience literature begins to focus on the suffering of, for example, Margery Kempe, as opposed to the learning and debating power of, for example, Catherine of Alexandria. The genre ends up supporting, just like most existing cultural material does, the view that women should be kept outside of conventional learning; the genre ends up supporting, just like most cultural material does, female victim-status by narrating examples of it repeatedly.[91]

The Mechanics of the Gendered Patience Narrative

Besides the general evolution of patience works toward narratives concerning more and more passive figures who endure more and more incredible and spectacular tortures, further changes in the patience narrative take place during its early stages. In order to construct a chart of these changes, I have consulted the generic divisions of earlier critics, but the existing breakdowns of early patience works (more often than not saints' lives) into a number of typical elements are now out of date because critical concerns have inevitably shifted. More recent scholars are less interested than earlier ones in trying to separate fact from fiction in the canon of martyrs and their *acta*, a task now recognized as impossible. Also, divisions between descriptors such as "court records," "narratives," and "visions" seem dubious, and several classifications of elements have declined in their usefulness (Musurillo, lii–liii). For instance, it is preferable to call the "court record" aspect of patience works the "Dialogue Portion." One cannot presume that a judicial hearing in a passio is based on an actual court record. And, of course, one needs to include secular patience works along with saints' lives in any consideration of the programmatic aspects of patience literature.

Major Division in Examples of Patience Narratives

Dialogue Portion. A dialogue between the protagonist and his or her persecutors is standard. Its purpose is to establish the victim's moral strength and to affirm the inevitability of his or her suffering. A secondary purpose that often occurs is to reveal or further reveal the negative characters of the persecutors (Musurillo, ed., 54–55, 66–67, etc.). For the earliest examples of patience literature, and particularly the accounts of martyrs, this Portion seems to have been more important that the Suffering Portion, which was often outlined much more briefly than the saint's conversations with his or her persecutors (42–47, 54–61, etc.). In early examples of secular patience literature, such as the Greek romances, Dialogues Portions typically concern love and marriage arrangements (Achilles Tatius 1.6.21, 2.11.75). Patience narratives normally proceed with at least one Dialogue Portion preceding at least one Suffering Portion. The two Portions often contain elements that parallel or refer to one another.

Suffering Portion: *hypomonê*. This is the only essential element of an example of patience literature. *Hypomonê* is detailed above (16-17).

Minor Divisions in Examples of Patience Narratives

Break with Authority. Almost all examples of patience literature include some justification for the suffering of the protagonist. Typically, he or she runs foul of a mistaken and/or unjust authority, for example, civil authorities or (more typically in examples of secular patience literature) parents (Achilles Tatius 2.12.79). The Break often happens before the action of the patience narrative has started and often helps to establish a decidedly legalistic tone within the Dialogue Portion (6.20.343; *LA*, 30,

113–14, 771–72, etc.). In some of the secular patience works, the Break seems very artificial, as for example, when pirates appear and kidnap the protagonist.[92]

Search. Not an essential part of any patience narrative, this element is more common in secular patience literature than in sacred (Achilles Tatius 5.23.289, 6.10.325). It is one of the few elements that involves shifts in location for the protagonist, and where such shifts are integral to the narrative. The major example is Polycarp (Musurillo, ed., 4–9). The Search element is more likely to apply to male protagonists, because women are typically discovered in their homes, whereas men habituate (their) public spaces. Nevertheless, female protagonists in the Greek romances travel (Longus 2.22.96–97, 2.25.102–03).

(Belief) Identification. The Dialogue Portion nearly always results in a statement of identification from the protagonists. For hagiography, this statement is an unequivocal expression of belief, but it only needs to be a (re)indication of the protagonist's Break with Authority, as when the heroine in the Greek romance *The Adventures of Leucippe and Clitophon* says "here is my body, burn it" (Achilles Tatius, 6.21.345; Shaw, "Body," 271). Often the Identification contains two kinds of statements: a (Belief) Identification and an urging of the "judge to perform his duty" (Musurillo, lii, and ed., 340–41). In the passios, many of the victims, male and female, seem to refer to Acts 4:24 (Musurillo, lii, and ed., 90–91, 146–47, etc.). They often go on to proselytize, an extension of their Belief Identification.

Martyrdom. Not an essential element. In examples of secular patience narratives, the figure of suffering usually lives (Longus 2.30.108–09). In the passios, a violent death is just about inevitable.

Minor Divisions That Occur in Later Examples of Patience Literature

Growing Complexity. The genre becomes a more and more literary one, so that conventions and traditions become more ingrained than previously. As a genre develops, its authors play with its elements more elaborately. Artificiality, abstraction, and self-consciousness increase. See the *Lives* in the *Legenda Aurea*, for example Cecilia, who sends her solitary expression up to heaven with the music in church (*LA*, 771–72).

Multiplication of Suffering. The focus of (really the justification for) the patience narrative becomes *hypomonê*, at the expense of other elements, such as the Search and even the entire Dialogue Portion.

Gendering. The suffering tends to be applied more to women than to men. Examples are Cecilia, Katherine of Alexandria, Lucy, Agatha, and Agnes. The perfect example of explicit gendering is the introduction of the brothel into the typical patience narrative. It is impossible to think of a man in the same situation; nor does the chastity of a man typically figure in the authority's torture of a male protagonist in the way that it does for a female one (*LA*, 94, 350). The brothel appears very early (in the passio of Irenê, Musurillo, ed., 288–91) and soon became commonplace. Most of the lives of famous female martyrs contain an attack on their chastity, frequently in a brothel. For examples, see the *Lives* of Lucy, Agatha, Agnes, and Cecilia.

By Ways. The intrusion of new places into patience works concerning women is remarkable. The typical patience narrative only requires two locations: the place of the Dialogue(s) Portion(s) and the place of the Suffering(s). These two can be the same place and often are. Both have judicial functions and atmospheres.[93]

The most important example of a new place that intrudes into gendered patience narratives is the brothel (Musurillo, ed., 288–91), but there are others. In *The Martyrdom of Saints Agapê, Irenê, and Chionê at Saloniki*, Irenê and the women with her escape to a high mountain before their capture (280–81). In the Greek romances, female protagonists are often removed to distant places (Achilles Tatius 6.4.311, 6.9.321). At Agatha's tomb, Lucy and her mother congregate in a kind of all-female society, inheriting their wisdom from a female saint (*LA*, 30). Cecilia and others negotiate their marriage status and chastity in their private chambers (318–19; *The Clerk's Tale*, line 330).[94]

Women's Space

In the ensuing chapters, I explain this general sequence in a more particular fashion through (in part) a focus on connections between conceptions of space and feminine expression. As soon as the possibility of a feminine language of endurance first appears, the possibility of an exclusively feminine space appears as well. In fact, one may characterize the chronology of gendered patience literature as

1. the emergence of feminine space,
2. the domestification of this space, and
3. the displacement of this feminine space into what can only be described as the Shrine.

Most obviously, each of the early martyrs' passios is a specifically made (or remade) obverse of the classical idea of space as a representation of Rome's imperial state and empire. If Rome and its public arenas represent (among other things) the Greek athletic ideals and militarism taken to a kind of apotheosis—as for many, including the Romans themselves, they did—then the martyrs usurp the political space of the arena by triumphing in it. The opening of "The Martyrs of Lyon and Vienne" points to another reason that images of space might appear in the passios. It prefaces its narrative with "we [Christians] were not only shut out of our houses, the baths, and the public square, but they [the pagans] forbade any of us to be seen in any place whatsoever" (Musurillo, ed., 63). In the face of this perception of complete denial of space to the persecuted Christians, it is not surprising that they then—metaphorically and in extremis—invent their own. For instance, one of the miracles of Polycarp's martyrdom by fire is that "the flames, bellying out like a ship's sail in the wind, formed into the shape of a vault and thus surrounded the martyr's body as with a wall," so that the very substance of his torture turns into a seemingly protective force, providing Polycarp with a space of his own and partially obscuring the spectacle that his execution is designed to represent (15). The final events of Blandina's martyrdom help to define the idea of new spaces even more clearly: "After the scourges, the animals, and the hot griddle, she was at last tossed into a net and exposed to a bull" (79). Her final space has sometimes been translated as "a basket."[95] More likely, she was stripped before going into the arena and then wrapped in a kind of netting which was the usual garment, both limiting and diaphanous (and thus spectacle-inviting), for women condemned to be thrown to the beasts. This mode of execution dress was reserved for women convicted of adultery and was meant to shame them in public, according to Shaw. But this netting is remarkable for being a garment associated with women only, and it therefore reemphasizes Blandina's femaleness at the climax of the narrative.[96] The possible translation "basket" also suggests a pun on the word $\gamma \upsilon \rho \gamma \alpha \theta \grave{o} \nu$ that would hint at the kinds of domestic tasks that a bondwoman like Blandina would typically perform in late antiquity.[97] Thus her garb, like the fire in Polycarp's story, stakes out a kind of individual, defining space for her. Of course, such metaphorical spaces for the martyrs could be interpreted as representations of a new (Christian) community (as Perkins notes) and as demonstrations of the connections that Jacques Lacan makes between language, "the locus of the Other," and the gaze.[98] More generally, when Elizabeth D. Kirk notes that the concept of patience is "redefined" in later medieval literature into "a new sense of man's place in a theocentric universe," she is observing a change that had already taken place (or at least been foreshadowed) much earlier.[99]

Feminist Methodology

The current backlash against feminism, particularly the backlash against *l'écriture féminine*, fits with the kind of events I see as happening during the gendering of medieval patience literature. When Cixous calls for a kind of writing that would be exclusively feminine, she would seem to sequester any literature previous to the writing of "The Laugh of the Medusa" from any newly feminine and revolutionary literary tradition. In other words, feminist studies of any age earlier than the twentieth century (some would say earlier than right now) "are haunted by a ... sense of the belatedness of their work."[100] *L'écriture féminine* can only begin once Cixous or another person has proposed the idea, and she seems to allow for only two contradictory positions: the creation of a new, female language at the present moment, or a fall back into a male, sexist language. Her concept cannot work in retrospect, and many would argue that it is essentialist, that its efficacy is questionable because its call has gone largely unanswered—that it is ephemeral and stale.[101] Meanwhile, Sheila Delany and others have rightly chastised critics who propose the existence of protofeminist streams of literature that would occur parallel to the traditional literary canon. Such proposals are far too idealistic.[102] No composition can exist outside of its context, and one must conclude (gloomily) that the traditional literary and intellectual canon is irrevocably sexist and hence deaf to Cixous's call.

Yet, if *l'écriture féminine* is essentialist, then patriarchy (a ludicrously simplistic term) is even more so. It is idle to define and hence dismiss any society as simply, monolithically patriarchal. For instance, critics often tend to interpret the objectification of women as a foregone conclusion in any works earlier than the twentieth century. Objectification is, however, both constitutive and reactive. Enormously complex, it continually changes into highly individual forms, which in turn tend to hide its baselessness. For instance, the end of Chaucer's *Clerk's Tale* in itself contains several objectifications of Grisilde, and many critics have remarked upon their complexity and their alienating effects, almost as if one were viewing the character of Grisilde through a kaleidoscope.[103] More generally, the objectification of women plays a part in individual societies' compulsive and obsessive debates concerning masculinities and femininities, when scholars cannot assume that such debates, especially during earlier periods such as the Middle Ages, are anywhere near stable, let alone complete. Meanwhile feminist critics can continue to expose, analyze, and interpret as protofeminist any of the inevitable frictions that occur during the many, successive reobjectifications of women down through literary history.

If patriarchy is merely a debate, then Elizabeth A. Castelli is justified in arguing that instances of profeminism are embedded in examples of medieval literature, even if sweeping feminist social movements or separate but equal textual traditions probably are not.[104] In other words, despite

Cixous's focus on the immediate moment as the obvious rallying point for her call for women's writing, the egalitarian idea behind this call has always existed, and occasionally it becomes overt or gains popular support. If these glimpses of egalitarian ideals, these brief engagements, these empathetic moments, arise from collapse-of-classes fantasies, as they certainly seem to do in early Christianity—and become manifest in events such as the exaltation of patience and the association of patience with God—then one can argue that *l'écriture féminine* is always immanent in language and in the literary canon because egalitarian ideas, once raised, can only be suppressed and ignored through deliberate and politically guilt-ridden acts of the will. The reassertion of masculinist traditions after such engagements is then a repression and hence a displacing of egalitarianism—of *l'écriture féminine*—into the "irruption of desire" inherent in all language, if one may adjust Derrida's theory of desire in language slightly.[105] Indeed, much analogous rearticulation and reassertion of the ethical aspects of language occurs in the work of Emmanuel Levinas.[106]

Cixous's (re)discovery, then, is not so much of *l'écriture féminine* but of a kind of moral amnesia and false consciousness that persist from the earliest historical periods through to now. Hagiography demonstrates the idea of moral amnesia very well through the almost obsessive neglect of such a significant genre by general reading audiences, and by, until recently, literary studies. In the traditional literary canon, saints' lives barely exist as representative works. The skewing of the canon toward ever more recent periods has deepened the neglect despite the recently increasing critical interest in hagiography. In the past, the prevailing view was that saints' lives failed to meet the canon's originality requirement; instead they typically seem to repeat the same narrative material, with slight variations, over and over.[107] But this repetition syndrome is not tautological. Collections of saints' lives obsessively announce and reannounce the passios' assertions of the breakdown of social distinctions, and hence continually rehearse specific equity issues. Moreover, such announcements gained authority in the late classical period by echoing scriptural passages and by seeming to fulfill predictions of the early Christian apologists. As the lives of the saints became contemplative texts with the approval of church authorities, the ideals in them (including egalitarianism) begin to be affected by their repetition. Familiar and memorable as narratives, the saints' lives became part of day-to-day activities and seasonal rituals, so that hagiography makes up, as any literary history of the Middle Ages will attest, a dominant discourse of the age, appearing in rituals, sermons, and calendars, with Jacobus's *Legenda Aurea* in all of its manuscript and printed versions the most widely read exemplar of patience works and one of the most influential compositions in Western literary history.[108]

Counterfeit Consciousness

However, patience literature can also be accused of complicity in a prevailing atmosphere of false consciousness concerning women in the Christian west: while advocating a release of women from traditional roles and rules of control, any sensible Christian accepts that worldly inequities are inevitable in a fallen world.[109] Women, like slaves, must resign themselves to taking comfort in the prospect of heaven, while free men can retain their "heroism" and wider social and expressive opportunities.[110] Yet, the obsessive repetition of the content of saints' lives belies the total dominance of this kind of consciousness. Repetition occurs precisely because egalitarian principles have been announced in these works but not enacted, exactly in the way that Cixous's principles of *l'écriture féminine* have been announced but not enacted.[111] Once society has heard of egalitarianism and spurned it through ongoing acts of the will, through reinstatement of the logic-defying commonalities of power, the ideal develops into a syndrome. It must reappear again and again. Then one may define the obsessive repetition and sidelining of such ideas—the combination of moral amnesia with repetition syndrome—as examples not of false consciousness but of counterfeit consciousness: covert and overt attempts to repress empathy and egalitarianism through constantly embedding an empathetic and egalitarian point of view, which is never acted upon, into the fabric of literary works and into the architecture of intellectual history. Counterfeit consciousness as a critical concept, then, begins with the arrival of false consciousness: the repressing assumption that certain inequities are justifiable or at least inevitable. Counterfeit consciousness is the duplication and reduplication of false consciousness concerning the genders in cultural material. As patience figures start to feature in ever more standardized narratives and images, so that the composers of these figures seem to be merely copying from one another in a mechanical fashion, these figures nevertheless retain their status as witnesses of the inequality that results when a virtue like patience is attributed to women more often than men.

Of course, inequality is embedded in the very idea of reduplication, of counterfeiting. Examples of this kind of inequity-within-reduplication occur right at the moment of the gendering of patience literature: in the martyrdom of Irenê, usually dated about 304, she is sentenced "to be placed naked in the brothel," a torture unthinkable for a man (Musurillo, ed., 291). This kind of sex-distinguishing punishment demonstrates that the gendering of patience literature occurs because "the feminine comes to represent the arena over which ... master-narratives have lost control" during the historical and cultural revolutions of late antiquity.[112] Such distinctions then become an almost inevitable feature of the later, more literary, and very popular passios that concern women, for instance, Lucy and Cecilia. Inequality between the sexes is also (re)asserted when, in most of the more literary lives of female martyrs, legal proceedings that take place in order to establish belief—the essential legal issue of almost every passio—become mixed in with marriage negotiations (LA, 27–28, 318–19).

Lucy and Cecilia represent and help to substantiate awareness of the inequities between men and women. Lucy's story begins in an exclusively female society that involves inherited traditions and values. She takes her mother to the tomb of Saint Agatha, an earlier female martyr, so that her mother's bleeding may be cured (27–28). This bleeding is an obvious image of the passing on of inherently female knowledge and progeny, which also, the story implies, comes from the previous martyr's blood. Cecilia, in the middle of her anxiety about her upcoming marriage, expresses herself in her own, exclusive kind of musical language, reminiscent of the ecstatic languages of Job's daughters in *The Testament of Job* (LA, 771–72). Then, reduplication develops through the Middle Ages as artworks and other representations of patience figures start to gain as much currency, popularity, and "efficacy" for audiences' desires as the patience figures themselves. Counterfeiting occurs to the extent that saints and other patience figures are often subsumed into images, relics, and other aspects of their cults.

The fact that a pool of ideas has been flooded by a mass-produced and empty currency (the obsessive repetition of egalitarian ideas, typically displaced into ideals such as heaven, a perfect world, the coming revolution, the next generation, or the university classroom) does not mean that the original currency has ceased to exist, though, of course, it has been altered through being imitated. It becomes an aspect of hegemony with no force—a haunting hegemony. Far from merely reemphasizing the inequities of a patriarchal age, the repetition of egalitarian rhetoric in the saints' lives marks "a historical crisis in the conceptuality of ... [wo]man as an *object* of regulatory power, as the subject of ... representation." Meanwhile, "only *within* the practices of repetitive signifying [does] a subversion of identity become ... possible."[113]

The repetition of hagiographical material from one composition to another is not then entirely negative. Reasons have been offered in the past for this repetition, suggesting an awareness by medieval authors that such "plagiarism" looked suspicious to certain readers, and any genre that features extensive, wholesale repetition of material can be accused of paralysis.[114] Critics have often judged saints' lives to be backward, tedious, naïve, and insignificant precisely because of this repeated material.[115]

Indeed scholars have persisted in branding the entire medieval era with similar accusations throughout much of its critical history.[116] However, one might describe what happens between one saint's life and another as (more specifically) mimicry rather than repetition: "ever ylike newe" as Chaucer describes worshipful love in *The Legend of Good Women* (F 56). For example, Gregory the Great notes a major change in the content of hagiography once the period of Christian martyrs has largely moved on from depictions of blood martyrdom to other modes. Later saints' stories reiterate the language and ideas of the early passios, but this repetition, as Gregory acknowledges, cannot be absolute and complete because of inevitable changes in historical context and circumstances.[117] Repetition must change to mimicry, "almost the same, but not quite"; must gain a certain measure of (among other things) irony. A mimicked act or work would seem to be non- or even anticreative, but the actions and effects of such mimicry, as Homi K. Bhabha argues, are instead ambivalent: "mimicry is ... the sign of a double articulation; a complex strategy of reform, regulation, and discipline."[118] The articulation is double, for instance, in the way that mimicry both affirms history by reiterating it, and wishes to annihilate history by drawing attention to its fundamental inequities. For instance, "the parodic repetition of gender exposes ... the illusion of gender identity as an intractable depth and inner substance."[119]

The Immovable Saint Lucy

If one takes the habit in saints' lives of mimicking one another as a motif, of which many hagiographers are perfectly conscious, then one may observe significant connections between the form and content of these works. For instance, hagiographers certainly seem to be aware that many saints, and particularly female saints, are monolithic and marmoreal in terms of their characterizations. This example occurs in Jacobus de Voragine's *Legenda Aurea* (c. 1260):

> Tunc Paschasius lenones fecit venire, dicen iis: invitate ad eam omnem populum et tamdiu illudatur, donec mortua nuntietur. Volentes autem eam trahere, tanto pondere spiritus sanctus eam fixit, ut omnino eam movere nequirent. Fecitque Paschasius mille viros accedere et manus ejus et pedes ligare, sed eam nullatenus poterant movere; tunc et cum viris mille paria boum adhibuit; sed tamen virgo domini immobilis permansit. (*LA*, 31)[120]

> Then Paschasius summoned procurers and said to them: "Invite a crowd to take their pleasure with this woman [Saint Lucy], and let them abuse her until she is dead." But when they tried to carry her off, the Holy Spirit fixed her in place so firmly that they could not move her. Paschasius called

in a thousand men and had her hands and feet bound, but still they could not lift her. He sent for a thousand yoke of oxen: the Lord's holy virgin could not be moved.[121]

The Roman authorities make further efforts to shift Lucy, and then intensify the violent attacks upon her body, but she remains fixed to the same spot. She is probably the most extreme example in the saints' lives of a martyr who brings his or her persecutors to a state of futility of further action, following Blandina's example (Musurillo, ed., 67). Most obviously, such immovability represents an acknowledgment that Christian beliefs and pagan Roman beliefs are mutually exclusive and must come to an impasse, and, equally obviously, such an image represents the saint's firmness of purpose. But these episodes of stasis also occur in early examples of secular patience literature (Achilles Tatius 3.15.167); furthermore, they connect with the egalitarian rhetoric of the first passios. For instance, once Blandina has driven her torturers to exhaustion, the renewal of interrogations causes her to say again "I am a Christian." Her fellow-martyr Sanctus then follows her into the arena and replies to the question of whether or not he is a slave or freeman with the identical answer, "I am a Christian," which he then repeats "again and again" (69). The egalitarian statements of Tertullian and the apostle Paul thus become part of the hagiographical motif of stasis joined with repetition, as if such mimicry is self-conscious, as if the hagiographers are aware that egalitarian attitudes (among other aspects of Christianity, of course) cause the mutual paralysis that seems to arise when Christians confront persecution. Lucy herself seems to hint at this self-consciousness about mimicry (doubling) when she answers Paschasius's threat of removing her to the brothel with *castitatis mihi duplicabitur ad coronam*, "my chastity will be doubled and the crown will be mine" (*LA*, 31; trans., 28).[122]

The stasis motif is more common in women's passios than in men's (cf. Musurillo, ed., 9, 11, 13, 17; *LA*, 293, 578, 621). "As a genre, in other words, the narrative of the virgin martyr becomes purely literary earlier than almost any other form of hagiography," as Maud McInerney observes.[123] One may then see Lucy's miraculous immovability as a symbol of lack of movement, not only because she represents convention within a literary genre, but also because she represents the egalitarian ideals of the early saints' lives: she is a dead weight in that her characterization varies little from that of the earlier Christian martyrs, in that she is no easier to understand or identify with than they are, and in that her life is merely a repetition of material that the vast majority of her audience must already know. Lucy can only attain authority through becoming, like Grisilde, the equivalent of a stone wall. But she also embodies the strongly profeminine and generally egalitarian attitudes on view in the early passios and early apologetic works when she maintains control over the space that she occupies, which eventually becomes a church dedicated to her. Then she explicitly usurps the power of the pagan Roman authorities through her speeches and actions as well as her stasis. She declares: *de regno suo Dyocletiano expulso ... ego civitati Syracusanae concessa sum interventrix* (*LA*, 32) [(the emperor) Diocletian has been driven from the throne ... I am given to the city of Syracusa as mediatrix (1.29)]. Clearly the mimicry in the *Passion of Lucy*, just like colonial mimicry, "poses an immanent threat to both 'normalized' knowledges and disciplinary powers," such as governmental and ecclesiastical structures. It thus quashes the accusation that it is non- or anticreative.[124] The repetition syndrome in saints' lives is not a benign and pointless "tape loop." It is instead a pattern of counterfeit consciousness that must occur if creative processes, for example, subsequent engagements with egalitarianism, are going eventually to occur. It is somewhat "playful repetition" replete with "reflexivity."[125] The pattern is frequent in writing by both men and women. For instance, the maiden in the Middle English *Pearl* is frozen at a virginal age and obsessively idealized, whereupon she becomes almost undistinguishable from 144,000 others during a vision of heavenly Jerusalem. Queen Heurodis in the Middle English *Sir Orfeo* is paralyzed in the exact position in which she was abducted by a fairy king, under a tree, but nevertheless appears again as part of this king's traveling retinue of 60 nearly identical women.[126]

Female writers typically dispense with the counterfeiting, but not the paralysis. Julian of Norwich begins her visions only when her illness causes her to be paralyzed from the waist down, and Margery Kempe has her first vision only once she has been put in a straitjacket. In subsequent paroxysms of ecstasy, Margery falls to the floor and loses control over her movements.[127] Here, then, is the ghostly tradition of women's writing running parallel to men's: not an alternate reality, an alternate canon, or an alternate intellectual history, it is instead best described as a phantom inheritance. Barred from gaining any substantial benefits in and from the mainstream, traditional, and canonical activities of their societies, women, for example, Job's daughters in *The Testament of Job*, occasionally receive emblems of their participation in such benefits. But these emblems, even at their most consequential, amount to only a disquieting double vision of the traditional literary and intellectual canon, at once an acknowledgment of this canon's inequities and of its inevitable dominance. One may perceive the double vision of phantom inheritance and the distress it applies to the canon through encountering mimicry in examples of hagiography, where the reduction of colonial forces like

Rome to "partial presences" comes about because "the representation of difference"—in the case of the early saints' lives, the difference between men and women as well as that between races and classes—is "always also a problem of authority."[128]

Plan of the Book

This book includes six chapters in addition to this introduction. Chapter 1, concerning mainly *The Passion of Perpetua and Felicitas*, deals with the most obvious and extensive protofeminist case to be made for a late classical work, though this text has proved controversial with regard to its profeminine attitudes (or lack thereof). Chapter 2 deals with Lot's wife in her role as the patience figure par excellence, despite the fact that she disobeys God and therefore hardly qualifies for sainthood. Nevertheless, her monumental qualities demonstrate how patience comes to be associated particularly with women, as one may see in depictions of the transformation of Lot's wife into salt in Old English works. Not only do patience attributes extend to women who are not saints and who are treated pejoratively in medieval literature, but these attributes also extend to female figures largely outside of the traditional sacred texts. Chapter 3 examines the *Legenda Aurea* in order to assess the attributes of patience literature at its height. Chapter 4 examines Chrétien de Troyes's *Cligés* in order to interpret the torture of the empress Fénice as a remarkably profeminine example of secular patience literature. In Chapter 5, I return to Chaucer's *Clerk's Tale* and explore other works by him in order to put forward, so far as is possible, his interpretation of—and satire of—the patience literature genre.

One of the ways in which patience literature develops is that the maternal space that comes as an inheritance to female patience figures becomes increasingly concrete, so, lastly, in Chapter 6, I define female patience figures more specifically through situating them in their "ideal" medieval milieu by the time of the later Middle Ages (and when Margery Kempe is writing her *Book*): the Shrine—an important context largely ignored by previous critics. Laura Mulvey's proposal for the occurrence of a specific combination of voyeurism and self-absorption during the screening of a film for a typically male audience fits the combination of female votive object together with male divine authority that goes into the iconography of many medieval shrines and other devotional objects, of Chaucer's *Clerk's Tale*, and of Margery Kempe's *Book*.[129] However, the Shrine nevertheless allows for surprising innovations by female patience figures, for instance, Margery's combination of patience, expression, and subversive activity.

CHAPTER 1

THE FEMALE PATIENCE FIGURE AS SPEAKER

> Wommen ful trewe, ful goode, and vertuous,
> Witnesse on hem that dwelle in Cristes hous;
> With martirdom they preved hire constance.
>
> —Proserpine to Pluto in Chaucer's *The Merchants Tale*,
> from Fragment IV of Chaucer's *Canterbury Tales*,
> lines 2281–83

The *Passio Sanctarum Perpetuae et Felicitatis*

A text that has long been acknowledged as a questioner and destabilizer of male-traditional attitudes concerning gender and the political structures of the Roman Empire is the *Passio Sanctarum Perpetuae et Felicitatis* (*Passion of Saints Perpetua and Felicitas*). This text is probably from the late second century.[1] Critics have mostly focused on the apparently autobiographical account of a young North African noblewoman in the passio, Perpetua, who experiences trials and visions just before her martyrdom. If the account is genuine, these events are related in her own words—an attribution that the narrator insists upon: *haec ordinem totum martyrii sui iam hinc ipsa narrauit sicut conscriptum manu sua et suo sensu reliquit* (108) [Now from this point on the entire account of her ordeal is her own, according to her own ideas and in the way that she herself wrote it down (109)]. With the prison-diary section possibly representing an extremely rare example of feminine self-expression from this period, Perpetua's passion has attracted much critical attention.[2]

This saint's life is unusual in its treatment of a woman who dominates all the other characters in the passio. Perkins notes another distinguishing aspect of Perpetua: the heroines of Greek romance may appear admirable for their independence and will and even come over as "unruly" but they always return to a subservient position in their societies. Instead,

"Perpetua's place turns out to be very different from that assigned to her by society." She "climbs to heaven; she cures others' pain; she vanquishes a strong and evil male opponent in a triumphal contest." I would add that, unlike most other female patience figures, she engenders mimicry as opposed to reduplication. In sum, she "fashions a powerful conception of herself,"[3] and the passio's primary narrator collaborates in the forming of this conception. He introduces Perpetua by singling her out for special treatment. A group of Christian catechumens is arrested, *Inter hos et Vibia Perpetua, honeste nata, liberaliter instituta, matronaliter nupta* (108) [and with them Vibia Perpetua, a newly married woman of good family and upbringing (109)]. None of the other martyrs, including the other female one, Felicitas, or any of the other major characters in the narrative is introduced with such detailed information. The audience learns both of Perpetua's names and hears about her family background, current family situation, lineage, class, and upbringing: *habens patrem et matrem et fratres duos, alterum aeque catechumenum* (108) [Her mother and father were still alive and one of her two brothers was a catechumen like herself (109)]. The phrase *inter hos* [with them] places her apart from the other detainees (mostly men) listed before her, and suggests that her arrest is more significant than theirs. Felicitas's introduction, on the other hand, which appears after that of the first slave in the list of catechumens, makes her seem of secondary importance, and being female, therefore, is not the sole identifying factor that would make Perpetua stand out from the others.

Despite the prevailing interest in Perpetua's autobiography, more recent critics, rightly in my view, have examined the diary portion together with other material that makes up the rest of this relatively lengthy composition.[4] Erin Ronsse has noticed, for instance, that not only do Perpetua's autobiographical sections of the narrative reveal many links with one another, but these sections also have strong links (presumably fashioned by the redactor and general narrator) with the surrounding material, including a prologue, an account of a vision by one of the male martyrs in the group, Saturus, and an account of the tortures and executions of the martyrs.[5] Ronsse concentrates mainly on an examination of the passio's rhetoric. Several of the critics who, in contrast, have examined the entire work in terms of its intellectual history have found it, not surprisingly, revolutionary in its profeminine stance. For instance, Ross Shepard Kraemer associates the work with ideas of the Montanist sect, often called the "New Prophecy." She concludes that the *Passio Sanctarum Perpetuae et Felicitatis* provides evidence for women instituting their own religious traditions exclusive of the masculinist ones.[6] Of the passio's other feminist critics, Castelli comes closest to my views concerning what happens in it with regard to gender issues. She writes that saints' lives such as Perpetua's "do not simply rearticulate the hegemonic gendered order, nor do they simply deconstruct it; rather, they stretch its boundaries and, if only for a moment, call it into question—even if, ultimately, things return to 'normal.'" She suggests that, in this particular passio, "the battle is between Perpetua and the forces of evil *and* between competing understandings of gender."[7] Certainly this saint's life deals to a remarkable extent with the needs and wishes of an individual woman. For instance, several of the seemingly bizarre events in Perpetua's visions can be explained rather convincingly as expressions of her (sometimes stated) desires. For instance, Shaw calls them "empowering experiences."[8]

The passio has received critical attention from feminists because any attitudes that might be construed as contradictory to traditional masculinist attitudes would be remarkable in a late antique work. Yet my reading of the *Passio Sanctarum Perpetuae et Felicitatis* differs from others because of its focus on expressive power, a neglected topic in the study of Perpetua's story. For instance, although her infant son plays an important role in the narrative as a catalyst for her progress toward the abandoning of earthly concerns such as motherhood and other family connections and toward acceptance of her new role as a martyred Christian, he is also crucial as a locus of communication, if only because interaction of infants with their mothers is often described as communication at its most "natural," "instinctual," and ideal.[9] Although the narrative never depicts Perpetua talking to her child, one may assume that she does so and that part of the reason for her extreme anxiety when she is separated from him in prison comes from being unable to communicate with him (108). A bribe from two deacons to prison authorities then allows Perpetua and her fellow catechumens to move to a more congenial part of the prison where they may receive visitors. Her family brings the infant there and she nurses him, an act that the narrative parallels with two other deeds that are presumably almost entirely verbal. Perpetua speaks to her mother and comforts the brother who accompanies their mother on the visit: *adloquebar matrem et confortabam fratrem* (108). Her mother is otherwise absent from the narrative, which implies that Perpetua wants to emphasize a particularly feminine tradition of interaction at this juncture. Presumably, for instance, the two women share information about nursing and about trying to comfort children—tasks typical of women in traditional roles.

Besides the general and obvious benefits of communication, one may assume that Perpetua also gains, through contact with her baby, the more specific benefits that Kristeva ascribes to an exclusive language that can only exist between mother and child: "the first echolalias of infants," which are "rhythms and intonations" and "premonitory sign[s]" rather than references to "signified object[s]." Kristeva calls this "anterior" communication between mother and child the "semiotic" stage in language. She calls the later, conventional language of "phonemes, morphemes, lexemes, and sentences" the symbolic stage. In psychoanalytical terms, the semiotic stage is "anterior to naming, to the One, to the father," and therefore must be "maternally" as opposed to patriarchally "connoted."[10] It is significant, then, that the introduction to Perpetua's autobiography juxtaposes the information that she is nursing her baby with the record of her authorship of the text that follows:

> habens ... filium infantem ad ubera. Erat autem ipsa circiter annorum uiginti duo. Haec ordinem totum martyrii sui iam hinc ipsa narrauit sicut conscriptum manu sua et suo sensu reliquit. (108)
>
> [She was about twenty-two years old and had an infant son at the breast. (Now from this point on the entire account of her ordeal is her own, according to her own ideas and in the way that she herself wrote it down.)] (109)

At this point, my argument would be mere assumption based on the existence of an infant as a character in the narrative were there not several junctures in the passio where the idea of an exclusive, feminine language comes to the fore. In fact, a contest between male and female language figures in the first major episode in Perpetua's narrative, a disagreement between herself and her highly emotional father. As Ronsse notes, the dialogue is best understood as a "type of confrontational debate or trial scenario." Thus it links thematically to Perpetua's upcoming appearance before the Roman legal authorities. The unnamed father, representing those legal authorities, his own status as head of a family, and (more generally) the idea that "transcendental mastery over discourse is possible, but repressive," to use Kristeva's words, tries to persuade Perpetua to renounce her intention of becoming a Christian.[11] His daughter then asks him *uides uerbi gratia uas hoc iacens, urceolum siue aliud*? ["do you see this vase here, for example, or waterpot or whatever?"] and, when he says *video* ["I see it"], he declares his attachment to the masculinist world of naming, as Perpetua notes by telling him she could no more renounce being a Christian than the vase could *alio nomine uocari potest quam quod est* (108) ["be called by any other name than what it is"] (109). In other words, his "take" on the vase affirms the "objectification of the pure signifier," where the "symbolic ... as opposed to the semiotic is [an] inevitable attribute of meaning, sign, and the signified object for [one's] consciousness."[12] Perpetua's father, then, must lose the debate with his daughter because he (and perhaps, any man) cannot speak both languages, semiotic and symbolic, at once. The passio proves this inability through a verbal parallel. Perpetua's use of *uideo* at the start of each of her visions (110, 114, 116) recalls her father's use of the same word (108) when he demonstrates his literalist thinking with regard to the vase. Perpetua experiences visions just in the way that her unbelieving father perceives only the "real world."

The vase-debate demonstrates Perpetua's rejection of her father's systems of language, values, and representation. She undercuts masculine language by saying *uas hoc iacens, urceolum siue aliud* ["vase ... or waterpot, or whatever"], as if the object's actual name were irrelevant to her. Her very phrase confirms that the object can be called by several different names. Her dismissal of the connection between name and object then must create, if one follows Kristeva's ideas concerning language, "a dissonance within the thetic, paternal function of language."[13] And, during the debate, this dissonance threatens to undermine all of language because (crucially) Perpetua does not use merely the *idea* of a vase as her example. She indicates a specific object to her father and apparently arrives at this choice through sheer chance: *urceolum siue aliud* ["waterpot, or whatever"]; so, any object is potentially subject to Perpetua's new kind of "language." The dissonance is also peculiarly resonant during the debate because the water pitcher, with its domestic and feminine associations, is the only identifying marker in the place where Perpetua and her father argue (108–09). Her use of this object defines the space—of language, of debate—as feminine space.[14]

Having undermined her father's system of language generally, Perpetua then invades it specifically through her use of the term "Christian." For him, this reidentification of his daughter is a "nonsense effect ... that destroy[s] not only accepted beliefs and significations," as the reference to the vase proves, "but, in radical experiments"—such as the [Christian] one now attempted by Perpetua—destroys "syntax itself, that guarantee of thetic consciousness (of the signified object and ego.)" Hence, the new term produces "a *discordance* in the symbolic function and consequently within the identity of the transcendental ego itself."[15] Appropriately, the father, as the representative of the transcendental ego in this passage, can then only act in a desperate, nonverbal fashion. He rushes at Perpetua in order to pluck out her eyes, when he *hoc verbo mittit* (108) [was so angered by the word ("Christian")] (109). His childish rage confirms that he is pedantically literalist, that he is superficial in that he is only moved by words rather than concepts, that he cannot even perceive her arguments despite how clearly and reasonably she puts them. He can only leave Perpetua for the moment. She says *et refrigeraui absentia illius* (108) [I was comforted by his absence] (109). Her intensifying beliefs, on the other hand, gradually move her beyond the limits of language into a more abstract world, as indicated by her capacity for dream-visions, and by her ability to assert her identity through an image partaking in the fundamental relations between objects and signs. Perpetua's use of the term "Christian" is a radical act of *desemanticization*.[16]

Of course Perpetua's renaming of herself also directly attacks her father's values, which are related to his system of language, as Ronsse observes. By changing her name, Perpetua renounces her family history. More specifically, by asking her father to imagine a situation, Perpetua invades "his thoughts." Her assertion of a new identity then abruptly "destroy[s] his mental image, ... flout[s] his argumentative prowess," and affronts his vanity and family pride. As for his system of representation, visual images of women are often connected with waterpots and vases by analogy with their body shapes. Such images support the masculinist idea, associated with commodification, of trying to present a woman's body as merely a vessel for developing (preferably male) children.[17] Perpetua smashes these images along with her father's image of her.

The vase-debate is a further affront to the literalism of Perpetua's father and a threat to traditional representations of women because her new assertion of identity as a Christian is so broadly artistic, so sweepingly and self-consciously poetic.[18] She connects this new identity to a vase when a vase is not only an object with a name, encountered by chance, or a domestic object replete with social history. A vase is also frequently an art object, like some of the images in her visions. Moreover, the pose of a woman carrying a basket, pot, jug, or vase is strikingly common in artworks from the entire history of art in the Western world.[19] But the vase-debate demonstrates that the male-instituted, so-called feminine world of water-carrying, where everything has a convenient, male-established name, is over for her. In addition, her distinctive treatment of language and of the pitcher as an object would encourage the audience of the passio to be ready for further artistic and rhetorical devices in the text, for further opportunities to exercise their powers of interpretation.

Such powers are soon put to the test: dreams—events traditionally seen as peculiarly in need of interpretation—will soon form much of Perpetua's narrative. In fact, the suggestion that her visions are poetic appears not only in their self-consciously artistic content but also in the text of the passio. The first instance of the verb *facio*, for instance, initiates a verbal pattern, as the passio sets up parallels between acts of seeing, praying, and making (110, 114, 116).[20] The saint's life and Perpetua seem to associate *facio* with the interpretation of visions as both works of art and works of God; as both miracles of Christian belief and miracles that lead to her individual (and highly artistic) transformation into a martyr.

Furthermore, Kristeva's ideas concerning poetic language suit the events of Perpetua's visions very well. Poetic language inculcates "a so-called new formal or ideological 'writer's universe,' the never-finished, undefined production of a new space of significance."[21] This "new space of significance," a By Way, is exactly what Perpetua evokes in her visions—and once even before her visions.

A new space appears explicitly when she announces the change to her prison:

> et usurpaui ut mecum infans in carcere maneret; et statim conualui et releuata sum a labore et sollicitudine infantis, et factus est mihi carcer subito praetorium, ut ibi mallem esse quam alicubi. (110)
>
> [I got permission for my baby to stay with me in prison. At once I recovered my health, relieved as I was of my worry and anxiety over the child. My prison had suddenly become a palace, so that I wanted to be there rather than anywhere else.] (111)

Not only is her reinterpretation of the prison a mental triumph over her oppressive surroundings and a declaration of ownership over an imagined space, but it is also a triumph over her father's overliteral interpretation of the world, which is apparent from his inability to imagine the name of an object as anything but its existing name. For Perpetua, the jail is a palace simply because she has decided to call it one. With the concepts of "prison" and "palace" both representing institutional authority in society, her renaming of the jail also "produc[es] interplay within the structure of meaning as well as a questioning process of subject and history." With her maternal and feminine status, she produces "[a] reinstatement of maternal territory into the very economy of language." For instance, she usurps the traditionally male power of naming, just as she did when she reidentified herself as Christian during the vase-debate.[22] Moreover, she has chosen a word for her dwelling that often in Latin literature means the residence of a Roman magistrate. A noblewoman in Roman times would typically have care of her household, so this new naming has consequences for conceptions of domestic roles. Her choice of wording thus allegorizes a usurpation of the Roman legal system, part of a usurpation pattern that occurs throughout the passio. Also, her prison becomes a kind of idealized haven because in it her family is narrowed down to a group untainted by paternal influence. Her baby, now returned to her and the direct cause of the renaming of her surroundings, is parallel to her father's refreshing absence. In a world made up of her child and herself, Perpetua has control over language and communication. More generally, the argument with her father and its location, together with the renaming of the prison, demonstrate that the traditional attitudes that tend to hide women away in domestic spaces while men openly interact with the outside world in public are entirely reversed in the *Passio Sanctarum Perpetuae et Felicitatis*.

After the baby causes the renaming of the prison, his role as an enabler of particularly female communication continues. For instance, he becomes the direct cause of Perpetua's first vision:

> Tunc dixit mihi frater meus: Domina soror, iam in magna dignatione es, tanta ut postules uisionem et ostendatur tibi an passio sit an commeatus, (110)
>
> [Then my brother said to me: "Dear sister, you are greatly privileged; surely you might ask for a vision to discover whether you are to be condemned or freed,"] (111)

whereupon the first dream follows immediately. The privilege to which Perpetua's brother refers is most likely her ability to be with her child in prison because this reunion occurs just previously in the narrative. Her almost ecstatic reaction to the return of her baby also implies that she feels privileged by this reunion (110–11). Presumably, the typical maternal relations with a child then take place: nursing, but also further signs of affection and communication between mother and child. These may even continue to occur while she experiences her first vision.

Generally, any vision can be connected to powers of expression. Dreams are often, for instance, interpreted as attempts to express repressed desires. In parallel fashion, Christianity is a repressed religion in the second century, so Perpetua's visions can represent a desire to proselytize this religion. More specifically, Perpetua's visions evoke the idea of direct communication in that she uses the "oracular" present tense during her descriptions of them, as Ronsse notices, a tense that implies an audience.[23] The idea that Perpetua dreams of powers of expression also makes psychological sense for a woman in her position. Detained because of her religion, she would primarily be nervous about her fate, but she has other reasons to be anxious. The prosecutors are very likely to call upon her to speak in public when Roman women rarely made such speeches. When she eventually expresses herself at her trial, a large crowd is present (112–13).

The first vision has received much attention by critics.[24] It clearly, like Perpetua's other visions, demonstrates her desire for a By Way, and thus connects women directly to the tendency for By Ways to appear in works that feature female saints. This first vision also concerns powers of expression in an obvious way. Near its end, Perpetua arrives at what is apparently heaven, where a pleasant-looking old man calls upon her to participate in a Eucharistic feast:

> clamauit me et de caseo quod mulgebat dedit mihi quasi buccellam; et ego accepi iunctis manibus et manducaui; et uniuersi circumstantes dixerunt: Amen. Et ad sonum uocis experrecta sum, conmanducans adhuc dulce nescio quid. (110–12)
>
> [He called me over to him and gave me, as it were, a mouthful of the milk he was drawing; and I took it into my cupped hands and consumed it. And all those who stood around said: "Amen!" At the sound of this word I came to, with the taste of something sweet still in my mouth.] (111–13)

Critics have observed that her vision of heaven and her eating of milk there (actually, cheese) have associations with education and learning in early Christian writings.[25] Even without such specific associations, the sweet taste in her mouth intimates that she has something new and immediate to say. In addition, Perpetua's experience recalls that of John, who eats a book that tastes like honey. He is then instructed to prophesy in the Book of Revelation (Revelation 10:9–11). John's experience in turn is based on passages from the Old Testament prophets and psalms (Ezekiel 3:3; Proverbs 16:24; Psalms 19:10, 119:103).[26] Sweetness in the mouth also brings to mind the Song of Songs 2:3 (see also 4:11), "his fruit was sweet to my palate," and thus also recalls the church fathers' commentaries on this hymn, as Giselle de Nie notes. The sexual image of Perpetua awakening with a taste in her mouth must then support, with its parallels in scripture, connections between semen and speech and the Word made flesh through the incarnation.[27] Equally, since Perpetua nurses her child and then is fed a milk product in paradise during her vision, speech must be associated in this passio with taste in the mouth from breast milk, an image of the passage of knowledge, speech, and language from mother to child. The most explicit commentary concerning these connections appears in the works of Clement of Alexandria (150—c. 215), who is so concerned with maintaining the tradition of God as the origin of knowledge that he portrays the Father with breasts:

> The Word is everything to the Child, both father and mother, teacher and nurse ... The nutriment is the milk of the Father, by Whom alone the littlest ones are fed ... and the Word alone supplies us children with the milk of love, and only those who suck at his breast are truly happy ... Thus, for Christ, nourishment was to do the will of the Father; but for us, the little ones, nourishment is Christ himself: we drink the heavenly Word. For this reason, seeking is called sucking: to those infants who seek the Word, the Father's breasts of benevolence supply milk.[28]

Ambrose in his D*e Virginibus* makes a similar assertion concerning Christ, whom he conflates with Mary. Christ is

> Virgo est ergo quae nupsit, virgo quae nos suo utero portavit, virgo quae genuit, virgo quae proprio lacte nutrivit ... Ergo a Christo non deficiunt ubera (5.22)[29]
>
> [a virgin, then, who married [us]; he is a virgin who bore us in his womb; he is a virgin who brought us forth; he is a virgin who nursed us with his own milk ... Therefore teats are not lacking to Christ] (79)

Hence, Clement and Ambrose seem to suggest a female line of inheritance for knowledge, language, and speech, which are passed along to children like breast milk, because these attempts to graft female breasts onto the masculinist tradition of knowledge that originates with God the Father results in images that are difficult to visualize. Evelyn Birge Vitz tries to justify the bizarre Father-with-breasts image by intellectualizing it: "This may well be a gendered transformation of the great martyrdom metaphor attributed to Tertullian, that 'the blood of Christians is seed'": a metaphor that is "agricultural and male." But breast-feeding "is a maternal and female metaphor," she rightly insists, even when "the virgin martyr's blood" is being described as "'pure and white milk' [that] nourishes the Christian community."[30] And, logically, if a mother were to nurse only girls with the milk of learning, then this knowledgeable community would consist only of women. Works later than Clement's support this idea of feminine inheritance. Hrotsvitha of Gandersheim (c. 973) depicts Saint Sapientia saying to her daughters as they go to be martyred:

> Ad hoc vos materno lacte affluenter alui, ad hoc delicate nutrivi, ut vos caelesti, non terreno, sponso traderum.[31]
>
> [Yes, it was for this you were nursed with so much of your mother's milk, for this I spoiled and fed you all your favorite foods, so that I might marry you to someone better than a man—a divine bridegroom.][32]

Vitz offers further examples of this idea, for instance, in "the Old French life of Christina, when the virgin's breast is cut off what flows out is not blood but milk."[33]

The idea of specifically feminine expression in the first vision of the *Passio Sanctarum Perpetuae et Felicitatis* also appears in the way that the dream is introduced. Perpetua is surprisingly confident about its occurrence: *et ego quae me sciebam fabulari cum Domino ... Crastina die tibi renuntiabo* (110) [I knew I could speak with the Lord ... "I shall tell you (her brother) tomorrow"] (111), while her brother defers to her completely.

For instance, he says nothing about the possibility of visions of his own. Her wording (*sciebam*) even implies that she has had visions before; certainly she feels remarkably close to God. Perhaps, she is aware that "in the early Church, female leadership had often been exercised through visions."[34]

The passio's major concern with speech continues from Perpetua's first dream to her first (presumably) public speech at her trial. Now that a taste in her mouth suggests that she has something to say, she says it—but not before her father has had another try at turning her from her belief. Significantly, one of the arguments that he makes to her during his second appearance in the passio is that *nemo enim nostrum libere loquetur, si tu aliquid fueris passa* (112) [None of us will ever be able to speak freely again if anything happens to you] (113). By mentioning one of the immanent effects of her choice of religion, that is, that it will silence the family, her father admits that she has completed and won the debate concerning this choice, and demonstrates that his typically masculinist thinking forces him (and his family, were his influence to continue) into a state of intellectual paralysis. His narcissism means that he can only perceive Perpetua's style of speech as akin to his own style: competitive and aggressive, perhaps in an oral-heroic fashion.[35] Then this kind of aggression, together with its purveyor, is held up to ridicule in the passio. At the tribunal, all of Perpetua's fellow catechumens confess their Christianity, and then, just before she is to speak, her father steps forward with her son, drags her from the stair in front of Hilarianus the governor, and commands her: *Supplica. Miserere infanti* (112) ["Perform the sacrifice—have pity on your baby!"] (113). Hilarianus then immediately repeats the exact sense of her father's words: *Parce, inquit, canis patris tui, parce infantiae pueri. Fac sacrum pro salute imperatorum* (114), he said ["Have pity on your father's grey head; have pity on your infant son. Offer the sacrifice for the welfare of the emperors"] (115). These two men, one a political authority and the other a head of a household, concur to a remarkable degree. Perpetua's father had asked her to have pity on his "head" earlier in the narrative (112–13). Their views also parallel the "paternal, sacrificial function" that Kristeva attributes to male-dominated discourse. For her, this idea of sacrifice for the sake of one's family becomes "more and more emptied of meaning" and soon arrives at "an insipid formalism": the mere parroting of long-standing attitudes.[36]

Such attitudes then receive a double ironic attack in the passio. First, the essential accusation against Perpetua, that she has no pity for either her father or her son—with the implication that women typically harbor such "feminine" emotions and therefore she is emotionally unnatural—is proved wrong. She records that she pities her father. She even specifically has pity for his old age (114–15), just as he demands. Equally, since she anxiously misses her baby when they are separated (108–09), she pities him too. Any reader of the account of her trials can discover these emotions, which the governor and her father are apparently too self-absorbed to sense from her. Nor do they seem to be able to conceive of the idea that Perpetua might experience pity and nevertheless make the choices that she has made; that she might separate emotion from action in a stoical manner. The heavily masculine discourse of the trial and of her father's demands blocks the expression of what she feels and, ironically, of what these two men want. The male discourse is revealed as counterproductive, as absurdly limited. It is blind to the courage of her choices, probably because courage is more expected from men than from women.

The second irony directed at the attitudes expressed by men during Perpetua's trial occurs when *staret pater ad me deiciendam, iussus est ab Hilariano proici et uirga percussus est* (114) [my father persisted in trying to dissuade me; Hilarianus ordered him to be thrown to the ground and beaten with a rod] (115). If at this juncture Perpetua's father is repeating, as seems likely, the arguments he has used already against his daughter, Hilarianus is in the ludicrously contradictory predicament of flogging a person for saying words and professing attitudes that he himself has just stated and advocated. Meanwhile, Perpetua has completed the pattern she started during the vase-debate by announcing *Christiana sum*, a brief speech that seals her fate, publicly reidentifies herself after her own desires, and professes ideas that transcend the male authority of her father and of the judge (114). For instance, Perpetua's declaration marks a victory of Christian language over the pagan statements of the governor.

Her second vision confirms the powers of expression that she is given in the first. Just before her second vision, Perpetua finds the word "Dinocrates" in her mouth, reminiscent of the sweetness that was in her mouth at the end of her last vision. Moreover, she comes across this word in the exact way that she encountered the "vase" earlier—supposedly by sheer chance. She blurts out the boy's name as if it were automatic speech delivered directly from a supernatural source. The parallel actions in the two visions suggest that this vision begins where the other ended, and the specific words that Perpetua uses during her intercession for Dinocrates follow Kristeva's language theory closely. Perpetua describes the prayers she begins for her brother soon after she first says his name in the passio as *et coepi de ipso orationem facere multum et ingemescere ad dominum* (114) [I began to pray for him and to sigh deeply for him before the Lord] (115). The sighs are emotional, nonverbal elements that evoke (among other things) sounds that pass between mother and child. They amount to semiotic language from the mother.[37] After the second vision when she realizes Dinocrates is suffering, her sigh-filled prayers take place with the regularity of breast-feeding and of other aspects of infant care: *et feci pro illo orationem die et nocte gemens et lacrimans* (116) [And I prayed for my brother day and night with tears and sighs] (117).

Although Perpetua's fourth and last vision is not so obviously about language or expression as her previous ones were, in one respect it represents rhetoric come alive. Since her last dream is not apparently inspired by another person or by any event except—one might guess—the prospect of her going into the arena, and since it seems to represent both allegorically and emotionally the events of a martyrdom, it would seem to be the most psychologically realistic vision in the passio. However, Tertullian refers to the martyrs as athletes in metaphorical terms many times in the course of his works;[38] so, with the appearance of the *Passio Sanctarum Perpetuae et Felicitatis*—a narrative supposedly told by a martyr in her own words—at nearly the same time as his treatises, one encounters a work that features a remarkably faithful visualization of his favorite metaphor. Moreover, this visualization goes to an extreme of specific detail, mentioning the crowd, seconds, antagonists, and the gates of life and death:[39]

> Et exiuit quidam contra me Aegyptius foedus specie cum adiutoribus suis pugnaturus mecum. Ueniunt et ad me adolescentes decori, adiutores et fautores mei ... et coeperunt me fauisores mei oleo defricare, quomodo solent in agone. (118)
>
> [Then out came an Egyptian against me, of vicious appearance, together with his seconds, to fight with me. There also came up to me some handsome young men to be seconds and assistants ... My seconds began to rub me down with oil (as they are wont to do before a contest).] (119)

The fourth vision forces the audience of the passio to consider the aptness and consequences of using the figure of an athlete allegorically: what happens when one of the contestants in a gladiatorial fight or an athletic event is a woman? The evocative wrestling match in this vision also helps to support Ronsse's idea that the passio represents not so much "authentic facts" as "early Christian rhetorical sophistication,"[40] and one cannot help but notice that this match is (among other things) a performance akin to a rhetorical performance. Perpetua demonstrates her control again when she pointedly winds her narrative up, announcing *hoc usque in pridie muneris egi; ipsius autem muneris actum, si quis uoluerit, scribat* (118) [So much for what I did up until the eve of the contest. About what happened at the contest itself, let him write of it who will] (119). Obviously no further narration will come from her, whereupon another narrator obediently takes over the discourse in order to relate the martyrdoms of the catechumens.

After the visions and during this narrative of the martyrdoms, there is one last demonstration of the powers of expression that appears to call up Kristeva's maternal, semiotic language. Another female martyr besides Perpetua, Felicitas, is heavily pregnant when she enters prison. Pregnant women were not allowed to be executed under Roman law. However, Felicitas wants to be martyred along with her comrades, so they send up a prayer: *coniuncto itaque unito gemitu ad Dominum orationem fuderunt ante tertium diem muneris. Statim post orationem dolores inuaserunt* (122) [And so, two days before the contest, they poured forth a prayer to the Lord in one torrent of common grief. And immediately after their prayer the birth pains came upon her] (123).[41] This group prayer, indicating unanimity of thought, is similar to the highly emotional prayers that Perpetua offers on behalf of Dinocrates. One may even see this entreaty as a community version of her earlier, individual prayers, so, her "language" has now found a wider audience and has helped to develop a community. One may also see the group supplication as, in a way, directed at the baby, which duly responds. Apparently, this kind of semiotic language (the text implies a nonverbal element to the prayer in its extreme of grief) results in direct communication. Moreover, the child is a girl, a kind of displaced version of Perpetua's child, with a sex more in keeping with Kristeva's ideal of semiotic language. Perpetua's child had to be abandoned to his fate because of Perpetua's convictions. He passes into his mother's family, where her father still has influence. Felicitas's child, on the other hand, is the daughter of a slave. One hears nothing further with regard to Felicitas's background or status. This baby can pass into a new life, then, uninflected by previous traditions, because she has no other family besides her mother, now intent on near immediate martyrdom. Unlike Perpetua's son, this child is not burdened with a grandfather (or father, apparently) who might bring her up as a non-Christian. Hence, the narrator's development of the *passio* seems to present Felicitas's daughter as ideally status-free. Perhaps, the *passio* goes so far as to recognize that the constraints of Roman aristocratic society are wrapped up in its male-centeredness, and is proposing that society in general is better off without them.[42]

Ronsse writes that the existence of Felicitas's baby means that "the cycle of interpretation [of Christian learning] and imitation [of Christian lives] will continue. The nameless daughter is the hermeneutic figure her mother uses to explain her faith [122–25] and the promise that future generations will continue to incarnate, and thereby model and teach, Christian practices." Certainly the idea of "heritage of the mother" as specifically female heritage seems to be suggested by the *passio*, which advocates a kind of female mimicry as opposed to the mere duplication of patience figures that feature so strongly in later examples of hagiography:[43] *Ita enixa est puellam, quam sibi quaedam soror in filiam educauit* (124) [And (Felicitas) gave birth to a girl; and one of the sisters brought her up as her own daughter] (125). According to Ronsse, *educauit* [brought up] implies intellectual education, and the passing on of Christian tradition brings the *passio* back full circle to one of the major concerns of its prologue.[44] This opening section is very concerned with the dissemination of *omnia donatiua administraturus in omnibus* (106) [all his (God's) gifts to all] (107). These gifts, presumably the stories, visions, prophesies, and examples of the martyrs (106), must be *digerimus et ad gloriam Dei lectione celebramus* (106) [set ... forth and ... ma[de] ... known through the word for the glory of God] (107). In fact, the *Passio Sanctarum Perpetuae et Felicitatis* is virtually unique in beginning with this lengthy prologue that justifies for posterity the work that follows as one that measures up to or even surpasses its earlier apologetic forebears (106–07). The *passio* is trying self-consciously to place itself within tradition, and the lengthy explanation of this process at the start of the work hints at some difficulties in its attempt to do so, perhaps, because of its female protagonist.

One may also note the continuing association between Perpetua's visions and expression in that, when the text of the martyrdom reverts to a male narrator, readers are shut out of what is presumably her last vision. After she is tortured in the arena for the first time,

> suscepta et quasi a somno expergita (adeo in spiritu et in extasi fuerat) circumspicere coepit et stupentibus omnibus ait: Quando, inquit, producimur ad uaccam illam nescioquam? Et cum audisset quod iam euenerat, non prius credidit nisi quasdam notas uexationis in corpore et habitu suo recognouisset. (128)

> [She awoke from a kind of sleep (so absorbed had she been in ecstasy in the Spirit) and she began to look about her. Then to the amazement of all she said: "When are we going to be thrown to that heifer or whatever it is?" When told that this had already happened, she refused to believe it until she noticed the marks of her rough experience on her person and her dress.] (129)

The *nescioquam* [whatever] that she uses to describe the heifer recalls the "whatever" that she used to describe the vase during the opening debate with her father, and her insensibility to pain suggests that her visions genuinely remove her to another world. But now this other world cannot be represented directly to the audience because Perpetua's narrative voice and text are absent. Indeed, the audience now has to assume the existence of another vision on the basis of her insensibility to the real world as opposed to basing their observations on an individual's discourse. The audience becomes aware of a narrative lack, entirely due to the loss of a particularly female mode of expression. By reducing her method of torture to a "whatever," when,

> Puellis autem ferocissimam uaccam ideoque praeter consuetudinem conparatam diabolus praeparauit, sexui earum etiam de bestia aemulatus, (128)
>
> [For the young women, however, the Devil had prepared a mad heifer. This was an unusual animal, but it was chosen that their sex might be matched with that of the beast,] (129)

Perpetua shows that any external comment concerning her sex is irrelevant to her. She rejects this attempted imposition of female attributes in the exact way that she rejected the vase-attributes. Her entire conception of herself is now extra-worldly.

Gender Roles in the *Passio Sanctarum Perpetuae et Felicitatis*

On the other hand, Perpetua's famous change of sex in order to fight the Egyptian would seem to imply a denigration of her sex and a presumption that women are incapable of active heroism.[45] One might argue for instance that, while Perpetua takes on leadership roles, these attributes come over as artificial. She is introduced as unquestionably the leader, or at least the most important member, of the group of catechumens who are arrested, and this pattern continues as she speaks to a prison guard directly and demands better treatment for her fellow prisoners (124), stares down the crowd in the arena, refuses to allow her group of martyrs to be dressed in pagan attire as they go before the multitude (126), and urges on the other catechumens to remain firm in their beliefs. Here she turns into a preacher, quoting Acts (14:22) and 1 Corinthians (16:13) as she admonishes her flock to "stand fast in the faith" (*Passio*, 129). These examples of leadership during the martyrdom itself, however, are related by the narrator rather than Perpetua and occur only once she has been "revealed" as a man, or a woman with the appearance of a man, during the wrestling scene.

But the text is not so straightforward, I believe, in its disposing of traditional gender roles;[46] nor are Perpetua's actions any more artificial than are those of the typical martyr. For instance, although her fourth vision contains male attendants who seem to see nothing out of place in preparing her and another contestant for an apparent athletic contest when a woman appearing in such a role would be highly unusual for second-century North Africa (118–19), the dream begins with *Pomponium diaconum ad ostium carceris et pulsare uehementer ... et dixit mihi: Perpetua, te expectamus; ueni* (116) [Pomponius the deacon came to the prison gates and began to knock violently ... And he said to me: "Perpetua, come; we are waiting for you"] (117). When he calls her by name, this immediate identification of her implies that the sex-change that she announces later cannot have already occurred. Indeed nothing at the start of this vision indicates change to her previous identity as it stands in the other visions or even in the trial-narrative: she begins this last vision in prison. Once in the arena, with her adversary and male attendants coming forward, *et expoliata sum et facta sum masculus* (118) ["My clothes were stripped off, and suddenly I was a man"] (119). The text does not suggest that she thought she was a woman until the moment that her clothes came off and then she suddenly realized that she was a man. Instead, her gender change apparently takes place right in front of the crowd. Moreover, since she is naked, the crowd would presumably witness this change as it takes place.[47]

It is possible, then, to identify the approach of the devil in the role of an Egyptian gladiator or wrestler as what provokes the gender change in Perpetua: a display of male militaristic traditions causes an (un)equal and opposite response in her. In other words, her sex-change takes place in the narrative simply because a woman in the role of an athlete would be so unexpected. So, if the narrator(s) (or Perpetua herself) wanted to present her as the principal martyr of the group in the act of wrestling with the devil, then a gender change was the only way that these narrators thought such an event could take place. But such an interpretation slights the fact that the Egyptian who would render the sex-change necessary is so obviously her enemy. The narrative represents him plainly as a negative character, and he is later revealed as the most negative character possible in a Christian work: the devil (118–19). Such a characterization thus implies—not approval of male-associated, aggressive, warlike activity as a regrettable but necessary measure under the circumstances but—outright disapproval of male-associated militarism and violence.

Another possible reason for the need for Perpetua's sex-change stems from the presentation of this change as a spectacle. One could argue that the gaze of the spectators, typically presented in the records of martyrdoms as a bloodthirsty mob, who in this instance are unable to accept a woman in the role of an athlete or gladiator, causes the change in Perpetua's sex.[48] Certainly the crowd demands a change when they first view the bodies of Perpetua and Felicitas during the account of the martyrdom:

> Itaque dispoliatae et reticulis indutae producebantur. Horruit populus alteram respiciens puellam delicatam, alteram a partu recentem stillantibus mammis. Ita reuocatae et discinctis indutae. (128)

[So they were stripped naked, placed in nets and thus brought out into the arena. Even the crowd was horrified when they saw that one was a delicate young girl and the other was a woman fresh from childbirth with the milk still dripping from her breasts. And so they were brought back again and dressed in unbelted tunics.] (129)

Meanwhile, Perpetua herself has indicated no explicit desire to become a man. Instead one may argue that her sex-change represents the crowd's vision of her, a vision that comes from traditional attitudes. Perhaps she can be accused of holding these attitudes herself because they appear to be an aspect of *her* dream. However, this vision depicts her as overmatching and overcoming them as well. She fights the Egyptian, wins easily, and receives (apparently divine) approbation (118–19). Later, she walks into the arena of her martyrdom *uigore oculorum deiciens omnium conspectum* (126) [putting down everyone's stare by her own intense gaze] (127). Through this gaze, the martyr "refus[es] objectification, refus[es] to be a spectacle for the crowd's gaze ... repeats once more her resistance to the normative gender-based hierarchy," as Perkins notes. Also, during the athletic combat of the fourth vision, de Nie notices that "The trainer/Father ... continues to speak of and address her as a woman," despite her new gender.[49] In fact, the trainer addresses the crowd using feminine pronouns for Perpetua, as if they should understand that this wrestler really is a woman, while the word *facta* in the phrase that describes her transformation is feminine. Apparently, her masculine form is merely how the bestial spectators irrationally see her for the moment, while the narrative implies that God and the audience of Perpetua's diary can identify her actual sex. This connection between the sadistic crowd and the desire for a masculine, militaristic figure hints at critical treatment of traditional, masculinist values in the passio.

Then her newfound masculine attributes do not cause her to win the fight. Such an outcome would dramatize an exaltation of these attributes. Instead, she finds that she has gained superhuman powers: *Et sublata sum in aere et coepi eum sic caedere quasi terram non calcans* (118) [Then I was raised up into the air and I began to pummel him (the Egyptian) without as it were touching the ground] (119). These powers, which would presumably manifest themselves whether she were male or female, give her the victory. In other words, although a gender change occurs at the crucial moment in this dream, masculine virtues in themselves are not promoted per se at this juncture. And she only becomes a man in her dream. The subsequent narrative of Perpetua's martyrdom, while it contains the typical metaphor that describes martyrs as athletes and notes her leadership qualities, insists that she is a woman, stresses her gender when the women enter the arena, and does not describe her as a particularly "mannish" woman. Thus, Perpetua's passing through the gate of glory as a man in her last vision indicates that, in respect of reputation, she has done everything a man can or would do. She awakens, and the male world of reputation, as a worldly matter, concerns her no more. This succession of dream and waking mark the reestablishment of her as a woman, and in the rest of the narrative, "a mother's, not a man's, body is central."[50]

Criticism of Masculinist Traditions in the *Passio*

The passio criticizes male-traditional attitudes elsewhere as well—to such an extent in total, that I am surprised at how generalized the feminist criticism of *The Passion of Perpetua and Felicitas* has been. Castelli is one of the few critics to note that certain aspects of the masculine world, particularly ones associated with Perpetua's father, are demonized during Perpetua's first vision.[51] In it, Perpetua sees

> scalam aeream mirae magnitudinis pertingentem usque ad caelum et angustam, per quam nonnisi singuli ascendere possent, et in lateribus scalae omne genus ferramentorum infixum. (110)
>
> [a ladder of tremendous height made of bronze, reaching all the way to the heavens, but it was so narrow that only one person could climb up at a time. To the sides of the ladder were attached all sorts of metal weapons.] (111)

Most obviously, Perpetua's ascent of this ladder is an affirmation of her power. But power over what, exactly? The implements attached to the side of the ladder might represent gladiatorial equipment, as Perkins supposes, but these items also recall the male world more broadly conceived, particularly the world of war. All of them, *gladii, lanceae, hami, machaerae, ueruta* (110), "swords, spears, hooks, daggers, and spikes" (111) are typically wielded by men in battle.[52] In addition, these metal items suggest the world of the sculptor and the smith, to which women of late antiquity cannot typically belong. One may then allegorize the implements, as Perkins and Rex Butler do, as representations of Perpetua's fear of what she will encounter in the arena.[53] But none of these weapons save the sword appear in the subsequent martyrdoms in the passio; nor do they appear (save the sword) in any of Perpetua's other visions, including, rather surprisingly, the dream of her appearance in the arena. The main action in this fourth vision is a wrestling match (118–19), and the martyrs at the end of the passio are offered to the beasts and then summarily executed with the sword, without any gladiatorial contests (126–29).[54] So, her passage through the implements, where *si quis neglegenter aut non sursum adtendens ascenderet, laniaretur et carnes eius inhaererent ferramentis* (110) [if anyone tried to climb up carelessly or without paying attention, he would be mangled and his flesh would adhere to the weapons] (111), seems less like a representation of her martyrdom and more like a representation of a careful and attentive passage through and beyond the masculinist world of military acts and arts. One might note that enduring torture requires more courage than care or attention.

Certainly Perpetua's courage is essential to her progress: *sub ipsa scala draco cubans mirae magnitudinis* (110) [At the foot of the ladder lay a dragon of enormous size] (111). The dragon tries to terrify anyone approaching the ladder, and Saturus, who ascends before her, warns her against the beast. It *desub ipsa scala ... eiecit caput* (110) [stuck his head out from underneath the ladder] (111). Nevertheless, for Perpetua, the ascent is easy. After the first appearance of the metal weapons on the sides of the ladder, they are not mentioned again. She announces that the dragon will do her no harm, and she is right. It seems afraid of her, and she uses its head as her first step onto the rungs (110–11). Like the implements, the dragon represents masculinity. The passio itself connects it with the Egyptian in the fourth vision and with the devil, while critics have linked the beast with Perpetua's father and have called it a phallic symbol.[55] A biting dragon and "mangling" implements suggest the masculine obsession with castration, a kind of mutilation that she does not need to worry about because she is a woman.

Perpetua's Domination of Men in the *Passio*

Another profeminine aspect of the narrative that critics have noticed is Perpetua's mastering of men in the passio. The most obvious candidate for this mastering is her father, and his story "underscores the reversed hierarchical world her conversion has brought into being," a conversion that "continues to defy both patriarchal and state authority," according to Perkins.[56] The father pleads with her, *ne me dederis in dedecus hominum* (112) ["Do not abandon me to be the reproach of men"] (113). His interventions have no effect on her decisions, and eventually he humiliates himself by groveling on the ground, both in front of Perpetua (112–13, 116–17), and in front of the entire assembly at the trial, where he is scourged like a child (114–15). He pulls out hairs from his beard (116–17). In the most famous instance of Perpetua's mastery over him, she notes *non filiam nominabat sed dominam* (112) ["he no longer addressed me as his daughter but as a woman (mistress)"] (113). (Her brother in prison also calls her *domina* [110].) The father's action is parallel yet retrograde to the other major characters: as Perpetua starts to lead the catechumens and intercedes for the welfare of her brother, Dinocrates, her father loses influence; as she goes up the ladder, her father goes down (throws himself to the ground); he acts like a child when she is concerned with the welfare of her own male child but nevertheless has made the difficult yet responsible decision to give this child up; her father is even feminized as she is masculinized, according to Castelli, and Burrus underlines his parallelism with Perpetua by calling him a "poignantly failed martyr."[57]

More generally, Perpetua's visions are, among other things, fantasies where men tend to be "benign, supportive, and beautiful, as opposed to ... hostile" like her father.[58] During her vision of (presumably) heaven at the top of the ladder, the roles of child and parent that exist for her in the real world are reversed, as she drinks cheese that is given to her by an elderly shepherd, who is a kindly opposite to her bullying father. The shepherd can certainly be interpreted as a feminized man: he offers a milk product (110–13). He is also a typical example of a kind of character particular to these visions: the male advocate who fulfills Perpetua's needs and then disappears from the narrative:

> Ascendit autem Saturus prior, qui postea se propter nos ultro tradiderat (quia ipse nos aedificauerat), et tunc cum adducti sumus, praesens non fuerat. Et peruenit in caput scalae et conuertit se et dixit mihi: Perpetua, sustineo te; sed uide ne te mordeat draco ille. (110)
>
> [And Saturus was the first to go up, he who was later to give himself up of his own accord. He had been the builder of our strength, although he was not present when we were arrested. And he arrived at the top of the staircase and he looked back and said to me: "Perpetua, I am waiting for you. But take care; do not let the dragon bite you."] (111)

Significantly, Saturus does not figure again in her account, though he appears several times in the frame-narrative, as a leader, visionary, and teacher.[59] Nor is he identified as one of the worshippers in heaven once she ascends the ladder, whereas she proceeds to the hereafter with him in his corresponding vision (118–23). In contrast, Perpetua names no-one among the thousands who appear in the first vision's heaven (110–13). Within this dream, Saturus's role is only to precede her, whereupon he disappears. The action again contrasts with Saturus's vision, where he names several other Christians, *Iocundum et Saturninum et Artaxium, qui eadem persecutione uiui arserunt* (120) [Jucundus, Saturninus, and Artaxius, who were burnt alive in the same persecution] (121) and who meet up with Perpetua (also named) and himself in the afterlife.[60] In contrast,

Perpetua's first vision concentrates on her personal fulfillment almost exclusively. After all, a mature, educated person—let alone a spiritually fulfilled one—no longer needs a teacher or guide, which is how she has described Saturus. Logically, he vanishes from her autobiography as no longer relevant, whereupon she becomes the principal teacher-figure of the remaining narrative.[61]

This narrative pattern of the disappearing mentor is repeated almost exactly in her fourth vision. Again, Perpetua is summoned to her destiny by a benign and supportive man whom she has known:

> venisse Pomponium diaconum ad ostium carceris et pulsare uehementer. Et exiui ad eum et aperui ei ... et dixit mihi: Perpetua, te expectamus; ueni. Et tenuit mihi manum et coepimus ire per aspera loca et flexuosa. Uix tandem peruenimus anhelantes ad amphitheatrum et induxit me in media arena et dixit mihi: Noli pauere. Hic sum tecum et conlaboro tecum. Et abiit. (116)

> [Pomponius the deacon came to the prison gates and began to knock violently. I went out and opened the gate for him ... And he said to me: "Perpetua, come; we are waiting for you." Then he took my hand and we began to walk through rough and broken country. At last we came to the amphitheater out of breath, and he led me into the center of the arena. Then he told me: "Do not be afraid. I am here, struggling with you." Then he left.] (117)

Pomponius does not appear subsequently in her narrative.[62] He is clearly a precursor and guide for her, like Saturus in her first vision. Pomponius even calls her by name and declares "we are waiting for you," just as Saturus says. The role of Pomponius in her narrative, even more than that of Saturus, suggests that Perpetua wants support from men at the start of her conversion process, but later finds that she can do without this support. Her fourth vision allegorizes this shedding of male influence. She gets help from male attendants during her wrestling match with the Egyptian, but these are unnamed figures rather than men from her former life such as her father, Saturus, and Pomponius. Once the fight is over, Perpetua walks toward the Gate of Life alone, apparently, whereupon she wakes (118–19). Again, her solitude together with the disappearance of a mentor implies that she has transcended male-centered, earthly existence. Certainly the vision concentrates on her personal fulfillment so much—the vision is, after all, her narrative—that the other characters in the dream (all men) fade into the background, as if men must eventually become absent if they are going to feature in her dream: she achieves more presence through male absence. A further example of this kind of character is Perpetua's brother in prison who is instrumental in her achieving her first vision and then drops out of sight. The most radical example of this kind of character is Perpetua's husband. He presumably exists or existed, yet never appears in either the frame-narrative or hers. Readers know of his existence only due to the mentioning of her married status and to the presence of their child.

Another aspect of Perpetua's relationship with Pomponius during her fourth vision hinges upon his words to her: *hic sum tecum et conlaboro tecum* (116) ["I am here, struggling with you"] (117). Since he leaves right after saying them, he must mean that he is "with" Perpetua allegorically during the fight with the Egyptian. It seems reasonable to see Pomponius as useful to her, as "struggling" with her during the battle, because she has internalized him in some way. Of course, other ways of reading Pomponius's "being with" Perpetua are possible. He could be the miraculously tall *lanista* [trainer] figure who appears at the wrestling match, but this figure is usually interpreted as Christ. One of the attendants who rubs oil upon Perpetua could be Pomponius, but they are unnamed and do not really "work" with Perpetua in the way that the term *conlaboro* implies. In the case of internalization, then, a way of dealing with the supportive men who disappear from Perpetua's narratives is to identify them as a kind of male identity that she has no external use for because she has internalized it. And then, logically, she "becomes a man" during her wrestling match with the Egyptian not so much because she is forced into taking on a male form in order to engage in the traditionally "masculine" pursuit of wrestling or combat but because she has internalized a male identity and can therefore logically (though miraculously) externalize it when she needs to do so. Masculine identity has become subservient to her identity.

Indeed, one may observe direct attacks on male identity in the passio. The two most obvious examples occur during Perpetua's entrance into the arena, *uigore oculorum deiciens omnium conspectum* (126) [putting down everyone's stare by her own intense gaze] (127), and during her battle with the Egyptian in her fourth dream, which describes her kicking him in the face when the face is the most important indicator of identity (118). The battle ends with *et cecidit in faciem et calcaui illi caput* (118) [He fell flat on his face and I stepped on his head] (119), actions that both spurn the Egyptian's face and obscure it from view. Since he ends the fight in this position and there is no mention of him standing up again, Perpetua seems to have almost erased his identity. Equally, her second and third visions may be interpreted as a reinvention of Dinocrates, a male figure, whose facial appearance she changes.

Gender matters are also important to the passio, as Shaw notes, when Perpetua is brought into the arena to be martyred with Felicitas. Shaw's reading of the scene is that the two women were carefully reserved as a finale to the public executions. Symbolic degradation was added to their punishment. They were to face a wild and savage cow (*ferocissima vacca*). The choice of the animal was unusual, but was a deliberate one on the part of the authorities.[63]

Shaw contrasts the use of a cow with a bull, the animal used against Blandina. A bull, he observes, is the traditional beast used to execute an adulteress publically in the Roman Empire. He then argues that the significance of the heifer is "to mock the sex" of the young women: "by analogy with a bull, it was implied that they were sexually shameful; but since a cow was employed, the inference was that they were not 'real women' enough to be guilty of adultery." Shaw's points regarding the suggestion of lesbian relations between the two women and concerning the obvious incongruities between an accusation of Christianity and that of adultery certainly ring true. But his judgment of Perpetua and Felicitas as not "real women" enough seems strange when the choice of heifer occurs precisely because, according to the text, they are female. In addition, as Shaw himself points out, women appear in the arena (regardless of their supposed crimes) much more rarely than men, and therefore have a spectacle-premium that might suggest in itself the unusual choice of beast for their punishment.[64] The text actually says *Puellis autem ferocissimam uaccam ideoque praeter consuetudinem conparatam diabolus praeparauit, sexui earum etiam de bestia aemulatus* (128) [For the young women, however, the Devil had prepared a mad heifer. This was an unusual animal, but it was chosen that their sex might be matched with that of the beast] (129). So, if nothing else the use of a heifer would further feminize the proceedings. Indeed, Burrus believes that the final scene in the passio, with its addition of Felicitas and the heifer to the narrative, "becomes almost parodic in its exaggerated—and rather explicitly eroticized—strategies of feminization."[65]

Perpetua, Felicitas, and Motherhood

Issues of egalitarianism arise with the displacement of Perpetua's motherhood onto Felicitas. Presumably, Perpetua could have been led into the arena alone and the crowd would have been horrified by the sight of *her* lactating breasts, as opposed to Felicitas's, were the story merely to omit the slave-woman and the dual miracle of the sudden weaning of Perpetua's child and sudden drying up of her milk (114–15). Instead the crowd sees Perpetua as a "young girl" and they are *horruit* (128) [horrified] (129) by the spectacle, apparently just as much as they are by the spectacle of Felicitas, obviously a new mother. The mob demands garments for both women, but it presumably does not know that Perpetua is a recent mother whose condition has been miraculously transformed. Perhaps, the spectators would assume that she is a virgin, as the terms *puellam delicatam* [delicate young girl] suggest. Thus, at the martyrdoms, the passio seems to want to present two conventional aspects of womanhood at once, maternity and virginity. Since both women, one a recent mother and the other (at least by appearances) not, then receive the same torture and the same reaction from the crowd to their bodies, the passio proceeds to undercut motherhood as the essential sign of female status, and traditional attitudes toward women consequently receive a further hit. More generally, the effect of forcing two women into the arena in order to face a deranged female animal is to suffuse the scene with the idea of being female, and the *Passio Sanctarum Perpetuae et Felicitatis* hence creates a world of "femenye"—in the most unlikely of places.

This pair of female figures put on display, Perpetua and Felicitas, also represent in a very schematic way the beginning of the process of saints mimicking other saints as hagiography becomes popular and perceived as an effective means to promote Christianity. But, despite the positive presentation of a kind of female instruction and inheritance in this passio, the seeds of duplication are in it as well. Felicitas, not nearly as developed as a character in the narrative as Perpetua is, is clearly a copy of the latter as opposed to a figure who would be able to stand on her own, and as opposed to earlier habits of repetition in the early martyrologies where *events* typically get repeated rather than characters within the same composition. Felicitas's motherhood is, in contrast, a clear imitation of part of Perpetua's biography. This pairing or mimicry suggests that a special genre of saints' life tailored to traditional representations of women could arise and it duly does (*LA*, 29–32, 113–17, etc.). Such lives usually contrast with the depictions of male saints who often, for instance, are not virgins and who often maintain abilities to participate in situations from which female saints are typically excluded. Hence, the *Passio Sanctarum Perpetuae et Felicitatis*, while it revels in images of female expressive power, contributes to and perhaps is an originator of the later counterfeiting of women's images in saints' lives.

Transvestism: The Virgin of Antioch from Ambrose's *De Virginibus*

My reading of the *Passio Sanctarum Perpetuae et Felicitatis* is unashamedly feminist. The fact remains, however, that, as Perpetua's dream metamorphosis into a man implies, this work can only be interpreted as feminist or even profeminine from a standpoint that is much later than its composition, while early Christian ideals regarding the relationships between the sexes are, even at their most extreme, egalitarian rather than partisan. With this egalitarianism in mind, verbalized most explicitly in Galatians 3:28 ("There is neither Jew nor Greek: there is neither bond nor free, there is neither male nor female. For you are all one in Christ Jesus"), one needs to consider briefly the issue of the gendering of patience literature within the context of early medieval attempts to provide narrative proof for the apostle's statement. The most obvious candidates for such narrative would be the many accounts of transvestite saints who live among men as women (or, much more rarely, vice versa) in order usually to promote ideals of chastity (*LA*, 603–05, 674–77).[66] The concept of transvestism would likely occur to early Christian apologists as a useful image of alienation: a Christian in a time of persecution, even an early Christian in the world generally, might feel like someone wearing the clothing of the other sex. But such stories also propose that saints can transcend their sexes, and that the assumption of the maleness or femaleness of any person is a socialized process based on role-playing and the exercise of certain social conventions. Moreover, patience works that profess or imply that gender differences simply do not matter at all have obviously progressed from those earlier works such as the passios that often declare or imply that women can behave like men and only then become numbered among the great heroes of the past.

There has been much recent interest in transvestite saints,[67] but I limit my discussion to Ambrose's story of a virgin of Antioch from his *De Virginibus*, one of his earliest works (c. 377), because the issues of transformation implied in transvestism reach the height of complexity in this narrative. For instance, a member of both sexes wears the other's clothes, and several characters discourse at length with others about the consequences of cross-dressing—rare events in these kinds of narratives.[68] There is also a kind of mixing of genders in the very language of early Christian texts such as Ambrose's *De Virginibus* that fits with the more general idea of transvestism. Mathew Kuefler notes that Ambrose and other early Christian writers "took advantage of the language of gender ambiguity in asserting their authority, describing themselves both as feminine in relation to God and as masculine in relation to other Christians."[69] The story of the anonymous woman of Antioch is significant in that it is one of the earliest of its kind and remained popular through the Middle Ages as one may see by its inclusion in the thirteenth-century *Legenda Aurea* (273–77), while Ambrose is one of the more influential church fathers. For the purposes of my argument, one may see development from the story of Perpetua to the story of this virgin, where the male writer seems to attack gender stereotypes, or at least seems to suggest that the gender divisions in society are merely human, traditionally conceived, and fallible.

The protagonist is an anonymous young woman of Antioch who shuts herself away from the male gaze (4.22). The result is that she becomes in McInerney's words "an erotically supercharged figure" to the pagan men who desire her. But at last *non iam amaretur, sed proderetur*, "she was no longer loved; instead she was betrayed" (4.22). She refuses to sacrifice to pagan gods, so she is taken to a brothel: the most commonly occurring By Way in the lives of female saints (4.26).[70] Such a beginning is thus quite standard for martyrdoms of a more literary bent than the earliest ones, but Ambrose's treatment of this By Way is uniquely complex. He presents the brothel as just as much a place of spectacle as the arena, complete with exceptionally strident speeches and actions: *Fit ingens petulantium concursus ad fornicem* [A huge crowd of curiosity seekers surged towards the bordello] (4.27). Indeed the actions of the crowds seem hypergeneralized in this work, while Ambrose in his moralistic vein can imply that the arena is a kind of brothel. In contrast to many of these kinds of narratives where the heroine attracts the desire of an individual, usually an official in the Roman government, here the lust is generalized to the point that it seems to be an attribute of all men. The generalized emotion together with its childish fickleness (lust turns to hate in the space of one sentence) underlines the worldly, illogical, and irresponsible aspects of it, though there is nothing particularly profeminine about Ambrose's treatment of male desire. He condemns all sexual desire as a worldly distraction (and, interestingly, he also condemns cross-dressing).[71]

The very generalized behaviors together with other aspects of the text demonstrate that Ambrose's story of the anonymous virgin of Antioch amounts to a highly literary interpretation of the earlier martyrdoms. For instance, Ambrose rewrites the typical heroine of a passio in order to make her more proactive and prophetic. The young woman of Antioch prays that the savage minds of men might be tamed and that she be able to exit the brothel still a virgin (4.28). This prayer is not as naïve as it might seem. Typical passios of this kind curtly refer to miracles that preserve the saints' virginity at this juncture (*LA*, 28, 114, 701), but Ambrose's narrative is an exception in that the "miracle" is very elaborate. A *vir militis specie terribilis* [man with the appearance of a fearsome soldier], surely one of the more ludicrously theatrical speech-makers in all of literary history, bursts into the woman's room in the brothel (4.28).[72] We learn almost nothing about him save for this description and his unexplained desires to rescue her and martyr himself. Just like the young woman, he remains anonymous. At least his literary origins are clear: the typical persecutor or executioner of the early passios who is converted to Christianity through coming to admire his victims (Musurillo, ed., 81, 135, 165, 207). Such tangential figures, however, are usually dismissed with the briefest of asides and rarely speak, while this legionnaire's entrance into the narrative is remarkably dramatic, his words are urgent, and his proposals are specific, though bizarre:

> Ne, quaeso, paveas, soror. Frater huc veni salvare animam, non perdere. Serva me, ut ipsa serveris. Quasi adulter ingressus, si vis, martyr egrediar. Vestimenta mutemus; convenient mihi tua, et mea tibi: sed utraque Christo. Tua vestis me verum militem faciet, mea te virginem. Bene tu vestieris, ego melius exuar, ut me persecutor agnoscat. Sume habitum, qui abscondat feminam: trade, qui consecret martyrem. (4.29)
>
> [I beg you not to fear, my sister. I have come here as your brother to save my soul, not to destroy it. Heed me, so that you may be spared. Having come in as an adulterer, I shall, if you wish, go out as a martyr. Let us exchange our clothing; yours fits me and mine fits you, but both fit Christ. Your garb will make me a true soldier; mine will make you a virgin. You will be clothed well and I shall be stripped better, so that the persecutor may recognize me. Put on the garment that will hide the woman and hand over the one that will consecrate the martyr.] (99)

Ambrose might be using this idea of exchange to take a common role-reversal motif to its logical conclusion. In fact, the story in general represents a very schematic role-reversal of not only the sexes but also persecutors and victims. He even seems to hint at an ideal mixture of attributes from both sexes in the same person when he connects the idea of a female virgin's escape to the idea of a man in a woman's role; yet the resulting masquerade often reads like a creakily formal bedroom farce.[73]

The rhetoric of this story comes over as extreme in part because of the disjunction between attitude and action that the soldier displays, as if Ambrose desperately wants to preserve this character's masculinity despite the transvestism. After all, the identifying phrase for this man that would most likely stick in readers' minds, absent any further identifying information, would be the description *vir militis specie terribilis* [man with the appearance of a fearsome soldier] that introduces him. He also comes over as hypermasculinized because he is an extreme version of the typical spiritual athlete of the earlier passios.[74] The man in the brothel, like a typical hero, immediately takes over the action. He spouts authoritative phrases in peculiarly formal rhetoric. Asserting that a garment exchange will make him into a *verum militem* [true soldier], he aggressively proposes and implements his plans. He orders that the woman strip, presumably in front of him, almost as if the implied sexual encounter at the moment of his entry were still going to take place.[75] But, after all the bombast, this fearsome soldier's chief activities are to don a woman's garment and perhaps to lie in a bed, and Burrus's argument that the story of the woman of Antioch demonstrates how fourth-century Christian apologists tend to sublimate and veil male aggression does not quite fit the situation.[76]

The soldier describes himself as *Quasi adulter ingressus* [having come in (to the bordello) as an adulterer] (4.29). By implying that the outside appearance that identifies him as a Roman legionnaire, emblematic of military conquest and hence of the traditional masculinist virtues such as glory in battle, is the same as that of an adulterer, and by radically repudiating his attire with an assertion that woman's clothing will make him into a true soldier, he associates typically masculine attributes with illicit sexual conduct and with lack of control over one's desires.[77] Ambrose has already put forward the idea of a brothel-customer as possessing less-than-human reasoning powers through the use of animal imagery: men as hawks, lions, sheep among wolves (4.27–28). Later the adulterer-clothes association becomes explicit as the legionnaire *chlamydem exuit, suspectus tamen adhuc habitus et persecutoris et adulteri* [remove(s) his cloak, which was a garment that until this time was suspected of being that of a persecutor and an adulterer] (4.30). His readiness to hand it over demonstrates the disposability of what it represents; its effectiveness as a disguise for the woman demonstrates its superficiality. A soldier's equipment is merely a hiding mechanism: *servetque pudorem; abscondat ora* (4.29).

Meanwhile, the woman's dress that she gives to her rescuer has the effect of identifying him as he would wish, a person deserving immediate execution—that is, a martyr. Presumably a prostitute would wear, if anything, a garment that would be easy to lift or remove, and hence probably too revealing to hide the wearer's sex very thoroughly (depending of course on other aspects of the wearer's appearance). Underclothing (or nakedness) is also the typical garment (or lack thereof) that martyrs are tortured and executed in, as the soldier demonstrates by assuming that the next client who enters the room will almost immediately identify him as a man *in spite of* what he is wearing, whereupon his executioner will immediately identify him as a condemned man *because of* what he is wearing—almost as if the next person into the room (likely a military man like himself) will be this executioner. Presumably, the discovery of the first man's sex would lead to his near instant condemnation because a client who expects to find a woman in a brothel and finds a man instead would be so offended that only the most extreme kind of punishment would suit the perpetrators of such a fraud. In the event, the garment exchange leads to this exact result, as Ambrose observes: *damnatus est pro virgine, qui pro virgine comprehensus est* [he who had been seized in place of the virgin was condemned in place of the virgin] (4.32), but it also causes the reader to reflect upon the idea of the sexes in one another's clothing.

Any feeling of offense and resulting condemnation depends completely on normative and regulatory sexual attitudes.[78]

There is further evidence that Ambrose's story undercuts traditional gender roles. For instance, the rescuer's disguise certainly causes confusion in the mind of the next person to enter the room, *Unus qui erat immodestior* [one who was less modest], who duly recognizes its occupant at once as a man. Then, in an example of astute psychological observation on Ambrose's part, the new arrival starts to talk to himself: *Quid hoc, inquit, est? Puella ingressus est, vir videtur* [he said, "What is this? A maiden went in but a man is here"] (4.31). Such self-address not only betrays the conflicting emotions in the character's mind that arise from his unexpected predicament but also confirms that the person that this man encounters in the bordello is a version of himself, almost as if he were looking into a mirror. The speech patterns of the two men are almost identical (the new client seems to take over from the soldier, who remains silent throughout their encounter), both of them start talking the moment they enter the bedroom, both exchange their desire for sex for a desire for chastity,[79] and the first one declares that his new garb will make him into a true soldier: a kind of "true man." Thus, Ambrose's fourth-century patience narrative seems to be party to the psychologically informed viewpoint that men who are hunting for presumed sexual goals are really hunting for themselves or aspects of themselves.

The theme of narcissism continues when the less modest man immediately comes up with a mythological reference: *Ecce non fabulosum illud cerva pro virgine, sed quod verum est, miles ex virgine* ["This is not that famous story of the hind substituted for the virgin. Rather it is a case of a maiden being transformed into a soldier"] (4.31). The allusion apparently is to the story of Iphigenia who is miraculously replaced by a hind, a sacrificial beast, at the moment when her father is about to slay her in order to appease the gods.[80] The context of this myth's retelling renders it much more resonant than the second reveller could know. For instance, his reading of the story together with his situation means that he parallels going to a brothel with an ancient pagan rite of human sacrifice. Ambrose could not ask for better guilt by association, while sacrifice of course connects with Christ, Isaac, other figures of Christ, and martyrs. A Christian audience would also know that, with the mythological reference, the "metamorphoses" of the virgin of Antioch and her rescuer are being compared to other miracles of transformation, even though the actions of the two characters (exchanging clothes) are hardly miraculous. In addition, the general connection of a love-object to a prey animal such as a hind means that this hunting analogy, a mainstay of classical myths and later of courtly love literature, starts to lose its dignity when its ultimate object is changed into a transvestite man in a bedroom, so Ambrose again makes his point about sexual morality. And, perhaps, the second reveller is more intuitive than he seems. The myth of Iphigenia describes the saving of a girl's life. The first man to enter the room has just saved the woman's life, so the second man seems to choose the story that he alludes to because he had some kind of impression of what has just happened previously in the bedroom that he enters. Certainly his mentioning of the myth suggests that he is genuinely and thoroughly reflecting upon what he has witnessed.

The second man's apparent epiphany, together with his allusion to a pagan myth of transformation, might lead readers to dismiss him as a naïve believer in pagan superstition and black magic. But he demonstrates familiarity with Christian scripture: *At etiam audieram et non credideram, quod aquam Christus in vinum convertit: jam mutare coepit et sexus* ["I had heard and did not believe that Christ changed water into wine, but now He has begun to change sexes as well"] (4.31; cf. John 2:9). His reading of the events is incorrect (there was no supernatural metamorphosis in the brothel) but his reading of the Christian God (from Ambrose's point of view) probably shows promise. The reveller also points one of the apparent morals of Ambrose's story: for God, the sexes are not important. They do not matter at crucial junctures in a believer's life such as conversion and martyrdom and are attributes that the Almighty can change at will. The viewing of a man in place of a woman is then, in this case, the first step on the road to the less modest man's conversion—or, rather, could be. This witness is prepared to believe but not yet to convert: *Recedamus hinc, dum adhuc qui fuimus sumus. Numquid et ipsa mutajus sum, qui aliud cerno, quam credo*? ["Let us get out of here while we still are what we are. Have I myself, who see something else than I can believe, been changed too?"] (4.31). Under stress, he comes up with the classic (and irrational) gay-panic defense for his actions. Seeing a man in a place of a woman, a "metamorphosis" he cannot bring himself to believe, the second reveller (in a psychologically realistic manner) turns the idea of transformation back upon himself. He imagines that he might be changing into a woman and/or might be changing into someone who desires men instead of women, and he clearly fears the prospect of such change. Also, like any deeply prejudiced person, he assumes that others share his views: in mid-flow he changes his self-addressed speech to a phrase that includes the cross-dressing soldier, *Recedamus hinc* ["let us get out of here"]. Or, more likely, the phrase indicates the split that is occurring in his mind as his conflicted desires and now conflicted views concerning Christianity come to the forefront. The text thus again parallels conflicted attitudes concerning faith with attitudes concerning the differences between the sexes and the differences between desiring a member of the opposite sex versus a member of the same one (with the latter desire analogous to Christianity). His fear demonstrates his solipsism and vanity. However, the results of the events are, in Ambrose's view, positive for him. The man says *Ad lupanar veni, cerno vadimonium: et tamen mutatus egrediar, pudicus exibo, qui adulter intravi* ["I came to a brothel, I see a pledge. And yet I shall depart changed, I shall go out chaste—I who came in unchaste"] (4.31). After his bordello experience, he seems to perceive something of the soldier's duty (why else mention "a pledge?"), he seems to have been frightened into chastity, and he seems to be able to serve as an example of a virtuous pagan. And his experience shows that in general the idea of change, *mutatus*, is connected here and throughout Ambrose's story with the idea of change from one sex to another. This patience story refuses to be content with the idea that a woman must become a man in order to enter heaven. Logically, the reverse idea must also be true. While the woman of Antioch wears the clothing of a man in order to get what she wants, equally the legionnaire wears the clothing of a woman in order to become a martyr and thus get what he wants: entry into heaven. As Burrus concludes, "a swapping of the sexes has become rather a fertile proliferation of feminized virtue,"[81] while Ambrose takes pains to apply the typical passio-images of athletic apotheosis to both of his protagonists equally: *vincerunt: nec divisa est corona, sed addita* (4.33) [both were victorious, and their crown was not divided but joined] (101). Finally, unlike Perpetua, Felicitas, and Blandina, the virgin of Antioch's method of execution is presumably of the same kind as her male counterpart (4.33).

The implied equality of the sexes that comes through in the sameness of the two protagonists' fates does not mean that Ambrose can ignore the traditional differences between the sexes altogether. He treats women as inferior to men when he compares his exemplum of the virgin of Antioch to another story that features only men: *hic una virgo, quae primo etiam sexum vinceret* [one was a virgin, who first overcame her sex] (5.35). The traditional hierarchy of sexes in the story is clear in that whereas the transvestite man seems to gain nothing from his new garments save that they *consecret martyrem* [will consecrate the martyr] (4.29), he describes the heroine as gaining important attributes besides rescue from rape through donning his outfit. For instance, by putting his clothing and equipment on she becomes an exemplar of two allegorical figures ultimately based on the armor of a Roman soldier: the *militem Christo* [soldier of Christ], as the transvestite man calls her, and the wearer of the armor of God (Ephesians 6:13–17), as this man immediately starts to interpret her.[82] (Ambrose elsewhere in the *De Virginibus* addresses female virgins as having *vos vestrae militiam pulchritudinis* [Book 1.6.30] [your own *soldierly* charm] [81; my emphasis]).

The anonymous woman bears the requisite allegorical arms such as the *scutum fidei* [shield of faith] (Book 2.4.29), according to the legionnaire, through taking up his equipment. She is masculinized in a similar way to Perpetua. But the woman of Antioch is only masculinized by a (temporary) outward state, as the clothing-exchange makes clear. Her inward qualities are maintained throughout the narrative and these presumably remain feminine. After all, she does not have to walk *into* the brothel dressed as a man, when braggadocio and other verbal manifestations of traditional masculinity would more likely be expected of her. A person leaving a bordello is, according to the story, more likely to slink away, avoiding notice as much as possible. The soldier describes a client leaving a brothel as typically embarrassed, *erubescere* (4.29).[83] The woman herself makes the point that dress has no significant effect upon her real nature when she later says *Tibi cessi vestem, non professionem mutavi* ["I have changed my clothing, not my profession"] (1.32). In contrast, the soldier's new attire indeed seems to affect his nature. His newfound chastity means that he has adopted at least one of her attributes and, after donning the woman's garment, his rhetorical bravado vanishes. When the next client enters the bedroom and speaks, the cross-dresser remains silent, though an attempt to convert this newcomer would seem to be both logical and, as it turns out, likely to succeed.

This succession of rhetorically domineering men, the usurping of the young woman's "place" in the bedroom by a soldier, and her dressing in military garb, all point to the dominance of masculinist attitudes. But the traditional hierarchy of sexes is disrupted when Ambrose continues the woman of Antioch's story beyond her escape and when the legionnaire, though generally a positive figure in the story, reveals his limiting sexism. While rescuing the woman, he concentrates on her desire to maintain her virginity: *Habes bonam militiam castitatis, quae stipendiis militat sempitcruis* ["You have accomplished much in the service of chastity, which fights for an everlasting gain"] (4.29). He apparently is blind to the fact that her ultimate goal is martyrdom. He assumes that his execution would simply substitute for her virginity without considering that she might want both her chastity *and* the crown of martyrdom. Her desire is clear when she runs to the arena (like an athlete) in order to secure death for herself and contradicts her rescuer when he presumes that her capital sentence has shifted onto him. Her assertions are so strong that they militate against any idea of this woman being from a weaker sex: *Non ego te mortis vadem elegi, sed praedem pudoris optavi* ["I did not choose you as a bondsman against my death but as a protector of my purity"] (4.32). The narrative becomes one "of female autonomy: she gets to choose her fate."[84] Her version of the events also vastly reduces his undeniably active role in them. She asserts that she chose him as her rescuer when the previous account seems to indicate that the soldier chose her as the means to his martyrdom. He provided the escape plan. She omits this detail. Apparently, she believes that her will must dominate: *Si pudor quaeritur, manet sexus: si sanguis exposcitur, fidejussorem non desidero, habeo unde dissolvam* ["If it is my purity that is being sought after, your obligation remains. But if it is my blood that is demanded, then I want no-one to assume liability for me; I have the means to pay my debt"].[85] Ruthlessly, she is prepared to use him or not depending on her circumstances. She then insists on her point of view, saying, *Cave, quaeso, ne contendas, cave ne contradicere audeas* ["Take care, I beg you, not to contend with me, take care not to dare to stand in my way"] (4.32). She silences her rescuer and any other opposition to her plan. She asks to be executed first, as if the proceedings were a race with heaven as the prize. Moreover, by interpreting her dealings with him as an economic relationship, as a legally binding contract (as the second client also seems to see when he interprets the transvestite soldier as a *vadimonium*, a "pledge"), she implies that men and women are equal before the law, just as they are in the early martyrdoms. She even openly challenges the authorities and onlookers: *quis me audet excludere? ... quis audet absolvere?* ["who would dare exclude me ... who would dare absolve me?"] (4.32). Her martyr-hero status permits her to speak so boldly, but she remains a woman—a "strangely masculine" one according to Burrus, but, significantly, issues of dress receive no mention during the martyrdom scene, as if they have ceased to matter.[86] In this scene, her gender transcends the fact that she is (presumably) still dressed as a soldier. The woman of Antioch fights for the crown of martyrdom with a male opponent (*contenderunt* [4.33]) and wins a small battle of the sexes because, against the odds in a man's world, she gets exactly what she wants, even while refusing help from a male rescuer.

Ambrose uses other means, besides the character of his heroine, to covertly undermine the traditional hierarchy of the sexes. For instance, having used a wolf and sheep analogy in order to indicate the differences between the sexes, *Ecce agna et lupus non solum* (4.30; 4.28), he then uses the same analogy to indicate the differences between persecutors and Christians: *ceu raptores ad agnam, ceu lupi fremere ad praedam* (4.31). On the surface, this parallel would seem to denigrate women by comparing them to lambs, typically associated with innocence and passivity. But, if the world may be divided into two animal groups by both sexual and moral attributes, then the sex-differences can be interpreted as moral, not inherent: changeable by God and via conversion. Ambrose's main point is that changing one's social role is as simple as changing one's clothing, as if sex-roles and perhaps other social roles in themselves were largely artificial and in the end insignificant. The only real solution to any gender identification problems of this world is the total collapse of gender distinctions in the next, as Ambrose confirms when he describes his two protagonists as *Addantur personae, miles et virgo, hoc est, dissimiles inter se natura, sed Dei miseratione consimiles*, [A soldier and a virgin—that is, persons unlike in nature but alike in God's mercy] (4.30). Meanwhile, statements such as "By the end of the fourth century, the legend of the virgin martyr had been rewritten from one that promised freedom from male domination to one that inculcated female submission to male authority, and especially female silence," need some qualification or perhaps a shift to a later time period.[87]

Denial of Any Sex: *The Vitae Columbani* of Jonas of Bobbio

The most idealistic connection between heroic patience and a collapse of the differences between the sexes occurs in the *Vitae Columbani* of Jonas of Bobbio (c. 645).[88] In his account of the royal abbess Burgundofara and the nuns in her convent, he takes the next logical step in the gendering of medieval patience literature, in idealizing patience as a gender-specific attribute, and in describing a female heroism of suffering when he associates patience with these nuns. In Burgundofara's convent, a young nun named Ercantrude repeats the example of Job, almost as if she descends from him:

> Tantaque tenera aetas flagella sustinuit, ut exemplum in eam Iob ex poenarum immanium multitudine crederes redundare. Sed mira in iuvenili aetate patientia repperiebatur. (262)
>
> [she suffered so many things in her tender years that, from the multitude of her sharp pains, you might believe that the example of Job was repeated in her. But behold what patience she found in her youth!] (165)[89]

Although the audience is invited to make the connection between Ercantrude and a patriarch, her patience arrives, according to the text, from an exclusively female tradition. The vita notes that she has grown up from infancy in the convent, presumably an environment completely free of men (262; trans., 164), before describing her mysterious suffering. The outward signs of her patience are recorded as athletic feats, as if she were a hero of the martyrologies: *Pollebat inter poene incendia virtus animae, manebat inconcussa fides, immobilis bonitas, inconparabilis lacrimarum ubertas* (262) [The strength of her soul stood firm in the fire of pain. Her faith held unshaken; her goodness was unmoved; the floods of her tears were incomparable] (165) ... *Gravibus ictuata vulneribus, flere coepit* [she began

to weep, wounded by the heavy blow (of being denied communion)] …
lacrimas et uberes rugitus ac crebra suspiria veniabilem (263) [tears and abundant groans and choking sighs] (165). Only after these sensational descriptions of her trials, reminiscent of the pains of childbirth and of Kristeva's feminine language, does Jonas introduce Ercantrude's attitude toward the sexes. The abbess Burgundofara

> Tanta custodia matris enutrita intra coenubii fuit septa, ut nullatenus inter sexuum noverit diiudicare naturam; aequae enim marem ut feminam putabat, aequae feminam ut marem. (262)
>
> [Nurtured her (Ercantrude) so carefully within the convent walls that she (Ercantrude) could not distinguish between our sexual natures: for she counted male and female the same; female and male just alike.] (165)

This innocence concerning sexual difference, which Jonas presents as a cultivated situation, as parallel to Ercantrude's endurance and therefore as a further pseudoheroic act, could be interpreted as merely a way of declaring that the younger nun had cast aside lust in general and as a way of comparing the ideal sheltered world of the convent to the constant buffets of the outside world. However, the text immediately follows the declaration concerning sex-differences with another encomium to Ercantrude's patience: *Exemplum etenim erat omnibus uberis conversatio, patientiae virtus, pietatis cultus, lenitatis affectus* (262) [Her behavior was an example to all of the rich power of patience, of pious worship, and loving gentleness] (165), confirming that Jonas wants his audience to connect the two virtues of patience and extreme sexual innocence. Also, Burgundofara's role in developing the ideal qualities of Ercantrude is crucial.

For instance, the older woman seems to make sure that her own unavoidable worldliness will not be reproduced in her student, and Ercantrude's suffering seems to represent a purging of this worldliness. The narrative thus implies that complete disregard for sexual differences can only come about through instruction from a member of the same sex to an individual who begins his or her learning process with a blank state. Since Burgundofara is a woman, and there is no parallel instance in this text of a man who rises to Ercantrude's achievement of total sexual innocence, this particular vita comes over as profeminine, while the narrative in general focuses on the differences between men and women quite strongly, in particular describing the abbess's struggles with various male authorities, most notably her father (241–43; 253). On the one hand, Ercantrude seems to represent the height of egalitarian thinking with regard to the sexes in patience literature. Her attitude marks obvious progress from the suggestion in the *passios* that women can behave like men and therefore become numbered among the great heroes of the past. The idea that, in contrast, gender differences simply do not matter at all is perfective. On the other hand, such idealism is never repeated in Jonas's work and it seems to be naïve. For instance, the concept that a person can achieve perfect chastity through not bothering with sex-differences implies that same-sex relations never occur.

Feminine Expression in the *Vitae Columbani*

Besides heroic patience and a suggestion of total equality between the sexes, Burgundofara's vita shares with earlier saints' lives a concern with feminine expression, though, interestingly, Jonas treats the idea of an exclusively feminine language with caution. One chapter of the life of Burgundofara tells the story of a young nun named Anistrude and an unnamed member of the abbess's convent who witness and describe one of the other nuns, Domna, as having *globus igneus candido fulgore rutilans micabat* (267), "a globe of white fire [that] shone, glittering and sparkling" (168) in her mouth when she sings after receiving communion. This image conflates the miracles of transubstantiation and of the Word made flesh and recalls the biblical traditions of divine language that Perpetua encounters in her first dream (Revelation 10:9–11; Ezekiel 3:1–5; Proverbs 16:24; Psalms 19:10, 119:103). Nevertheless the description is an ambiguous act because Domna succumbs to the sin of vanity upon hearing of the miracle ascribed to her, and both of the witnesses of Domna's miracle come down with a fatal illness, whereupon one of them begins *una earum inaudita auribus humanis carmina* [to sing a song unheard by human ears], reminiscent of the women's language in *The Testament of Job*: *dulcia modulamina pio ore canere, orare conditorem miris sermonibus, inauditis precibus, ineffabilibus sacramentis* (267) [Sweet harmonies issued from her pious mouth praying the Creator with wonderful words, unheard prayers, ineffable mysteries] (168). Since the globe in Domna's mouth is a gift from God and appears when she is singing, it represents not only the miraculous body of Christ but also language: He is the Word. The witness's deathbed language must be a legacy from Domna to her, as if she inherits a divine language that is exclusive to young women. Despite the fact that Domna never reappears in the subsequent narrative, she presumably retains the potential to receive the ability of miraculous language from God if only she were free of sin. Perhaps, had she resisted the temptation of vanity, the entire convent, an exclusively female community, could have adopted her new language. This miracle of language and other attributions of peculiar powers to women in Jonas's work probably also reflect general attitudes toward women that are a feature of Burgundofara's era and locale. The editors of the most recent English translation of these stories from Merovingian France, *Sainted Women of the Dark Ages*, put the lives of Burgundofara and her followers into the context of a culture where royal decrees had "placed women in a favorable position in the inheritance system" and made such women into "valuable repositories of wealth" (159).

Of course, the very ideas of transvestism, feminine language, and the collapse of gender differences altogether, not to mention a female martyr who possesses the expressive power of Perpetua, trigger during the early Middle Ages a variety of responses. Besides the increasingly literary idea that female patience figures could imitate one another, these responses also include a backlash similar to the reaction against *l'écriture féminine* that persists among much literary criticism to the present day. This backlash has a part in the early medieval conceptions of the personified patience figure.

CHAPTER 2

THE FEMALE PATIENCE FIGURE
AS FROZEN SPEAKER

> *The insignificance of language, of the properly linguistic body: it can only take on meaning in relation to a* place.
>
> —Jacques Derrida, *Shibboleth: For Paul Celan*, trans. Joshua Wilner,
> in Derrida, *Acts of Literature*, ed. Derek Attridge
> (New York: Routledge, 1992), p. 407

Much evidence for the gendering of patience literature appears in late classical and early medieval discussions of patience that employ personification and allegory: widely used rhetorical techniques in these periods. Very quickly and almost unvaryingly these discussions present patience as a female figure,[1] and the monumental qualities of even the earliest of these personifications demonstrate that writers conceived the personification process, at least partially, as a marking out of space—as might be expected when this process casts abstract concepts into the forms of statue-like representations. But marking out spaces would be an unusual activity for late antique or early medieval women. Consequently, as patience literature develops and mimicry of patience figures changes into duplication, many female figures of patience start to occupy and define spaces that early medieval writers identify more and more specifically as "appropriate" ones for women.

The Christian tradition of the female personification of patience almost certainly originates in the *de Patientia* of Tertullian, probably the most famous treatise from the early church fathers concerning this virtue, written around the year AD 200. This treatise offers clues regarding the monumental aspects of allegorized patience, but it is surprisingly inconclusive with regard to this figure's gender. Prudentius's personification of patience in his *Psychomachia* also has its surprising aspects, though the allegorical figure of Patience that he creates is certainly part of the tradition of perceiving patience as a typically feminine attribute. Indeed, this tradition was probably involved in the tendency of medieval writers such as the author of the Old English *Genesis A* to reimagine certain Old Testament characters into patience figures. For example, Lot's wife becomes—rather unexpectedly—a particularly important patience figure.

Tertullian's Personification of Patience

Although the Western Christian tradition of presenting a personification of patience as female probably springs from Patientia's depiction in Tertullian's *de Patientia*, as a whole this allegory involves a surprisingly complex combination of attitudes toward gender.[2] When he begins his description of a personification of patience, the noun *patientia* (gendered feminine in Latin) does not appear until several sentences into the description, as if Tertullian were reluctant to assign the virtue to a sex-specified figure.[3] This delaying tactic echoes the rhetorical technique that he has used just previously to introduce another character. Job appears first as *illum* [that man] three times before Tertullian finally names him, well on in the paragraph and well after relating many of the events in Job's life (315; trans., 218). By omitting to name a famous patriarch until the last possible moment Tertullian is probably trying to distinguish, in a subtle fashion, a Christian understanding of patience from the morally dangerous idea of taking pride in this (or any) virtue: true Christians should not exercise patience in order to seek glory for their names, so at first no name appears. But this device teases the reader by inching the description along in a rather coy and frustrating manner.

This same manner characterizes the introduction of Tertullian's personification of patience, who like Job is introduced obliquely and with a masculine pronoun, *eius*. Indeed, the introduction is so oblique that readers might be unsure of Tertullian's exact intentions and meaning until the description is well underway:

> Age iam, si et effigiem habitumque eius. Conprehendamus: uultus illi tranquillus et placidus, frons pura nulla maeroris aut irae rugositate contracta; remissa aeque in laetum modum supercilia; oculi humilitate, non infelicitate deiecti; os taciturnitatis honore signatum, color qualis securis et innoxiis, motus frequens capitis in diabolum et minax risus; ceterum amictus circum pectora candidus et corpori inpressus ut qui nec inflatur nec inquietatur. Sedet enim in throno spiritus eius mitissimi et mansuetissimi qui non turbine glomeratur, non nubilo liuet, sed est tenerae

serenitatis, apertus et simplex, quem tertio uidit Helias. Nam ubi deus, ibi et alumna eius, patientia scilicet. (15.4–6)

[If you will, let us try to grasp the features and appearance of patience. Its countenance is peaceful and untroubled. Its brow is clear, unruffled by any lines of melancholy or anger. The eyebrows are relaxed, giving an impression of joyousness. The eyes are lowered, in an attitude rather of humility than moroseness. The mouth is closed in becoming silence. Its complexion is that of the serene and blameless. It shakes its head frequently in the direction of the devil, and its laughter conveys a threat to him. The upper part of its garment is white and close-fitting so that it is not blown about or disturbed (by the wind). It sits on the throne of its spirit which is extremely mild and gentle and is not whipped into a knot by the whirlwind, is not made livid by a cloud, but is a breeze of soft light, clear and simple, such as Elias saw the third time. For where God is, there, too, is the child of His nurturing, namely, patience.] (220)

Through most of this description Tertullian persists in identifying the figure with vague pronouns, for example, *illi* [its], instead of with a name. He thus refuses to come out and say explicitly that the personification of patience is female, despite the prevailing gender assumptions concerning this figure in later criticism.[4] Readers coming across the passage for the first time then will almost certainly assume by default that the figure is masculine, just as an earlier *eius* turned out to be Job. Consequently, they must rely on particular aspects of the character's description, for instance, *oculi* [eyes] that *humilitate* [are lowered] and clothing: *ceterum amictus circum pectora candidus et corpori inpressus* (15.5) [the upper part of its garment is white and close-fitting] (220), in order to guess at the figure's gender, due to the vagueness of the passage's pronoun referents; but, even with these clues, Tertullian's personification of patience remains curiously generalized.[5] He invites readers to interpret its gender only through the (re)activation of gender assumptions based on preconceived social attitudes concerning outward appearances—while here asserting no such assumptions himself. Nor is this delaying technique typical of Latin prose style. He suspends resolution of the question of the identity of this figure to such an extent that translators typically insert the word "patience" much earlier in the paragraph, as the translator above does, so that the reader is more likely to make sense of the passage. This lengthy delay of identifying material has the effect of spotlighting the attitudes concerning gender and other aspects of a person that would typically lead readers to make identifications. A further curious aspect of the personification is that, until its last sentence, there is nothing particularly Christian about it. The description recalls others of idealized, modest, statuesque women in classical literature.[6]

Previous interpreters have further contributed to the assumption that Tertullian's personification of patience is simply and traditionally female by taking the passage out of context. In the paragraph just previous to the one that invites the reader to "grasp the features and appearance" of patience, the virtue is also personified, though not as extensively as later. Here patience performs a series of activities. If one accepts for the moment the traditional presumption that activity is typically a male attribute while passivity is typically female (Shaw, "Body," 279),[7] then this personification is most likely male:

> fidem munit, pacem gubernat, dilectionem adiuuat, humilitatem instruit, paenitentiam expectat, exhomologesin adsignat, carnem regit, spiritum seruat, linguam frenat, manum continet, temptationes inculcat, scandala pellit, martyria consummat. (15.2)
>
> [it strengthens faith, governs peace, sustains love, instructs humility, awaits repentance, places its seal upon the discipline of penance, controls the flesh, preserves the spirit, puts restraint upon the tongue, holds back the (violent) hand, treads under foot temptations, pushes scandal aside, consummates martyrdom.] (219–20)

In this sentence, the abstract idea of patience begins to take on a vaguely human aspect once the verbs start to denote actions typically performed by people: *frenat, inculcat*. Yet, just as in Tertullian's slightly later description of a figure of patience, he relies on the audience to assume a gender for the personified figure while declining to assert any gender identification himself. The apologist then ends this paragraph with *In omni sexu, in omni aetate formosa est* (15.3) [in both man and woman, at every age of life, (patience) is exceedingly attractive] (220), an even-handed treatment of the two sexes.[8] Thus, with his discussion of patience, Tertullian is able to promote two major themes of his writings: martyrdom as the ultimate manifestation of patience and endurance, and, more subtly, the early Christian ideal of egalitarianism.

A further aspect of Tertullian's famous personification of patience that has been ignored by critics is that, having sketched in a feminine figure through detailing its clothing and demeanor, Tertullian proceeds to muddle this provisional gender identification and then abstract it beyond all gender. He describes the figure, still indicated by *eius* [it], as *Sedet enim in throno spiritus* (15.6) [sitting on the throne of its spirit] (220), a rather chimerical mixture of abstract and concrete images. He further defines the personification as *tenerae serenitatis, apertus et simplex, quem tertio uidit Helias* (15.6) [a breeze of soft light, clear and simple, such as Elias saw the third time] (220), a contradiction in terms that conflates the figure of patience with an enigmatic vision of the (male) Lord Himself: in the biblical prophet Elijah's third vision, God appears, after wind, earthquake, and fire, as "a whistling of a gentle air" (1 Kings 19:12). This representation undercuts the previous identification of the patience figure as female. Only after these rather bewildering suggestions and 12 lines into the description does Tertullian conclude *Nam ubi deus, ibi et alumna eius, patientia scilicet* (15.6) [For where God is, there, too, is the child of His nurturing, namely, patience] (220), whereupon readers may at last ascertain the name and gender of the personification plus its exact relationship to God; but only after so much game-playing by the writer concerning the issue of gender that few readers would be comfortable with a conclusion that pinpoints patience as an unambiguously and purely feminine virtue—though, strangely, this has been the conclusion of almost all interpreters of this passage.

For Tertullian to be profeminine is uncharacteristic. He announces in this same treatise that patience *feminam exornat, uirum adprobat* (15.3) [adorns a woman, perfects a man] (220), as if women were material, not capable of perfection, and men were abstract; as if women typically do not strive for the traditional virtues in the ways that men do (perhaps, Tertullian thinks, in the ways that men must); as if only men have reason. He composes an influential treatise disparaging the supposedly ostentatious and provocative dress of women, attacks their authority as speakers, and seems to fear their sexual desires.[9] But his personification of patience refuses to equate or burden femininity with passivity openly, his attitudes toward the female body is much more positive than the attitudes of many contemporary thinkers, and certainly his text refrains from constructing a figure of patience out of broad, sex-based stereotypes.[10] Rather, Tertullian sketches her in as female using the lightest of touches. So, although the tradition of patience personified as a woman begins very early in patience literature, examination of at least one of the foundational texts of this tradition betrays the fact that the sexism of later interpreters is more responsible for this tradition than the early writers themselves.

Another very influential personification of patience in the early medieval period, from Prudentius's *Psychomachia* (c. 400), is also ambiguous with regard to the gender attributes of its protagonist, due primarily to the consistently and elaborately warlike presentation of Patientia herself (lines 124–40). Generally, the personified virtues, all female, of the *Psychomachia* bear a resemblance to Ambrose's transvestite martyrs, bellowing away in their resolutely moralistic and faintly ridiculous manner. In sum, all three Latin writers have trouble integrating the masculine and feminine attributes of patience into one character. Tertullian distinguishes himself from the other writers in that his touch is light. Ambrose's and Prudentius's are heavy.

Loth's Wife in the Old English Tradition

Despite their obvious differences, these two early medieval patience figures from Tertullian and Prudentius share one disquieting aspect: both personifications are reminiscent of statues, when readers often associate a tendency to view women as artworks with the objectification of women, with the growing paralysis of the early martyrologies' egalitarian thinking, and eventually with counterfeit consciousness. This monumental quality strongly influences future manifestations of patience figures, and is particularly significant for medieval discussions of the fate of Lot's wife, a highly individual patience figure, first described in Genesis 19:26. Since Old Testament narratives often depict suffering women who are neither saints nor figures from the heroic tradition, it is also important for my argument more generally to examine early medieval versions of such bible stories. The occurrence of such anomalous patience figures demonstrates that patience literature is indeed a distinct genre in Western Europe and Britain, even in the early Middle Ages, if only because it maintains an existence outside of hagiography.

Generally, there is more tension between histories, genders, and traditions in Old English scripture-based poems than would appear to be the case at first glance.[11] In particular, with the depiction of events concerning Loth's wife in the Old English verse *Genesis A*, evidence emerges for women being famous for patience precisely in the way that men are famous for the traditional heroic virtues. There is only one manuscript copy of this relatively neglected work, which appears as the first item in MS Junius 11 in the Bodleian Library, a manuscript that dates from AD 1000 to 1025. *Genesis A* seems to be one of the earlier Old English compositions: A. N. Doane dates it to the eighth century, roughly contemporary with *Beowulf*.[12]

In the middle of describing Loth's wife's transformation into salt, the narrative voice of *Genesis A* interrupts the story in order to announce *þæt is mære spell* (2568b) [this is a famous story], when these kinds of substantive additions to the poet's scriptural sources are relatively rare. Paul G. Remley observes that, except for the poet's expansion of three episodes, the capture of Loth, Abraham's war against the five kings, and the destruction of Sodom and Gomorrah, the Old English writer follows the Vulgate-Genesis rather closely.[13] Through additions such as *þæt is mære spell*, and through the retelling of the story of the cities of the plain more generally, the poet of *Genesis A* produces in Loth's wife a patience figure par excellence who also betrays a remarkably subversive quality that comes through in her message and her legacy. Her legacy takes the form of statements by her daughters and by Abraham's wife, Sarra (2560–74; 2599–614)—like Loth's wife, strong-willed women—that seem to suggest that women are able to secure audiences for their speeches despite disobedient behavior and attempts to silence them. The play of oppositions (oppositions between men and women, between oral tradition and written history, between sanctioned acts and unsanctioned acts) that occurs in *Genesis A* results in a reiteration of God's authority but also in examples of *mægðe sið*, literally the "journey [or undertaking] of women," which, rather surprisingly for such an overtly pious work, subvert God's and scriptural authority.[14]

On the surface, the women of *Genesis A* have little chance for expression; they contrast with the overtly male messengers of God's word. The start of the poem credits the Almighty with the origin of language and with the authority within language (6, 104, 111), and God's frequent conversations with Abraham and statements such as *waldend usser þurh his word abead* (1771), "The Lord commanded [Abraham] through His Word" reaffirm this accreditation throughout the entire Abraham story. In contrast, Loth's wife is silent and nameless through her entire episode. She seems to be an utterly passive character. Loth leads her into various lands and situations, but her feelings with regard to these major events in her life go unrecorded. During the territorial wars, when Loth and his family require rescue by Abraham and his army, women are reduced to the role of mere possessions when they are carried off like booty (2090b). Once, they are even paired with rings as if they *were* booty (2085–87).

Besides the overtly sexist attitudes in the *Genesis A*-account of Loth's wife, modern readers presumably have even more fundamental reasons to interpret her story in almost all of its popular versions as a pernicious example of double standards and of the habitual scapegoating of women. By being turned into salt for disobediently looking at communities that are being punished by God for the sexual sins of their inhabitants (Genesis 19:26), she represents the blame that is unjustly placed on women for the sexual activities of men. The guilt and shame that often flare up arbitrarily after instances of male sexual aggression are irrationally displaced onto the female body of Loth's wife, as if that body were somehow a more appropriate outlet for the expression of guilt and shame—perhaps of suffering more generally—than a man's body, often associated instead with control of the emotions.[15] Certainly, a woman petrified for being disobedient would seem to be an archetypical figure of subservient roles for women in a patriarchal society.

But such scapegoat figures, as certain attributes of patience literature make plain, are not as passive as they might seem at first. In *Genesis A* when God changes Loth's wife into "salt-stone," the poem makes it clear to readers that she offers a message in the precise moment that she makes her way into a By Way and is petrified:

> Þa þæt fyrgebræc,
> leoda lifgedal,   Lothes gehyrde
> bryd on burgum,   under bæc beseah
> wið þæs wælfylles.   Us gewritu secgað
> þæt heo on sealtstanes   sona wurde
> anlicnesse.   Æfre siððan
> se monlica   (þæt is mære spell)
> stille wunode,   þær hie strang begeat
> wite,   (2562b–70a)

[When Loth's city-wife heard the noise of fire, the death of the people, then she looked back at the slaughter. The scriptures say to us that she at once turned into a figure of salt-stone. Ever afterward this likeness (this is a famous story) has remained there, still, where she received this harsh punishment.]

The Old English words that the poet uses for the transformed state of Loth's wife, *anlicnesse,* "figure" and *monlica,* "likeness," express not only the idea of a statue, as the Latin Vulgate text does with *respiciensque uxor eius post de, versa est in statuam salis* (Genesis 19:26) [and his wife, while glancing behind her, was changed into a statue of salt], but a figure or image: that is, an object with a particular message.[16] Certainly, the word *spell* in the phrase *þæt is mære spell* can mean "message" rather than "story." Also, the pronoun *þæt* in the phrase could have as its referent the word *monlica,* as opposed to being a reference to the events of the transformation more generally. With this more precise referent the "likeness" of Loth's wife would then embody the story that the narrator here relates. Two questions then come up due to the poet's indication of a message from Loth's wife: what is that message, and how does the figure express it? Obvious answers to the questions are that she must (at least primarily) represent patience, because she makes manifest, with the events of her metamorphosis, both suffering and a near immortal existence. Unlike the biblical account in Genesis, the poem emphasizes that she exists, after the events of her transformation, for *Æfre* [ever]. She thus perfectly represents what Kristeva calls "monumental" or "women's time."[17] Moreover, because of her disobedience to God, she represents a kind of patience that must be distinct from that of the saints.

Lot's Wife: Interpretations

But a more crudely literal interpretation (or noninterpretation) of the message of the story of Lot's wife has, rather surprisingly, prevailed in much of the criticism of the transformation scene that a scholar is likely to encounter first when researching this narrative. When one looks up the entry for Lot's wife in bible encyclopedias and dictionaries, it often includes a photograph of a rocky feature in the desert by the Dead Sea, with a caption by the writer averring that, traditionally, this rock has been called Lot's wife. The Internet offers many examples of such images. I have always found the inclusion, content, and presentation of these photographs extremely puzzling.[18] How do they help a reader to understand the story? The rocky formations in them never even remotely resemble human beings. Without these stone objects' (probably arbitrary) connection to the account of Lot's wife, there seems to be no reason to anthropomorphize them: they would seem to suggest nothing in particular to, and have no particular appeal for, a viewer. In other words, they look like nothing except rocks (see Figure 2.1).

If one accepts any one of their identifications as indeed Lot's wife, any identity that she might have, beyond the most reductive kind, is obliterated.[19]

A glance through several of these handbooks and encyclopedias and the many images on the Internet would seem to take this obliteration

Figure 2.1 Lot's Wife. Public Domain.

even further because very few of the rocks identified as Lot's wife have any authority (if they had any to begin with) beyond that of the books or websites that include them. Almost all of these "pillars" look completely different from one another. This bible story thus seems to have caused an embarrassingly large number of (usually male) biblical scholars or their agents to head out on a pilgrimage into the desert in order to find a physical marker that has been named Lot's wife—an absurdly limited understanding of the story in the first place—only to accept, in a gullible manner, something that is not even recognizably human, let alone recognizably female, as that marker. The large number of seemingly possible candidates shows the utter futility of such a task. It also illustrates how far away from objectivity critics are willing to wander in their searches for so-called objective information. The displacing of this naïveté onto "tradition" merely reveals a patronizing attitude toward certain peoples and traditions. Yet, this approach to Lot's wife prevailed not only because these biblical scholars supported the "pillar of salt" tradition, as the King James version puts it, as opposed to the "statue" tradition for denoting Lot's wife in her transformed state,[20] but also because—I think—it is a way of (subconsciously?) limiting interpretation of her and her story: of ignoring the uncomfortable consequences that arise if one were to consider this "pillar" as not a pillar but an explicit representation of a woman, obviously feminine in form, as the vulgate text suggests with its term *statuam* and as *Genesis A* makes even more clear with its nouns *anlicnesse* and *monlica*.

Lot's Wife: Meanings and Representations

A more practical way than the absurdly literalist one of discovering the message of Lot's wife would be to familiarize oneself with approaches apparent in the early medieval depictions of this image. Unfortunately, the illustrator of the manuscript that contains *Genesis A*, MS Junius 11, did not arrive at the requisite section of the Genesis story and the "illustration" is a blank page.[21] Cotton MS Claudius B. iv in the British Library (c. 1053), on the other hand, includes a finished illustration of the transformation scene related in its corresponding text, an Old English prose translation of the Book of Genesis. Moreover, there is much evidence in this manuscript that its text and illustrations are closely in concert with regard to what they intend to depict, as opposed to the disparate relations between illustrations and text in many other medieval manuscripts.[22] The transformation scene, a panel on 33r of the manuscript, shows Loth's two daughters under the arch of a building. Such a representation means that they are indoors and therefore, in the context of the fire and brimstone that rain down upon Sodom and Gomorrah, safe. These women would seem to know something of their mother's fate because one daughter holds her right hand up to her face in a typical gesture of sadness. Loth, a little to the right of center in the illustration, raises his hands in the typical posture of a person expressing fear (Figure 2.2).[23]

He seems to be the dominant character in the panel, although his role in this illustration is plainly to respond to a miraculous event. Loth's wife, at far left, though clearly unlike any other figure in the manuscript, is nevertheless recognizably human. This representation of her seems to follow the "statue" tradition, a significant decision by the artist because this particular Old English translation avoids the vulgate's word *statuam* and instead states only that Loth's wife changed into *anum sealtstane*, "a salt-stone."[24]

The artist would seem to have outlined this figure so that the representation is certainly that of a woman (her robe is typically a woman's garment), and then filled in the outline with a white pigment. An effect of this application of paint, presumably performed in order to resemble salt, is to obscure many of the features that such a drawing might be expected to have, and this effect is magnified by the subsequent darkening of the pigment on the figure, almost certainly because of oxidization.[25] Many human characteristics are therefore barely discernible, for instance, her hands. However, one may observe that she is holding these hands toward Loth, and her feet are also pointed toward him, so that her body appears to be facing in his direction. The angle of the outline of her head, on the

Figure 2.2 BL Claudius B.iv, 33r. © The British Library Board.

other hand, suggests that she is looking away from Loth, over her shoulder. Comparison with other drawings of women in the manuscript shows that the artist meant to depict her chin as facing left (Figure 2.3).

In addition, the entire transformation panel recalls other panels with angel-messengers in the exact position of Loth's wife, at the extreme left

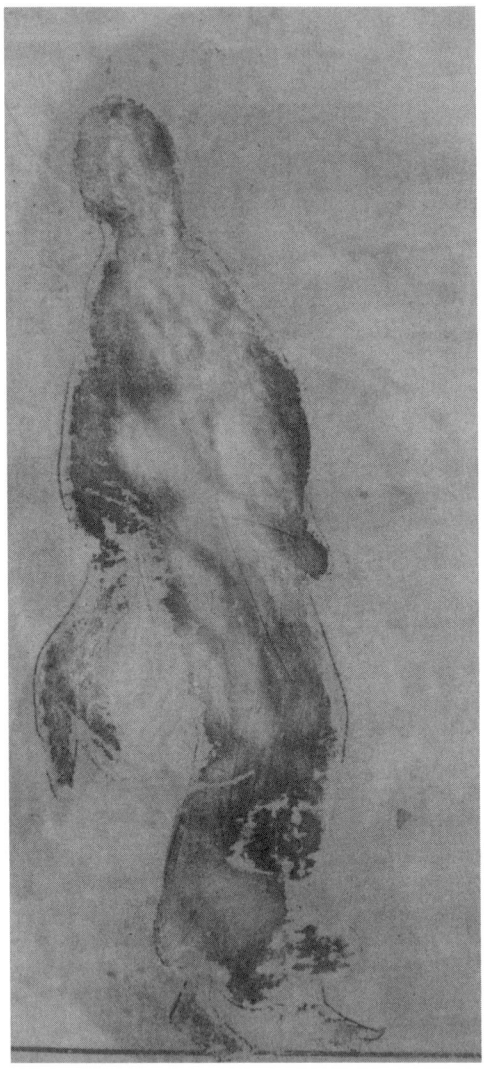

Figure 2.3 BL Claudius B.iv, 33r. © The British Library Board.

of the scene, so the artist seems to be intent upon suggesting her role as a messenger.[26]

The position of the transformation panel in relation to the larger illustration of the fate of Sodom and Gomorrah on 32v of the manuscript, a panel which includes depictions of dead city-dwellers lying on the ground, means that the image of Loth's wife seems to be looking back to this illustration. She thus illustrates her disobedient act in an iconographic way (Figure 2.4).

The nearest illustration to the scene of Loth's wife's reembodiment in *Genesis A*, then, considering date, language, and content, presents her image as retaining most of her bodily features during and after her transformation. Such an image accords with most other early medieval representations of this scene: the general site of Sodom and Gomorrah includes a statue of a woman looking at a ruined paradise that becomes, and in much medieval tradition remains, hellish (Figures 2.5, 2.6, 2.7).[27]

Recent criticism of literary depictions of the Sodom and Gomorrah episode match the early medieval artists' typical presentation of the landscape of these destroyed cities. For instance, Allen J. Frantzen has implied that the destruction of the cities of the plain is a penetrating use of language by God that imitates the sex-acts of the male Sodomites in its penetration of the earth.[28] So, if Loth's wife is turned to stone at the very moment that she looks over her shoulder, as the *Genesis A*-account and the illustration of the scene in Cotton Claudius B. iv indicate and as the Middle English poem *Cleanness* states explicitly,[29] then she becomes a statue in the pose of a person responding to sound. A likely interpretation of the events surrounding this figure would be, then, that sound itself turns her to stone. However, one could equally say that she responds not so much to a sound as to a disjunction between one sense and another, hearing and sight, a kind of "crisis ... of signification," as Martin Harries calls it.[30] One may see her as in the middle of such a crisis when the sound of the cities' destruction reaches her: *Þa þæt fyrgebræc, / leoda lifgedal,   Lothes gehyrde / bryd on burgum,   under bæc beseah* (2562b—64) [When Loth's city-wife heard the noise of fire, the death of the people, then she looked back].

Her backward look, then, would be an attempted "reification ... from the loss of self," as Harries describes it because we know virtually nothing about her save this look. We lack knowledge of any happiness (or lack thereof) that she might take from her husband and family, for instance. The look then tries to "undo ... the rift between observation and impulsive force" that God's prohibition of looking back at the cities implies. But the result is merely alienation in a different form, a further loss of self, because Loth's wife is literally spoken by God into a new substance.[31]

Figure 2.4 BL Claudius B.iv, 32v and 33r. © The British Library Board.

Figure 2.4 Continued.

Figure 2.5 The Hague KB 78 D 38 I, 23r. National Library of the Netherlands.

Figure 2.6 The Hague MMW 10 B 34, folio 32r. Museum Meermanno.

Figure 2.7 Lot's Wife Canterbury Cathedral. © Sonia Halliday Photographs.

By analogy with the cities that God attacks through penetration with His language, the sound penetrates her. God, with this transforming act or pronouncement, thus insists upon His system of representation in language. Since the new salt-stone version of Loth's wife is both herself and a representation of herself at the same time, an object that is both an original and its copy—an antisimulacrum[32]—she is part of (and demonstrative of) a (re)duplicating language that only God can speak.

If Loth's wife ends up with God's (new) language and message inside her, then the idea that her statue must offer some kind of message in the moment that she is frozen in time gains even more strength. Other Old English versions of her story confirm this message-role. The *Old English Heptateuch* says that when Loth's wife *unwislice*, "unwisely" looks back, she changes *to anum sealtstane, na for wiglunge ac for gewisre getacnunge*) [to a salt-stone (not because of black magic, but in order to be a wiser symbol)] (43).[33] By using the word *getacnunge*, the Old English translator seems to be almost insisting on a message-role for Loth's wife. He calls upon readers to understand the symbol by appealing to their wisdom. The *Heptateuch* version omits to explain further, but it hints at a moral message in the story by verbal parallelism: *gewisre* recalls *unwislice*. These two terms imply a contrast between the presumed lack of wisdom of Loth's wife and the wisdom of a reader able to interpret symbols. Meanwhile the reader cannot help but recognize that this particular *getacnunge* is a person like him- or herself because only a person (versus an object) can be "wiser."

In Ælfric's Old English version of Alcuin's *Interrogationes Sigewulfi Presbyteri*, Loth's wife is again described as a *getacnunge*. This time the text spells out the message that she offers: *þæt nan man ne sceal seðe wile synnu ætberstan. ⁊ to godes þeowdome gebugan. Beseon underbæc. þæt is þæt he ne sceal gewilnian þa woruldlican þing* (106) [that no man should look behind him who would escape sin and bow to God's service. "Look behind": that is that he must not desire earthly things].³⁴ Although this writer's moral imposition on the Genesis text might come over with a bit more force to readers of this work than the comments of the *Heptateuch* translator—because the *Interrogationes* are presented explicitly as a commentary upon Genesis as opposed to a translation of it—the message remains prescriptive rather than substantive.³⁵

The moral musings of such Old English writers follow the examples of earlier Christian authorities. The apocryphal Book of Wisdom refers to the burning of the cities of the plain and then mentions a "pillar of salt" that is a "monument to an unbelieving soul" and a "reminder of" mankind's "folly" (10:7–8).³⁶ Clement of Rome implies that the faith of Lot's wife was too weak. She was "double-minded," according to him, and she wavered.³⁷ In his commentary on Luke's Gospel, Bede says,

> Uxor Loth significat eos qui in tribulatione retro respiciunt et se ab spe diuinae promissionis quertunt. Et ideo status salis facta est ut ammonendo nomines ne hoc faciant tanquam condiat cor eorum ne sint fatui.³⁸
>
> [Lot's wife signifies those who in tribulation look back and turn themselves away from the hope of divine promise. And so she became a pillar of salt to warn people not to do that so as to harden their hearts, and not to be foolish.]³⁹

Ambrose, in his *De Virginibus*, says, *memor uxoris Loth quae naturam suam, quia in impudicos licet castis oculis respexit, amisit* (4.29) [Remember Lot's wife: she lost her natural condition because, even though her eyes were chaste, she looked upon lewd men] (99). In other words, the message that Loth's wife conveys—appropriately, if she has been penetrated by God's language—is much more His than hers, according to influential (male) interpreters of her symbolic role.

The penetration of God's message into Lot's wife also invites connections between semen, speech, and the word of God. Such connections in turn link with the theme of fertility that is crucial to the Genesis and Abraham story. The apparent message of her new substance, then, is a warning to the Judeo-Christian faithful, parallel but opposite to the promise of Abraham's prosperity. She becomes a parody of fertility: salt brings to mind artificial preservatives, thirstiness, dryness, mummification, even abortion through saline solution; the crumbliness of salt-stone suggests dead, hardened, spermatozoa. On a more practical note, a statue of a woman cannot reproduce. Salt-stone, one of the softer varieties of stone, would visibly wear away over time, enacting a further parody of fertility. Lot's wife would eventually lose the sculptural details that would identify her individually, then the details that would identify her as a woman, then the details that would identify her as human—and this is the version of her that the male writers of encyclopedias and bible dictionaries would seem to prefer. Eventually she would disappear into the landscape of the lifeless "Dead" Sea and its surrounding desert, which is an ironic inversion of the land-inheritance that men typically receive. This desert is often described as not just barren but as miraculously so by early Christian authors.[40] In other words, her fate after her transformation seems to imitate in a very attenuated fashion the worldly existence of the body: decline, decay, and disintegration. She is a vastly attenuated *memento mori*.

Proof of the new composition of Lot's wife's body would come through tasting part of her, an action that again demands her fragmentation. In other words, a transformation into salt seems to invite one to commodify and consume her, an eventuality that later writers and artists found appealing, perhaps because of its sexual connotations. An illustration in MS The Hague MMW 10 A 11 (Book 4, 1) presents Lot's wife in the same humiliating terms as the Middle English poem *Cleanness* does: *And alle lyst on hir lik þat arn on launde bestes* (1000) [and all earthly beasts want to lick her] (Figure 2.8).

Augustine calls her a *condimentum*, a "seasoning" for the faithful in his *Civitas Dei*, where he emphasizes the moral message of her story: obey God.[41] Her new substance and the economically charged verb that he uses to describe her purpose, *praesitit*, "supplied" to the faithful, seem to warrant the carrying off of parts of Lot's wife's transformed body as relics that would distribute her "famous story"—presumably the moral message—around the world. But I do not believe that such a version of her representation (which implies the gradual erasure of that representation and therefore of her) as Augustine interprets it, can completely drown out her communicative power. She may be petrified, but she still speaks.

Figure 2.8 The Hague MMW A 11 (Book 4, 1), folio 178r. Museum Meermanno.

For instance, *Genesis A* affirms that any message she might convey will not erode, be lost, or consumed. Instead, it will persist as long as any earthly story can last:

> Nu sceal heard and steap
> on þam wicum wyrde bidan,
> drihtnes domes, hwonne dogora rim,
> woruld gewite. Þæt is wundra sum,
> þara ðe geworhte wuldres aldor. (2571b—75)

[Now, hard and towering in that spot, she [Loth's wife] must wait for her fate, the Lord's judgment, when the world has finished its days. This is one of the miracles which the Lord of Glory has performed.] (cf. Genesis 19:26)

The mentioning of the end of time, of her awaiting her fate, and of a miracle by God ("miracle" is also suggested by the term *getacnunge* that appears in the other two Old English versions of her story because the term sometimes means "miraculous portent") imply that Loth's wife exists in a state of suspended animation. Certainly, she is not simply killed in the way that the Sodomites are. Harries notes that her punishment is similar to the classical idea of metamorphosis rather than death and that this kind of change has positive as well as negative associations. Early medieval works often imply or state outright that *dicitur et uiuens* [still is she said to live] inside her statue.[42] Petrification in itself suggests that her transformation is reversible because she is changed to one of the hardest known substances on earth (crumbly, in her case, but still much more lasting than human flesh). Her hardened substance also recalls the miraculous physical powers of the many martyrs who cannot be harmed by their torturers.[43]

Presumably, one aim of such a transformation is to produce a lasting image, and many interpreters of her story concur with this aim. One of the very earliest interpreters, Clement of Rome, writes:

> [Lot's] wife, who was of a refractory nature and not in complete harmony with him, joined him in going forth, yet she was made a permanent memorial: she was turned into a pillar of salt to this day. It was to be made known to all that the double-minded and those who question the power of God become a warning example of condemnation to all generations.[44]

Bede seems to agree that the message of Lot's wife makes more sense in a Christian era as opposed to in a much earlier Old Testament time.[45] The Middle English poem *Cleanness* says *and so ho* [she] *yet standes* (984), while the *Genesis A*-poet mentions explicitly that she gains for her story the kind of fame (*þæt is mære spell*) and immortality (*Æfre siððan*) that a warrior in heroic verse might long for.[46] In fact, the early medieval tradition of the immortality of Lot's wife in general contradicts the later, literalist tradition that has prevailed and that assumes the eventual obliteration of her feminine identity. An anonymous third-century Latin poem, *Sodoma*, presents her as maintaining her immortality in a miraculous fashion, presumably with God's help:

> durat enim adhuc nuda statione sub aethra;
> nec pluuiis dilapsa situ nec diruta uentis.
> quin etiam siquis mutilauerit aduena formam,
> protinus ex sese suggestu uulnera complet.[47]
>
> [And still in her unprotected place she endures beneath the sky, unmelted by the rains, unscattered by the winds. If some foreigner mutilates her form, she binds up the wounds from the place within herself.]

Her miraculous healing abilities are like those of a saint or a saint's relic. The poet seems to be basing this understanding of Lot's wife upon a passage from Irenaeus (c. 180). Not only does the latter affirm her immortality and present her as a message-giver, but he also seems to interpret her as a partly positive rather than an entirely negative symbol. For Irenaeus she represents the church:

> uxor remanserat in Sodomis, jam non caro corruptibilis sed statua salis semper manens ... Ecllesia, quae ext sal terrae, subrelicta est in confinio

terrae, patiens quae sunt humana; et dum semper auferuntur ab ea membra integra, perseverat atatua salis, quod est firmamentum fidei, firmans et praemittens filios ad Patrem ipsorum.[48]

[Lot's wife remained in Sodom, for she was no longer mortal flesh, but a permanent statue of salt.... the Church, which is "the salt of the earth," is thus left in the ends of the earth, suffering the accidents of man's condition. Whole limbs are from time to time removed, but the statue of salt continues: it is the support of the faith, and strengthens the sons of God and sends them on to their Father.][49]

Obviously, the immortality of Lot's wife, melded with a message that conveys (among other things) her suffering, marks her as a patience figure par excellence, particularly if she can represent humanity in general allegorically, as Irenaeus proposes when he connects her to the idea of the church. If Perpetua is the female patience figure as speaker, Loth's wife is the female patience figure as frozen speaker. Besides suffering, she embodies the other essential aspect of the modern understanding of patience: time, that is, unfulfilled desire.

She is also the epitome of a gendered patience figure because her message is a kind of epitome: it would seem to transcend the conventional means of communication. If one were to travel to the site of the cities of the plain in order to look at the statue of Lot's wife, her fame and immortality would be conveyed in a uniquely physical way, not by oral or written means. Her new substance, salt, immortalizes and fixes, as no other substance can, the weeping and suffering that art so often portrays as feminine and patience attributes. She is transformed into solidified tears, like Niobe.[50] Also, unlike writing in a book, her message cannot be separated from her body, as the *Genesis A*-poet makes plain by including the term *lic*, "body" within both words that the poem uses to describe her salt-stone image, *anlicnesse* and *monlica*. The corresponding idea that her body cannot be separated from her message comes through when the word *spell* in the phrase *þæt is mære spell*, "this is a famous story," connects her to the *spellboda* who are the messengers of God's instructions to Loth that he should quit Sodom, taking his wife and family with him (2946a). Thus, in spite of being voiceless and motionless, Loth's wife offers a formally unique and God-originating message, and the pronouncement that she exists in the same spot until doomsday means that her audience is virtually limitless because, once future audiences discover her, they can presumably always find the immovable place from which this communication originates.[51] Also, by becoming a place, she represents a shift by an object to the symbolic plane, as Lacan would have it: the abstraction of desire. The sound penetrates her, and, in her instance, changes her very substance, her "psychic space," to use Kristeva's phrase. She represents perfectly what happens when a woman tries to "assimilate the supposedly paternal law."[52] A statue with an embedded desire also represents perfectly the psychoanalytical principle that the Other is a place, the "locus of Speech," as Lacan puts it, from which the self gets its desires directed back at it.[53] Her *anlicnesse*, her "alone-likeness," is a site of witnessing, of pilgrimage, of the reception of messages.

Certainly the connection between Loth's wife's transformation and language is clear from the content of *Genesis A*'s next few lines after it relates this reembodiment. Abraham goes at dawn to the place where he is accustomed to speak with God (2576–79a), but no speeches ensue. Instead, the patriarch sees the pseudospeech that is the ruin of Sodom and Gomorrah written out upon the ground, as if the earth were God's page to write upon.[54] A kind of writing here replaces the divine word that Abraham is accustomed to hear at this site. One could then argue that, as an example of one of God's miracles, the reembodiment of Loth's wife in the Old English *Genesis A* enacts the poem's approval of the coming of the new order of writing and of literary versus oral traditions: a freezing in time of the creative word that is emphasized by means of an accompanying reference in the poem to written sources at the very moment of her transformation: *Us gewritu secgað* (2565b). After all, the Bible promotes God's rules as written texts, and at one point his rules appear upon stone tablets—almost the same substance as Loth's wife in her transformed state.[55]

Yet, there is no mention in *Genesis A* of Abraham seeing Loth's wife. The text has only that *he geseah from foldan up / wide fleogan wælgrimne rec* (2579b–80) [he saw slaughter-grim smoke rise up greatly from the earth], when, for almost all versions of the Sodom and Gomorrah story, she is part of the record of the lost cities: a crucial part of this written text for future viewers of the message-landscape. Moreover, Loth, like Abraham seems to be oddly impervious to any "message" that his wife's transformation might offer. Some bible commentators try to explain his sex-acts with his daughters with the excuse that he was acting under the drunken delusion that his partner during these episodes was his wife (Genesis 19:31–38). Such a mistake would indicate the most fundamental lack of understanding of the message of his wife's reembodiment, at least while his seduction is taking place. But, perhaps, Abraham and Loth, as God's favorites, do not need the communication that she imparts, which is probably directed primarily at the story's audience.[56]

By stressing the visual attributes of the lasting, so-called miracle of Loth's wife, and by presenting Abraham as a kind of audience, the *Genesis A*-poet invites readers to visualize the aftermath of God's intervention at this stage in the poem. On this score, the writers of bible dictionaries and encyclopedias were correct: the descriptions of the statue's situation in *Genesis A* and in its analogues read almost like parts of a travelogue. The authors almost seem to be mapping out a pilgrimage site so that members of their audiences can visit this site more easily. And Lot's wife appears as an important landscape feature of the holy land in Wisdom 10:7, in Josephus's *Antiquities*, in the earliest medieval encyclopedias, for instance, that of Rabanus Maurus in the tenth century, and in the later *Travels of John Mandeville*. Such mapping-out is also significant because patience figures tend to receive this kind of interpretive treatment.[57]

Lot's Wife as Part of the Landscape

In one possible visualization of the scene of Sodom and Gomorrah after the reembodiment of Loth's wife, one must stand on the path going to the cities in order to look at the face of her image. One may see her face, but surely her pose would make any viewer inclined to look back at what she is looking at, and thus imitate her and become complicit in her desire—the reversal of the supposed moral message that she is meant, according to the patristic tradition, to convey.[58] If nothing else, the action of a backward glance would seem to indicate some kind of desire. The poem omits to specify this desire but, since the figure that one is visualizing is female, the desire is not a man's desire, and apparently it is not God's desire (at least so far as His instructions would indicate). In fact, the solitariness of the salt-stone image suggests that her desire is unique. After all, she is neither rescued like the rest of her family, nor punished in the way that the other city-dwellers are. This singling-out implies that her desire was not sexual or not fully sexual, at least not in the way that the Sodomites' desires seem to have been, or she presumably would have been punished in the same way that they were (Genesis 19:1–9).

When one tries another vantage point and attempts to look at her from the front, as one would for most statues, one must come so close to her that she fills one's vision or, more likely, look back toward where she looks while one looks at her. Again one looks at the remains of the cities of the plain with the same effects of complicity, particularly if this location remains hellish long after her transformation, as it does in many medieval accounts of the story. One's third option would be to face away from her and hence away from Sodom and Gomorrah; but then one does not see the so-called famous story: one excludes oneself from the "text."[59] The image of Loth's wife in *Genesis A* thus insists on recognition, insists on the process of a viewer discerning a message, and insists on the recognition of this story as a woman, that is, the body of a woman. If one wants to get the message, one must see the statue; one must acknowledge that, unique as the message of Loth's wife may be, it is the communication of a woman. An early medieval viewer of this figure would also probably be impressed with its antiquity and its endurance over time, and as a consequence link its message to patience. In fact, one early medieval work makes the connections between time, suffering, message, and the body of a woman absolutely clear by noting that Lot's wife, after her transformation into a nearly immortal statue, continues to menstruate:

> dicitur et uiuens, alio iam corpore, sexus
> munificos solito dispungere sanguine menses.[60]
>
> [It is said that she is still living, and, with her new body, discharges with the customary blood the monthly offerings of her sex.]

If her message is her menstrual blood, then she has converted God's message-semen-speech into a feminine language of blood.[61]

So far, I have assumed that the viewer of the figure of Loth's wife goes to this pilgrimage site in order to have certain ideas confirmed. Such a viewer arrives at this site already knowing at least part of her story and therefore knowing at least part of her message in a way, or perhaps knowing the message of a poem like *Genesis A*, whatever that message might be. In fact, a visit to any representation of Loth's wife implies some prior knowledge of her story. Perhaps, more generally, as a communication "written" upon the landscape, she participates in the Bible's overt promotion of the authority of written texts. But one needs to consider the possibility of the solitary traveler who comes upon the scene of Loth's wife without having heard, seen, or read her story. A statue of a woman looking over her shoulder in such a lonely spot would be one of its most arresting features.

An artistic representation of a person on a path implies that there will be some kind of community in the immediate area, probably just a little further up or down the way, and the representation of Loth's wife is life-size, stressing its connection to other people.[62] But this image announces not the existence of a city and culture but their absence. No man is in sight (except the viewer if the viewer is male). Because of its stance and expression, the statue also tends to resist canonical or immediate interpretations. The woman represented is not posed as a traditional love-object. She indicates no need for male company. She is outside of the traditional location of the home, when such dislocation is relatively unimportant for men of the antique and early medieval era as compared to women. A man outside of a town could be a wanderer, scout, guard, prophet, or baptist, to take several examples available from Old English literature. This woman's situation and stance, in contrast, are peculiarly provocative. She looks at a ruined city, perhaps hellish, which speaks of lack of humanity, defeat, Troy. Viewers ignorant of the bible story might even imagine, turning their gazes to the ruins of the cities of the plain, that she destroyed these settlements, and suspect that they themselves might be in danger. A viewer ignorant of—or unfaithful to—God's rules prohibiting worship of other gods and of graven images might even decide, because of the power implied in her apparent ability to lay waste her surroundings, to worship this "idol" and therefore break one of God's taboos right on one of His message-sites.[63]

The City-Wife

With her defiance of God, a political act, Loth's wife is a reverse analogue to the civic monuments to women that one meets elsewhere in Old English literature.[64] The statue of her represents the sweeping away of the cities of the plain and replacement, in some ways, of those communities with her. Certainly, words such as *heard and steap* [hard and towering] that describe her after her transformation suggest that this reembodiment marks the appearance of a new stronghold. Changed into (literally) a *bryd in burgum* (2564a), she expresses physical aspects of the city at which she looked back, when cities represent in their turn, particularly through their associations with laws, a kind of textual authority, sometimes quite literally. A living statue would be the smallest kind of city, it is true; yet, a community of one is nevertheless a community. Indeed, one could see a sole figure on the landscape as representing the kind of definition through independence and struggle that city-states often tried to achieve.[65] On the other hand, when the traditional and highly artificial moral message drops from Loth's wife, her image conveys abandonment of the ancient city-state and of masculine culture. By disobeying existing law, she creates her own law. Such spurning and possible independence remain only some of the consequences, in this case, political, of her actions, and they fail to elucidate the mystery of what exactly she was thinking when she turned back. Also, significantly, both proposed viewers of her representation, the one who knows her story in advance and the one who does not, would have to admit ignorance of what the figure depicted in the statue desires.

What Is This Woman's Desire?

There have nevertheless been many influential guesses concerning this question.[66] The most reasonable one would seem to be the idea that Ælfric puts forward in his translation of the *Interrogationes Sigewulfi Presbyteri*. Loth's wife's backward look implies an interest in *weorold þingum* [worldly things], Ælfric declares and repeats (106). She presumably looks back because she is reluctant to leave something behind in her home. This interpretation gains credence from Jesus's injunction to remember Lot's wife, a warning that Ælfric quotes and translates in the *Interrogationes* (106). Christ uses her as an example of a person who looks back when God comes in judgment: the individual who stops to gather possessions in a house or who looks back at the field in which he or she was working will be left behind. But the Savior omits to explain what is in Lot's wife's mind when she disobeys (Luke 18:31–32). Equally, Ælfric provides no specifics concerning her desire (what worldly things exactly?). One can only conclude that, whatever her desire is, it seems to be feminine. Her desire has become fixed in her new embodiment. More specifically, if Lot's wife wants to take in the spectacle of a city being destroyed by fire from heaven, this desire is feminine in that the towering cities of the Bible such as Sodom and Gomorrah must represent male-dominated culture.

When she hears the *fyrgebræc, / leoda lifgedal* [the noise of fire, the deaths of people], Loth's wife in *Genesis A* looks back at, not the city, which would imply a desire for her previous life there, but the slaughter, *þæs wælfylles*, of the people in the city, as if these deaths were what she desires—or regrets.[67] In the latter case, she empathizes with people's suffering, and being turned into a salt-stone for one's empathy seems a very harsh punishment. In the former case, her desires would seem to concur with God's, and her fate would therefore seem arbitrary. In fact, the extreme punishment for her and for the cities of the plain raises the question: are God's actions in this instance clearly and entirely positive? Many critics of the poem, for instance Bernard Huppé, would certainly declare "yes" and would use commentators such as Bede and Alcuin to explain her transformation as just, as a moral lesson. Malcolm R. Godden observes that "On the whole, Christian tradition accepted [the] narrative logic" of Lot's story in general as a salvation story: "Lot [i]s the elect of God, the faithful individual who is saved when all others are destroyed."[68] Yet, the need for commentators to elucidate the story of Lot's wife suggests that questions concerning the severity of her punishment persisted. Alcuin's *Interrogationes Sigewulfi Presbyteri*, for instance, includes the question: *Cur uxor Lot in statuam salis conversa est* (105) [Why is Lot's wife changed into a statue of salt?]. To be sure, the questions in this work are in all likelihood artificially conceived devices meant to allow Alcuin to produce the kind of Genesis commentary that he intended; however, the existence of the question in itself intimates that the biblical account of the events is vague enough to provoke doubts. Furthermore, Ælfric seems to think that Alcuin's answer, *Ad condimentum fidelium; quia punitio impii eruditio est justi* (105) [As a condiment for the faithful; that is, punishment of the impious is a lesson to the just], which echoes Augustine, would benefit from expansion.[69] In addition, Ælfric reduces the *Interrogationes* from 280 to 69, which implies that his retention of this particular subject-matter might be significant, particularly when he amplifies Alcuin's commentary concerning Loth's wife so much.[70] First, he adds details to the question: why was she changed to salt-stone, *þapa god sende his twegen englas to ahreddene loth ⁊ his wif ⁊ his twa dohtra of þam fyre þe þa fif burga forbærnde* (104–06), "when God sent his two angels to warn Loth and his wife and his two daughters of the fire that would burn the five cities?" Ælfric's Sigewulf seems to be asking not only about her punishment but about the individuality of her actions. By including the other protagonists of the story, the question seems to be concentrating on the issue of why she individually chose to look back when all of the members of her family did not, though all got the same warning. Second, Ælfric enlarges Alcuin's answer, and expansion seems reasonable when Alcuin's response is so terse. For instance, would a general audience really benefit from his cryptically expressed metaphor *ad condimentum fidelium* or pick up on it as an allusion to Augustine? And Ælfric's need to fill in details suggests that at least some believers found something lacking in Alcuin's response—perhaps some even felt that the issue of the justice of Lot's wife's punishment was still open. *Genesis A* hints that this point is debatable when it notes that her punishment is *strang* (2569b–70a). The scriptural story in general certainly raises questions, such as would Lot's wife have been spared had she decided to bargain with God, as Lot and Abraham do when faced with God's pronouncements (Genesis 18:23–33; 19:18–21)?[71] And why are other punishments in the same story, for seemingly worse crimes, so much milder, for instance, the blinding of the Sodomites who try to force their way into Lot's house (Genesis 19:11)? In fact, the sins of the Sodomites, as they are first related in *Genesis A*, do not seem to warrant much punishment. Their "general vices" come over as those "of a prosperous city-dwelling society where people drink too much and become arrogant," as Godden explains—until a few of these citizens abruptly demand sex with two angels (*Genesis A* 2581–85, 2459–61).[72]

In the end, Ælfric's additions to Alcuin's question and response concerning Lot's wife are more illuminating than the source, but not much. For instance, one cannot help but notice that the attribution of worldly desire to Loth's wife (her look indicates a preoccupation with *weorold þingum*, "worldly things" [106], according to Ælfric) is mere speculation.

No more than anyone else can Ælfric have access to her thoughts, and his inclusion of Jesus's injunction to remember her—when Christ, being God, might uniquely indeed have access to these thoughts—only underlines the fact there is no proof of Ælfric's guess concerning her desires. These additions also call to mind the analogies, which Jesus uses to describe the coming of the kingdom of heaven, that immediately follow His abrupt injunction to "Remember Lot's wife" in the gospel. Jesus's warnings merely underline the point that God seems to act in an arbitrary way on occasion: "Whosoever shall seek to save his life shall lose it: and whosoever shall lose it, shall preserve it. I say to you: in that night [of judgment] there shall be two men in one bed; the one shall be taken, and the other shall be left" (Luke 17:33–34).[73] *Genesis A* also helps to indicate the arbitrariness of God's punishments (in this case, for illicit sex-acts) by adding the Sodomite's wine-drinking to the narrative.

Not only, then, does the transformation of Loth's wife into a nearly immortal image virtually immortalize her patience, but it also virtually immortalizes an act of God which presents Him as seemingly arbitrary, a reverse creator, a vengeful destroyer.[74] One also cannot help but notice that her punishment for seeing this obverse of God prevents her from ever describing what she sees, as if God might feel guilty about this seemingly negative aspect of Himself. Such ambiguous attributes mean that the symbol of Loth's wife transformed differs from any other in *Genesis A* or in the bible stories. The rainbow after the flood, for instance, is a promise by God that He will not destroy. Paradoxically, the statue of Loth's wife is a promise that God *will* destroy—even beyond death, as the poet reminds us by referring to the day of judgment. And comparisons of the story of the flood to the fate of Loth's wife are likely to occur to theologians and other readers because Christ Himself treats these events as analogies for doomsday (Luke 17:26–30).[75]

Meanwhile, although the statue proclaims a warning of God's power, it also embodies contradictions. Harries proposes that Lot's wife's offense is perhaps simply a desire to get close to God's actions. It is certainly true that He seems to place limits on proximity elsewhere in the Bible, to Mary Magdalene and Moses, for instance when, according to Harries, "there must be distance between the divine and what one can see"— hence God's prohibition of graven images. And yet the salt-stone figure, a work of God, is a graven image. Its creation, as Harries notes, implies a "return to totemism," the antithesis of belief in a unique, all-powerful, abstractly conceived divinity.[76] And although the statue is a warning and the blasted landscape of the plain would seem to be meant to discourage any viewer from trespassing, who would not want to approach and examine the only remotely human part of this landscape and exceptional and arresting evidence of divine handiwork, the statue of Lot's wife? Since she is a kind of reverse version of the moment of creation and control that marks the first act of God's creation through the Word, she would surely represent the pinnacle of artistic representation. She nevertheless remains a human being, made out of dust (particles of salt) and in the Creator's image as emblematically as Adam is. So, by reembodying her, God insists upon the direct representation and message-making of his unique and original acts of creation. Yet, the ambiguities of this message undermine the idea of representation.[77] Although the statue indicates God's power, it cannot help but be a tribute to *her*. It intimates a power inherent in her, despite her silence, and such interpretation of her memorial might occur whether one knows the Sodom and Gomorrah story or not. A sign of this inevitable identification with her is that the kind of solitary monumental figure that Loth's wife becomes, like the Colossus of Memnon, often has an accompanying myth that asserts that the statue still emits sound. The Colossus, for instance, "utters a sound like the breaking of a lyre-string every day at sunrise." Such inarticulate speech associated with a figure of a woman would affirm the repetitious image-making of counterfeit consciousness. Indeed, there is much scholarly work to be done concerning the connections between visual representations of Loth's wife and of the many medieval and early modern emblems depicting personifications of patience that I do not have space for here.[78]

Mægðe sið: The Inheritance of Lot's Daughters

Loth's wife in *Genesis A* also represents a patience figure because, like Job, she passes a legacy on to the next generation. In all complete versions of the story of Lot's family, the daughters mourn the loss of their mother as—above all—a break in the family line, and they quickly try to fix this break:[79]

                Hie dydon swa;   druncnum eode
seo yldre to   ær on reste
heora bega fæder.   Ne wiste blondenfeax
hwonne him fæmnan to bryde   him bu wæron,
on ferhðcofan   fæste genearwod
mode and gemynde,   þæt he mægða sið
wine druncen   gewitan ne meahte.
              Idesa wurdon eacne,   eaforan brohtan
willgesweostor   on woruld sunu
heora ealdan fæder.   Þara æðelinga
modor oðerne   Moab nemde,

> Lothes dohter,   seo on life wæs
> wintrum yldre.   Us gewritu secgeað,
> godcunde bec,   þæt seo gingre
> hire agen bearn   Ammon hete.
> Of þam frumgarum   folces unrim,
> þrymfæste twa   þeoda awocon.
> Oðre þara mægða   Moabitare
> eorðbuende   ealle hatað,
> widmære cynn,   oðre weras nemnað,
> æðelinga bearn,   Ammonitare. (2600–20)

[They did thus with the drunken man ... the elder of the two went first to her father's bed. Nor did the gray-haired man know when the two maidens ... were with him in the manner of a bride, fast bound in heart, mind, and memory, drunken with wine, so that he could not escape the enterprise of the maidens. The young women became pregnant, and the devoted sisters brought men children into the world, sons to their old father. One of these children was called Moab by his mother, that daughter of Loth who was the elder in years of life; the scriptures tell us, the sacred Books, that the younger called her son Ammon. From these princes sprang numberless people, the glories of two nations: one of these nations all earth-dwellers call Moabites, a widely famed race; men and the sons of heroes call the other Ammonites.] (cf. Genesis 19:30–38)

Genesis's theme of inheritance is clear in that these two women usurp the role of patriarch. When God promises to Abraham that his descendants will be famous and numberless (Genesis 17:2, 4; 18:18; 21:12–13, 18; 22:17), he and the witnesses of the prophecy would presumably conclude that (despite doubts concerning the outcome of the promise that might arise because of the advanced years of Abraham and Sarah) any descendants that would be produced would come directly through the male line as they eventually do; yet the daughters of Loth act as if they too are party to the covenant. They steal a march on Abraham (and God seems to trick him as well) by producing descendants before he does. They also take on a patriarchal role when they give names to their "famous" children who will people the world, according to the poem. The daughters have no explicit instructions from God to take matters into their own hands, but apparently He approves, for the Ammonites and Moabites thrive, though later scripture records them as enemies of Israel (Deuteronomy 23:3; Psalm 82). *Genesis A* treats them simply as famous peoples. The poem's phrases such as *þrymfæste* and *widmære cynn* [secure in glory] and [widely famous kinsmen] could be describing tribes in *Beowulf*. Indeed, various Genesis-commentators, notably Alcuin, defend the incestuous acts of Lot and his daughters as the only way to secure the future of their tribes and, as Godden observes, the *Genesis A*-poet does not seem to be particularly troubled by the idea of incest.[80]

Although Loth's daughters become pseudopatriarchs, they do so without much fanfare. *Genesis A* and any of its apparent sources omit to name these women. The *Genesis A*-version of the story does not even include any speeches by them: there is a gap in the manuscript where the daughters would speak as they do in the scriptural account. Nevertheless, just like their mother, they secure a huge audience for their "speech" (which in *Genesis A* is reported speech): the naming of their children. *Eorðbuende* [Earth-dwellers], according to the poem, know of the *þrymfæste twa þeoda* [glories of two nations], by the names that the women choose for their sons, Moab and Ammon. So the daughters' power and story extend, together with their progeny, down through the generations and all over the world, like orally transmitted stories of heroes. Nameless, these women take over the word-activated, creative power of the nameless God, most obvious at the onset of creation and when Adam names the animals. And one might well conclude that the inclination for independent action that these two women display is a trait inherited from their mother.

Certainly the story of Lot's daughters in general and in the *Genesis A*-version in particular is remarkable for its depiction of independent female will. The poem stresses the (temporary) transfer of power from men to women with the phrase *mægða sið*, "the undertaking of women" that it uses to describe what the daughters do. *Sið* means "journey," "undertaking," "fate," or "period in time."[81] This word is used elsewhere in the text to indicate events where men take the lead, such as the travels of Loth (2516a) and the military expeditions of Abraham (2023b, 2114b). During Loth's seduction, in contrast, he comes over "as an unconscious, passive victim-figure."[82] Corresponding to the oral fame that the daughters secure for their descendants (who are also an audience for their *sið*) is the silence of their father whose soul and memory are "fast bound" during their sex with him: *fæste genearwod / mode and gemynde* (2604b–05a). Indeed, the women usurp his position remarkably thoroughly. They seem to completely overshadow his will. Although this section is missing from the manuscript, the narrative in Genesis depicts Lot as so incapacitated that his daughters seduce him in turn, on two successive evenings when they ply him with drink. Why did the first occasion not raise his suspicions? Then, no indication appears in the story as to when or even if Lot finds out who fathered his daughters' children, and apparently he leaves the naming of them entirely up to the women. The narrative gives the impression that, from the moment of Lot's first incapacity, his loss of will continues indefinitely, or at least until the end of the narrative that concerns his family. *Genesis A*'s stressing of this loss is significant because it is downplayed elsewhere in Old English. Godden notes, for instance, that Ælfric's translation of the episode suggests that he "cannot quite accept the Bible's implications of male passivity."[83] Apparently the *Genesis A*-poet can.

Sarra's Speech

The narrative of the destruction of Sodom and Gomorrah as presented in the poem seems to be a center-point for a remarkable number of women who express themselves individually, so that the statue of Loth's wife comes over as not only a patience figure and patience site, but also as a representation of female expression more generally, whether one chooses to treat its message negatively or positively. For instance, the statue's relationship to Sarra is made even closer by the *Genesis A*-poet than it is in the original vulgate account through a pattern of displacement and response to speeches. Sarra's response to God's promise that she will bear a son in her old age, which she overhears from inside a tent when God speaks to her husband in person, is laughter:

>   Þa þæt wif aloh   wereda drihtnes
>   nalles glædlice,   ac heo gearum frod
>   þone hleoðorcwyde   husce belegde
>   on sefan swiðe.   Soð ne gelyfde,
>   þæt þære spræce   sped folgode.
>   Þa þæt gehyrde   heofona waldend,
>   þæt on bure ahof   bryd Abrahames
>   hihtleasne hleahtor,   þa cwæð halig god. (2382–89)

[Then the wife laughed at the lord of the people, not in the least joyfully; instead, she, wise from age, covered the prophecy with scorn in her heart. She did not believe the truth: that results would come from this speech. When the ruler of heaven heard that the wife of Abraham in her private room sent up hopeless laughter, holy God spoke.] (cf. Genesis 18:13–14)

In this poem, as compared to other accounts, the description of the laughter makes Sarra's emotions absolutely clear: her disbelief leads her to express scorn and a hard-hearted rejection of God's plan. She thus relates to Loth's wife and comes over as particularly disobedient, as Jonathan Wilcox notes. Other versions of the story try to excuse Sarra and Abraham by describing the laughter as more innocent, but here it seems to be at least partly motivated by Sarra's wisdom, and hence should possess some worldly credibility.[84] Like the disobedience of Loth's wife, Sarra's disobedience in *Genesis A* triggers a response. God at once promises Isaac to Abraham (2394–97). Then, in an addition by the poet to the source's account, the two angels who are accompanying God while He visits Abraham *feran* [journey out] from the "place of prophecy," a place that seems to be parallel to where Sarra "covers" God's prophecy in her heart. The poet indicates the parallelism with verbal echoes: *hleoðorcwyde* (2384a), *hleahtor* (2389a), *hleoðorstede* (2401a):

> "Þonne ic þas ilcan   oðre siðe
> wic gesece,   þe beoð wordgehat
> min gelæsted.   Þu on magan wlitest,
> þin agen bearn,   Abraham leofa!"
>   Gewiton him þa ædre ellorfuse
> æfter þære spræce   spedum feran
> of þam hleoðorstede,   halige gastas,
> lastas legdon,   (him wæs leohtes mæg
> sylfa on gesiððe),   oðþæt hie on Sodoman,
> weallsteape burg,   wlitan meahton. (2395–404)

["When I visit this same dwelling another time, my verbal promise will be fulfilled. You will be able to look upon your own child, Abraham my dear!"
    They went immediately after this speech, eager to depart from that place of prophecy, the holy spirits proceeded (the power of light was inside their selves) until they could see Sodom, the high-walled city.] (cf. Genesis 18:14–16)

The appearance of the term *hleoðor-* for a second time when the first refers to Sarra implies that, for the moment, she has displaced Abraham from his prophecy-spot. Isaac is (among other things) a reply to Sarra's incredulity as well as to Abraham's presumed paternal desire, and God seems here to speak in direct reply to Sarra's laughter, as if He were in dialogue with her. The biblical passage, in contrast, describes Sarra's laughter as only occurring in her heart. God hears it miraculously (Genesis 18:13–14).

Another displacement occurs in this passage. The immediate motion of the angels right after God's prophecy and the very positive description of them (*him wæs leohtes mæg / sylfa on gesiððe*) lead readers to assume that these messengers bear the news of Isaac's birth and are going to Sarra as pseudoannunciators, as the bringers of God's promise of fertility—again, in direct response to her laughter.[85] Instead, they go to Sodom and secure its destruction,[86] as if God's promise of a child to Abraham were the same as a command to level this city and as if Sarra's laughter were that of a

Sodomite, committing an offense against God that is so extreme that it causes Him finally to lose patience with the city-dwellers. Sarra's future pregnancy then not only represents the promise of a new society that will replace the one at Sodom and Gomorrah but it also, as a kind of bodily transformation, parallels Loth's wife's dehumanization through transformation. The reembodiment of Loth's wife occurs, the poem notes, *þæs heo wordum   wuldres þegna / hyran ne wolde* (2570–71a) [because she would not heed the words of the warriors of glory], that is, the angel-messengers, just as Sarra refuses to heed their words. These two refusals result in parallel but opposite miracles. In turn, Sarra's role is parallel to that of Loth's daughters, who ensure the future of their father's line. So, her laughter is another example of a woman's *sið*, of an undertaking that, typically for this poem, presents women's speech as at odds with God's authority. Nevertheless, these restricted, even silenced, voices of women in *Genesis A* gain audiences. Not only does God respond specifically to Sarra, but He also creates a new "prophecy-site"—a patience site—when He transforms Loth's wife.

Lot's Wife as a New Dwelling Place

In sum, then, the salt-form of Loth's wife consolidates law and disobedience, a woman's voice (hers) and a man's voice (God's), women's stories and men's stories, female inheritance and male inheritance; but it also consolidates female space and male space, private space and public space, domestic space and the city's meeting places. This idea of a new place, a patience site, being created through her transformation is clear from two more phrases in *Genesis A* besides the already mentioned *anlicnes*. The first is *bryd on burgum* ["city-wife" or "wife in the city"] that describes Loth's wife at the very moment that the community she previously dwelled in with her family is being destroyed:

>   Ða þæt fyrgebræc,
> leoda lifgedal,   Lothes gehyrde
> bryd on burgum,   under bæc beseah
> wið þæs wælfylles.   (*Genesis A* 2562b–65a)

[When Loth's city-wife heard the noise of fire, the death of the people, then she looked back at the slaughter.]

The obvious reasons for the poet to use this phrase at this juncture are its identifying and prophetic aspects. If Loth's wife looks back at Sodom because it is where her desires are inclined, then *bryd on burgum* is an apt way to define her. The phrase is prophetic because she is changed immediately into something like a city or a city wall: a "city-wife" in the most literal sense. But another obvious interpretive strategy would be to consider the idea of a city-wife more broadly in Old English and hunt for possible analogues. For instance, the epithet "city-wife" would seem to suit the heroine of Cynewulf's *Elene* (c. 950) when she takes over the authoritative position of the city of Jerusalem for her own purposes of refashioning the law and other state powers. She means to force an assembly of Jewish intellectuals to reveal the whereabouts of the true cross (lines 264–75, 332, 377–85, 411–12).[87] Both *Genesis A* and *Elene* present the speaking power of a woman as subversive to dominant male ideas, and, in their very different ways, as coming from a woman's usurpation (for the moment) of civic authority.[88]

The other aspect of the transformation passage that is important for defining feminine space besides *bryd on burgum* is the word *wic*. A look at the requisite dictionaries and the *Old English Concordance* demonstrates that generally the term can refer to a villa, a small collection of buildings, or even a village. However, unlike rough synonyms such as *burh*, *wic* typically refers to a "dwelling place" or "private quarters," that is, a space much smaller than and more obviously domestic than a military camp, a palace, a large city, or a fortification. In *Beowulf*, the term often appears in passages that relate a homecoming. This tendency suggests that *wic* has connotations of emotional security.[89] In any case, the term is an unexpected choice for a description of the location of Loth's wife in her transformed state:

> Nu sceal heard and steap
> on þam wicum   wyrde bidan,
> drihtnes domes,   hwonne dogora rim,
> worulde gewite.   Þæt is wundra sum,
> þara ðe geworhte   wuldres aldor. (2571b—75)

[Now, hard and towering in that spot, she [Loth's wife] must wait for her fate, the Lord's judgment, when the world has finished its days. This is one of the miracles which the Lord of Glory has performed.]

Even if one accepts the fanciful idea that she exists in a state of monumental suspended animation, to consider her as "dwelling" in her salt-stone *anlicnesse* is surely a leap of the imagination. That said, later descriptions of her transformed state confirm the idea. For instance, *The Travels of John Mandeville* says that *at þe riȝt side of* [the Dead Sea] *dwelliþ Lothis wyf a stoon of salt*.[90] The unexpected use of *wic* in *Genesis A* then intimates that an investigation of instances of feminine and/or feminized space would prove useful, particularly if this kind of space could be contrasted with male-oriented spaces such as the city with its emphasis on commerce, laws, and other modes of authority.

As noted above, the very word *anlicnesse* that describes Loth's wife in her reembodied state in *Genesis A* seems to suggest that, for early English society, a likeness of a woman standing outside the walls of a city had associations, rather unexpectedly, with civic duty and ideas of government. Such images are unlikely to represent an actual ability by women to govern: Anita R. Riedinger notes that, for instance, the Old English *Apollonius of Tyre* insists that its story is of Apollonius and of his success and that it ultimately must support the traditional idea that only men can inherit city-states and rule over them.[91] But neither are the images, statues, and tombs in *Apollonius of Tyre* representations of silent, passive women or of merely items of exchange. Instead these representations are paradoxically active exemplars of law and government, even in the moments that the women they depict are made monumental and hence paralyzed and eventually counterfeited.

Conclusion

As its use in *Genesis A* makes clear, the Old English term *wic* does not merely indicate a traditional division between men's and women's spaces, but instead helps to shed light on instances of what I call performative politics, of, in particular, the ways in which women perform political acts such as disobedience and conquest in spaces marked out by them but also claimed (as all space typically is) by men. For instance, in *Genesis A*, *wic* tends to appear when women have set out on journeys under their own volition and have become in some measure independent, like Hagar, Sarra, and Loth's wife and daughters. Loth's wife in particular stands out on the landscape as a kind of protest against the male God's cities, laws, speeches, judgments, and textual authority even though her image and new *wic* also help to demonstrate the influence of His power, scripture, attributes, and pronouncements. She is seemingly punished for disobedience and is therefore subservient to men and may serve as a negative example of the dominance of patriarchy. But *Genesis A*'s use of *wic* also demonstrates that the traditional dwelling places associated with women, if they apply to Loth's wife during her reembodiment, are subsumed into the monumental image in which she lives, and consequently are nowhere in sight in the landscape around her. She has performed a *mægða sið* [an undertaking of women] that is transformative, profoundly political, and declarative of her sex. A patience figure, because of her wait until doomsday with her identification as female clear and with her desire intact, she helps to gender patience literature by defeating typical male desires almost completely. Men want her to serve as an example of disobedience but she does not, men want her to be an object but she is not, men want her to be consumed but she is not, men want her to be merely an unindividualized rock but she is not, men want to fix her with their gazes but they cannot. Her transformation is at once both a subversion of the city and a creation of one. Later examples of the female patience figure, as mimicry gives way to duplication and reduplication of such figures, typically express more muted protests against male attempts to define and encapsulate women and the traditional virtues associated with them.

CHAPTER 3

THE FEMALE PATIENCE FIGURE AS COUNTERFEIT

Let us examine him by outrages and tortures that we may know his meekness and try his patience.

—Wisdom 2:19

Take all that shall be brought upon thee: and in thy sorrow endure, and in thy humiliation keep patience.

—Ecclesiasticus 2:4

The Apex of Patience Literature: Jacobus de Voragine's *Legenda Aurea*

The compiling of Jacobus de Voragine's *Legenda Aurea* announces the height of the patience literature genre. The years 1260–70, when Jacobus's compendium first appears, also work well as a rough marker for the apex of patience literature because the criteria for sainthood, and consequently attitudes toward saints' lives, underwent significant changes during this decade as the cults of Francis, Dominic, and others began to transform the previous definitions of saints and began to reach into hitherto uncharted political territory.[1] Of course Jacobus did not invent the later medieval attitudes towards the content of saints' lives. As the revolutionary rhetoric of Christianity began to lose its immediacy and as the hierarchy of the church began to take an increasing interest in and control over the making of saints, the typical vitas and passios had already undergone many changes in the centuries before 1260, and, as a compendium of hagiography from well-established sources, the *Legenda Aurea* must partake in movements such as the feminization of suffering and the gendering of patience as an attribute that had rapidly increased between 300 and 1260.[2] Ambrose had turned Agnes's body into a fetish of male fantasies, such as youth, virginity, modesty, and unquestioning loyalty, all miraculously preserved at the moment of martyrdom (*De Virginibus*, 1.2.5–4.19); Prudentius had turned Eulalia's body into a manuscript leaf, upon which spectators could read her sensational wounds like the text of Prudentius's *Peristephanon* itself (*Peristephanon*, 3.131–40);[3] the anonymous writer of the fifth-century *Life of Syncletica* had turned Syncletica's body into a *memento mori* of abjection: putrefaction, stench, disintegration, and absence.[4] In addition, the *Legenda Aurea* exhibits a tendency towards the abstraction of characters and situations and,[5] as a collection of "readings" concerning saints' days and other notable festival days of the church, this work tends to absorb, synthesize, regularize, and ritualize such attitudes, so that the individual lives of martyrs become items in a comprehensive and generally approved homiletic encyclopedia. Daily use of this work by many believers means that its influence was immense. Indeed, hailing the manner and scope of the *Legenda Aurea*'s reputation, availability, and reception as unique in literary history has become a standard critical refrain.[6]

The Patience Attributes of Later Medieval Saints

Despite the many changes from early hagiography to late that one may observe in the *Legenda Aurea*, the patience attributes of the figures in this collection exhibit many of the traditions of the early martyrologies. For instance, Jacobus retains the connections between martyrs, soldiers, and arena-style athletes established in the early passios (245, 293–94, etc.), and the saints in the *Legenda Aurea* often gain the "crown" of martyrdom—often referred to as simply a crown, with the idea of martyrdom implied—at the end of their lives (129, 204, 264, 704, etc.). Yet, despite the inclusion of many contemplative figures, bishops, and popes in the *Legenda Aurea*, when such figures would be expected to mitigate the more blood-drenched lives of the martyrs, motifs of violence, suffering, and endurance dominate this collection as compared to their incidence in the early passios.[7] For instance, Jacobus ratchets up the competitive machinery of sainthood by representing the many martyrs in his collection as contending with one another for glory, just like oral-heroic figures, but by means of suffering instead of battle-exploits. He even names a winner of the contest: *Notandum, quod passio beati Laurentii inter caeteras sanctorum martirum passiones excellentissima esse videtur … Primo in passionis acerbitate* (496) [It may be noted that the passion of Saint Laurence is seen to stand out above the passions of the other martyrs … (for) the bitterness of his sufferings] (2.70), a reference to this saint being roasted on a gridiron. Such competitiveness seems to be standard even if the results of the contest come over as dubious at best. Among so many martyrs in the *Legenda Aurea*, whose acts of endurance seem so similar to one another, the singling out of one sufferer seems arbitrary, as Jacobus admits (496), and Saint Vincent, for instance, is also roasted upon a griddle (118–19). Meanwhile, women seem to be disqualified from this particular competition—and only because it is a competition. Blandina, who in her passio reached an apotheosis of endurance in a much more convincing fashion than Laurence (an early martyr, she faced less competition than he does for the patience crown) by explicitly besting her mistress and her male companions, is not even mentioned in the *Legenda Aurea*.

Jacobus's version of the passion of Perpetua and Felicitas also signals many changes to hagiographical material as the patience genre evolves. The story of the women is now framed by the story of a man, Saturninus, whose biography dominates in the calendar. Unlike the original passio, this version allows Perpetua's husband to appear, and her assumption of the narrative voice is omitted. Only her first dream is related, which now glorifies a male character, Saturus, when he enters heaven (798). The dream ends with his encouragement of her to follow. She imperiously casts her baby aside along with the rest of her family, and therefore comes over as a much less sympathetic character than the protagonist of the original passio. She is given the immovability attribute, *vero immobilis stabat*, and is sent to the lions like a typical martyr. The feminizing mad heifer fails to appear. The female aspects of Felicitas are also reduced. She is burdened with a family relationship, and gives birth to a male child, so the original passio's motif of female inheritance is lost (799). In other words, mimicry by female patience figures is giving way to duplication, to adherence to a program, and most critics would probably agree that the result is an evisceration of Perpetua and Felicitas's original story.

A further telling indication of alterations to the passios in later hagiography is that patience has become so characteristic of the saints that the virtue is conflated in the *Legenda Aurea* with eternal reward. Instead of striving for the martyr's crown, as in the passios, Agatha strives for *coronam patientiae* (172) [the crown of patience] (1.156). Eugenia is anxious lest she and her companions lose *fructus patientiae* (604) [the reward of our patience] (2.166). Significantly, this explicit conflation occurs only for female saints, who are becoming increasingly abstract.

The trials of Saint Jacobo interciso, "James the Dismembered," probably represent the most overt example of the major changes that have occurred to the general content of martyrdoms between 300 and 1260. His life has become an opportunity to engage in a largely literary exercise concerned almost entirely with torture, while the other details of his life-story seem quite incidental. The writer seems uninterested in appealing to an audience's sense of realism or in contributing much to a reader's understanding of the history of early Christianity (though, of course, such attitudes are absent from much medieval hagiography, and one can hardly blame a work for being what it is versus what one desires it to be). The Dialogue Portion of this passio is minimized to two sentences describing the circumstances of James's soured friendship with the Prince of Persia (799–800), while the tortures make up a full two-thirds of the narrative. Besides changes to the standard plot, later hagiography also registers changes to the saint's character. Unlike most of the earlier martyrs, James seems to know exactly what becoming a saint entails, and his dialogue with his persecutors is highly self-conscious. As each of his body parts is cut off, he deliberately uses the occasion to reflect upon numerology, scriptural allegory, or other parts of his belief. He reads his fragmented body as if it were a book.[8] A further sign that he is a later saint is that the very method of his torture promises the distribution of relics throughout the Christian world (800–02). Yet, despite Jacobus's apparent tolerance of grotesque, artificial, and faintly absurd spectacles such as James's torture, this compiler's touting of patience as the most important and characteristic attribute of most saints is remarkably consistent.

Female Patience Figures in the *Legenda Aurea*

With patience so characteristic of the saints in the *Legenda Aurea*, several women-positive themes unsurprisingly continue from the early saints' lives into Jacobus's collection. Many of his entries describe female saints or their devotees inheriting traditions and knowledge from women (115–16, 136, 138, 364, 365, 444–45, 702). Saint Paula's knowledge that she passes on to her daughter is associated in particular with language, as if vestiges of Perpetua's highly expressive life were preserved in the later literature (139). When threatened with torture or execution, saints of both sexes welcome such trials, often call on the persecutors to do their worst (31, 114, 171, 402–03, 420, 794), and occasionally retain their powers of speech in miraculous fashion during their torments (32, 202, 421, 776). Like men, women best their pagan persecutors in debate (420, 776, 790–92) and would seem to hold a kind of political power over cities, or even nations (32, 172, 173, 421, 444, 634). On rare occasions, women even seem to dominate men, as when a male saint's *Sed hoc ideo inseritur, ut hystoriae sororis suae, cujus festum praecipue hic recolitur, haec quoque hystoria conjungatur* (577) [story, however, is given here simply as an adjunct to the story of his sister Savina, since the feast is celebrated principally in her honor] (2.142). More generally, Martha Easton notes that the *Legenda*

Aurea demonstrates that certain women, like some of the early female martyrs, "could leave behind their culturally constructed gender roles."[9]

Easton also notices that in the illustrations to the Huntington Library's manuscript of the *Legenda Aurea* men are much more likely to be summarily decapitated than women, whose executions involve more "public stripping," more treatment of the female body as spectacle, and more "pseudo-rape" (*LA*, 798–99). The later depictions of martyrs have more obviously pornographic aspects than the earlier ones, a tendency that has been noticed in the works of Ambrose, Prudentius, and Jerome.[10] Several women in the *Legenda Aurea* have their breasts severed (171, 203, 421, 794), a torture not specified in the earliest passios; nor do persecutors usually target any particular body parts of men. Jacobus never depicts castration, a torture that is significant in hagiography for its absence. A more sweeping observation about the women in the *Legenda Aurea* is that the later female saints to be included, most obviously Elizabeth of Hungary, tend to be more passive in character than the earlier ones (752–71).[11]

Jacobus's compilation also gives a strong impression of the rise of counterfeit consciousness. Sensational sufferings are inventoried at length; yet, they are very similar to one another, as if the lives were evidence of a very resilient repetition syndrome. The paralysis that occurs as a result of moral amnesia is widespread in the *Legenda Aurea*. Easton notes many "frozen moments of passivity and bodily display"—of "erotic stasis," to use McInerney's phrase—when the martyrs are female.[12] Also, the frequent pairings of female saints suggest that women are more readily copied and hence less individualistic than men, though men appear in pairs also (*LA*, 115, 343, 503, 578). Besides the onset of counterfeit consciousness, one may also note sexist treatment of female martyrs that is different from their treatment in earlier hagiography. In the *Legenda Aurea* women are often associated with domestic spaces. For instance, they are tortured in hot baths more often than men are (178, 402, 636, 776), women's houses and lodgings are mentioned much more often than men's (293, 339–40, 343, 490, 504, 776–77, 784), and female protagonists are associated with places of childbirth (137, 401, 402, 420), cooking (48, 168, 203–04, 248), and gardening (49, 223, 445).

Perhaps the most telling proof that the gendering of patience has become a commonplace by the time of the *Legenda Aurea* occurs when the reader observes that the seven brothers of 2 and 4 Maccabees change into female characters on two occasions in the collection. Seven followers of Saint Blaise are tortured and executed for their loyalty to Blaise as bishop. Though this passio includes motifs from other lives of typical female saints (168), there seems no particular reason in the narrative why they would need to be women.[13] In the life of Saint Sophia and her daughters, the narrative pattern of the seven sons in Maccabees appears once again (this time with three siblings)—again with the sex of the children transposed. The tortures are particularly bloody, as if sensationalism were particularly associated with female figures (203–04). In yet another transposition of the seven brothers story, the main characters remain male, but their mother (here Saint Felicity) is physically tortured, unlike the mother in 2 and 4 Maccabees (*LA*, 396).

Such habits of gender-blind reduplication are hardly new. As early as Prudentius's *Peristephanon*, not only is the typical description of a female martyr "both sensual and highly artificial" according to McInerney, with Eulalia turned "into a work of art, her limbs painted [*picta*] with her own blood," but also "the narrative has become generic" and "formulaic," so that "identity [is] almost entirely effaced."[14] Mary's entirely erased identity in "The Assumption of the Virgin" from the *Legenda Aurea* is the most extreme example of counterfeit consciousness in this collection. In one miracle story from this sermon, Mary protects a boy who has been thrown into a furnace while she, *in specie imaginis, quam puer super altare viderat* (*LA*, 516) [look(s) like a painting that the boy had seen on the altar] (2.87). The boy is converted as a result of his experience. The narrative is one of the Miracles of the Virgin, a subgenre of hagiography where simple stories often describe the faith of their protagonists as naïve, dangle the reward of heaven in a fairy-tale manner, and—not incidentally— feature many references to images of the Virgin.[15] Indeed, the boy's story in the *Legenda Aurea* demonstrates how saints and the images of them start to become interchangeable in the minds of some believers, compilers, preachers, and artists once ideas of incipient revolution start to fade. The saints' efficacy can be embodied in reproductions of them, and therefore any remaining identity or individuality that they might have can be leveled and whitewashed.

In another miracle from "The Assumption of the Virgin," a knight is saved by the Virgin from ministrations of the devil. While the knight's virtuous wife sleeps after praying to an image of Mary alone in a roadside chapel, the image comes down from its place above the altar and replaces the wife on horseback behind the knight. He recognizes the Virgin only once she has vanquished the devil, but the patriarchal message of the episode has been delivered in the meantime: any virtuous woman is a less powerful (and in this case quite passive) version of Mary, readily replaceable by her; any virtuous woman is a work of art, merely a copy of an already existing (and unmatchable) ideal, made up out of the desires of men in order to serve them (*LA*, 514). The story also indicates that, in works of art like the *Legenda Aurea*, an image of Mary in turn may give rise to further works of art, the Miracles of the Virgin being the most obvious example. Such reduplication implies that any actual figure of the saint may be eventually discarded as a simulacrum, as Blandina is discarded from the *Legenda Aurea*.

Counterfeit Consciousness in Chaucer's *Prioress's Tale*

A similar miracle story to the two concerning the Virgin from the *Legenda Aurea* connects Marian saints' lives to the works of Geoffrey Chaucer and connects the idea of miraculous patience to what can only be described as miraculous knowledge. A seven-year-old boy, the "clergeon" of Chaucer's *Prioress's Tale* (Fragment VII of *The Canterbury Tales*), has his throat cut unto the "nekke boon" and yet continues to sing and speak in a miraculous fashion just like Cecilia and other saints, and thus must relate to earlier patience figures (649). The knowledge that he gains in order to perform his characteristic act of singing the hymn *Alma redemptoris* through the Jewish part of an unidentified Middle Eastern city on his way to and from school, and the process of acquiring such knowledge, are painstakingly described in detail by the Prioress. The child learns to sing the hymn by rote, and the distinction between imitating the sounds of a passage or song as opposed to knowing a work's meaning is made abundantly clear by the narrator (545). Critics such as William Orth and Lee Patterson have rightly emphasized that the child is therefore never allowed to progress from rote knowledge to mature understanding, and thus, if one supports the Prioress's apparent point of view, one then must value "ventriloquism, impersonation, reproduction, duplication, parody, and mimicry" over more analytical kinds of teaching and learning— when memorization and parrot-like repetition as educational methods were under attack even as early as Chaucer's day.[16] In terms of acquiring knowledge, the boy represents a translator who has managed to find a vernacular term for only the first word of his text, *Alma* (555–56). Meanwhile, the only character in the story who actually deals in "sentence," that is, meaning as opposed to mere repetition, is the devil (563).

What critics such as Orth and Patterson ignore, however, is that the first item that the boy learns in the *Tale* is that he kneel down and say his *Ave Maria* whenever he sees an image of Christ's mother, a duty "taught" to him, presumably by his own mother (505–08).[17] An image like the ones of the Virgin in the miracles from the *Legenda Aurea*, then, with their associations with duplication, is the starting point of the boy's rudimentary knowledge and his ritualized methods of (non)learning. Chaucer thus indicates sensitivity to counterfeit consciousness. After all, the *Prioress's Tale* ends with the coining of a new martyr and saint from the image of Mary mentioned at the start of the narrative (a transmutation of the sexes), and the idea of rote learning in the *Tale* parallels the idea of replaceable images. For instance, the Prioress interrupts her introduction of the story's hero to say "whan I remembre on this mateere, / Seint Nicholas stant evere in my presence," using terms that recall physical replacement (513–14).[18] Even the phrase "This litel child, his litel book lernynge" suggests that a person and a body of learning (here a book) are interchangeable (516).

However, any parody by Chaucer here of works inclined to counterfeit consciousness is covert. The Prioress tells her *Tale* clearly and succinctly, and one can certainly argue that the clergeon's method of learning gains validation when he miraculously encounters, not an image of the Virgin, but Mary herself after his death and when he commends book-learning of Jesus's life to the monks who question his reanimated corpse, as if his knowledge has increased through his experience (652, 659–60). This new knowledge is symbolized in the miraculous "greyn" that the Virgin places on his tongue and that causes him to sing after death (642).[19] But the communicative power of this grain is lost at the end of the *Tale*. The abbot takes the grain out of the boy's mouth—as he must do in order for the child to go to heaven as Mary promised—yet, neither the abbot nor anyone else thinks to put this miraculous object on his or her own tongue. The narrator never again refers to this miraculous object, and the clergeon's death only causes the abbot to fall silent and to imitate the death and the stasis of the *Tale*'s martyrological hero: the abbot "fil al plat upon the grounde, / And stille he lay as he had ben ybounde" (675–76). Whether or not one decides to rebound the idea of rote learning back upon the Prioress and argue for Chaucer's harsh satire of her attitudes,[20] the repetition at the heart of such learning and belief dominates the *Tale*, relates to gender performance, and leads to apposition of the miraculous with stasis. A movement from mimicry to mere duplication is clear and, in the case of Chaucer, described self-consciously.

CHAPTER 4

THE FEMALE PATIENCE FIGURE
AS FROZEN EMPRESS

The bryde was broght abedde as stille as stoon.

—Chaucer, *The Merchant's Tale* (Fragment IV, line 1818)

One would expect to find patience in saints. But patience literature cannot work as a distinct genre unless there are secular works that apply heroic virtues of patience to women who are not saints—ideally for my argument, not even saintly. Chrétien de Troyes in his twelfth-century French poem *Cligés* supplies an important example of such a nonsaintly patience figure in the character of the empress Fénice, an analogue to Griselda. Chrétien is (among other things) an important contributor to the profeminine side of the debate concerning roles for women that arises during and after the "courts of love" described by Andreas Capellanus and that runs all the way to the fifteenth century and beyond in Western Europe.[1] In *Cligés* the empress Fénice falls in love with the titular character, a Greek prince. The lengthy interior monologue concerning her emotions is parallel to the Dialogue Portion of the passios, where a declaration of belief, a kind of self-identification, is the primary aim (4364–529). As frequently occurs in Chrétien's works, her passion is also described, in typical courtly love fashion, as an illness. Fénice cultivates and uses this love-sickness as a way to attract her beloved (2947–61; 4295–529).[2] Proactive, brave, and resourceful, she commissions her servant Thessala, a female magician and herbalist, to prepare a potion for her mistress that will simulate death so that Fénice can get out of her marriage to the emperor and instead set up a secret life with Cligés (5272–305; 5372–402).[3] In addition, Chrétien nudges the reader toward allegorical interpretation of this episode because the empress's name means "phoenix," a creature often connected to Christ by medieval authors (2685–91), though at least one "death-and-resurrection" of a secular heroine occurs in examples of early patience literature (Achilles Tatius 3.17.171).[4]

Of course this death-drug episode demonstrates sexist attitudes. For instance, for a woman to realize her desires, the most extreme possible obliteration of her social identity is required. She must cut herself off from and then hide herself away from society completely.[5] Such obsessive secrecy is necessary because the supposed infidelity of an empress of Byzantium is not merely a personal issue but a political one. Any relationship between her and *Cligés*, despite the elaborate attempts to keep it secret, would represent a kind of shadow imperial court, and ultimately Chrétien's poem seems to support the traditional political order—any court poet would need to be wary of suggesting otherwise.

At first her faked illness and death convince the courtiers, who mourn her in extravagant terms and proclaim her perfect (5717–42). However, three doctors arrive in the capital and volunteer to test the empress in order to see if she is merely feigning death (5743–823). Presumably, one reason for the convenient arrival of these physicians is to displace suspicion of the empress onto them as opposed to the emperor, who then can retain some positive attributes. The testing of a lady in a courtly love narrative is rare; Fénice here reverses the tradition of the knight who must prove himself in order to gain reward, often a lady like herself.

The chief physician, who senses life in her, vows to the emperor that he will restore her or the emperor may hang him if he fails (5828–30). The emperor agrees and the three doctors begin to "test" the empress.[6] They *mire ont descosu / Le suaire la dame a force* (5860–61) [roughly ripped open the lady's shroud].[7] The roughness is gratuitous, suggests rape, and betrays their desire to inflict violence, despite their protestations to the contrary. They then try to trick Fénice into revealing herself by making promises of loyalty, but to no avail:

> Lors la gietent fors de la biere,
> [Si la fierent et si la batent
> Mais de folie se debatent
> Car por ce parole n'an traient
> Lors la menacent et esmaient.][8]
> Et dïent, s'ele ne parole,
> Qu'el se tanra ancui por fole;
> Que il feront tele mervoille
> De li qu'ainz ne fu la paroille
> De nul cors de fame cheitive. (5882–87)

[They took her out of the coffin and beat and struck her. But this was madness, for they could not get a word from her. Then they threatened her and tried to frighten her, saying that if she refused to speak she would soon regret her folly because they would do to her such unbelievable things the likes of which had never been done to a wretched woman's body.] (196)

By reducing the empress to only a "wretched woman's body," the physicians set up an alternate position to the mourners' assessment of her as perfect, while her abilities to pretend come over as far superior to theirs. She is unlikely to believe their declarations of loyalty when their first approach to her is so harsh and insulting. Also, this kind of attempted persuasion followed by threats is parallel to the threats of sexual attack that female martyrs often endure, and Chrétien's phrasing seems to be openly advertising sensational material (see *LA*, 31, 115, 401). There are other similarities between the passios and the empress's ordeal. Most explicitly, she declares that she would rather be dismembered than shamed (*Cligés*, 3125–28; 161), her torments are described as a "martyrdom" (5941; 197), and her tomb-builder says

> ... qu'il en a apareilliee
> Une molt bele et bien tailliee;
> Mes onques n'ot antencion
> Qu'an i meïst se cors sainz non
> Quant il la comança a faire,
> "Or soit en leu de saintuaire
> L'empererriz dedanz anclose,
> Qu'ele est, ce cuit, molt sainte chose," (6005–12)

> [he had a very beautifully carved [tomb] ready, though when it was begun he had intended it only for the body of a saint. "Instead of a holy relic, let the empress now be placed within it, for I believe she is a saintly woman,"] (197)

an opinion that must read as ironic (or, at the very least, Chrétien here describes profane love in terms of the sacred) when Fénice is faking her death in order to set up a secret love-nest. But the relic analogy points to a further reason why the three doctors need to attack her body. The empress has created an artistic representation of herself and, traditionally, only men are allowed to make artistic "copies" of (idealized) women.[9] She is a transgressive figure because her feigned death has the purpose of reinventing herself as *Cligés*'s lover, and she succeeds in her subversive designs when her plan eventually works.

During the empress's trials, the torturers primarily engage in trying to make her speak, the same kind of attack on powers of expression that happens at the martyrs' trials, when the persecuted Christians often display miraculous powers of speech or silence (cf. *LA*, 3). In this case, however, the content of anything that she might say is largely irrelevant to the advancement of the plot because any utterance would betray her. The implication of her predicament and of the tomb-builder's assessment is then that she is perfect because she is dead and silent (see also Chrétien 5727–30), and any further speech by her would spoil this illusion. Chrétien is therefore directing satire at excessively idealistic portrayals of women in courtly love literature here, and is implying that any conception of perfect womanhood is dead, just as the death potion he includes in the episode is implicitly a corrosive satire of the love potion in the Tristan and Ysolt story.[10]

Like many of the Roman authorities in Jacobus's accounts of female martyrs, the physicians try to tempt Fénice and claim to have her best interests at heart:

> "Bien savons que vos estes vive,
> Ne parler a nos ne daigniez;
> Bien savons que vos vos faigniez,
> Si traïssiez l'empereor.
> N'aiez mie de nos peor.
> Mes se nus vos a correciee,
> Einçois que vos aïens bleciee,
> Vostre pleisir nos descovrez,
> Car trop vilenemant ovrez;
> Et nos vos serons en aïe,
> Ou de savoir, ou de folie."
> Ne puet estre, rien ne lor vialt. (5888–99)

["We are positive that you're alive and will not deign to speak to us. We are positive that you are faking death in order to deceive the emperor. Don't be afraid of us! You have already felt our anger so now, before we've hurt you more, tell us your plans, for your behavior is reprehensible. And we will help you in any undertaking, whether wise or foolish."
But it was no use, for she would not be moved,] (196)

just as Lucy may not be moved (*LA*, 31). The empress has reached a state of paralysis that means the possibility of counterfeit consciousness, and ironically the physicians merely contribute to the image of Fénice as perfect by employing physical tortures that recall those of a typical martyr:

> Lor li donerent un assalt
> Par mi le dos de lor corroies;
> S'an perent contreval les roies,
> Et tant li batent sa char tendre
> Que il an font le sanc espendre. (5900–04)

> ....
> N'en porent il ancor rien faire,
> Ne sopir, ne parole traire,
> N'ele ne se crosle, ne muet. (5909–11)

[Then they struck her again with their straps, raising welts all down her back, and beat her tender flesh until the blood poured forth ... still they could not get even a moan or word from her, nor did she stir or move,] (196)

while her stillness and immovability again recall the attributes of female martyrs (*LA*, 31).

Fénice moves further up the ladder of perfection when the doctors' next torture recalls not only the martyrologies but also Christ's crucifixion:

> Ensi afolent et confondent
> La dame le felon ribaut,
> Qui le plonc tot boillant et chaut,
> Si com il l'ont del feu osté,
> Li ont anz es paumes colé.
> N'encor ne lor est pas assez
> De ce que li plons est passez
> Par mi les paumes d'outre en outre,
> Einz dïent li cuivert avoutre
> Que, s'ele ne parole tost,
> Or endroit la metront an rost,
> Tant que ele iert tote greslie. (5918–29)

[These course scoundrels tortured and abused the lady by pouring the hot, boiling lead straight from the fire into her palms. But it was not enough for them that the lead burned right through her palms; no, the dastardly cowards said that if she did not talk soon they would put her on a grate until she was grilled to a crisp.] (196)

This proposed torture marks a turning point in the narrative. Such burning would not only recall the tortures of saints such as Saint Vincent but also would mar her looks in a most debilitating fashion. Unlike the previous tortures, this one is an attack on, as well as Fénice herself, the essence of male fantasies of women; beauty is a crucial part of the typical courtly lady's attributes. Moreover, this eventuality is surely one that the emperor had not contemplated in allowing the physicians to test their theory. They had promised to restore her to him intact.

The physicians' threats and tortures also demonstrate an important change in the female patience figure. As opposed to the tendency in earlier hagiography to discount sexual desire so that Lucy, for instance, protects her chastity through becoming immovable, Fénice's predicament makes it clear that an inability to move is a negative development, rather than the marking of an apotheosis together with an invitation to counterfeit her ideal virtues as if she were a saint. When a patience figure lacks sacred status, immovability merely allows persecutors like the doctors to torture their victim as they please. They can use one of the properties of the immovable, ideal body to attack the courtly love ideal, to attempt to prove its opposite. The drugged Fénice enacts the male fantasy of a woman who cannot say no, the rape victim who cannot struggle or escape. Therefore, one is tempted to conclude along with Brigitte Cazelles that, like the many French hagiographic romances of female saints that appear at almost exactly the same time as Chrétien's poems, these kinds of depictions of courtly love women amount to a violation of the female body.[11]

But an intervention takes place at this point in *Cligés* that firmly suggests that male fantasies cannot always dominate and that the sexes form separate, highly partisan communities:

> Cele se test, ne ne lor vie
> Se char a batre n'a malmetre.
> Ja la voloient el feu metre
> por rostir et Por graïllier,
> Quant des dames plus d'un millier
> Des genz se partent et desvoient;
> A la porte vienent, si voient
> Par un petit de roverture
> L'angoisse et la malaventure
> Que cil feisoient a la dame,
> Qui au charbon et a la flame
> Li feisoient sosfrir martire. (5930–41)

[Still she remained silent and sacrificed her body to their beatings and abuse.
  They were about to stretch her over the fire to be roasted and grilled when more than a thousand ladies who had been waiting outside the great hall came to the door and saw through a small crack the torture and suffering being inflicted upon the lady by those who were martyring her with the coals and flame.] (196)

The small crack in the door underlines the sensationalism of Chrétien's material because it points to voyeurism and to the erotic desires of the audience of the poem. The crack imitates a bodily orifice, while the secret vantage point of the ladies also suggests an attempt to discover illicit lovers in the act.¹² Then, taking on the typically knightly and masculine role of rescuer, and arming themselves with implements associated with men, the court ladies

> Por l'uis brisier et desconfire
> Aportent coigniees et mauz.
> Granz fu la noise et li assauz
> A la porte brisier et fraindre. (5942–45)

> [Brought axes and hammers to break down and pulverize the door, and there was a great racket as they attacked the door to hammer it down and destroy it.] (196)

These female partisans become like the armies of Greek, Saxon, and German warriors that fight one another and engage in tournaments elsewhere in the poem (2831–917). In fact, Fénice's entire scheme may be compared to battle deeds, while her endurance is a kind of physical combat, as the text indicates with words like *assalt* (5900) and *batent* (5903, cf. 4754). Earlier the crowd that mourned her had described Death's dealings with her as a *bataille* (5735), while her ruse amounts to a kind of masking, an important martial theme of the poem. *Cligés* uses a succession of disguises in order to hide his identity while engaging in a tournament, and the hero's father Alixandre fools his enemies by putting on the arms of a dead rival and entering the enemy's stronghold under false pretences (4660–78; 1815–28).

The ladies' partisanship then seems to become infectious. The narrator explicitly relishes the turn in the plot when they arrive at the empress's bier, the women's revenge, and the striking sex role-reversal that this revenge involves:

> S'or pueent les mires ataindre,
> Ja lor sera sanz atandue
> Tote lor desserte rendue.
>   Les dames antrent el paleis,
> Totes ansanble a un esleis,
> Et Tessala est an la presse,
> Qui de rien nule n'est angresse
> Fors qu'a sa dame soit venue.
> Au feu la trueve tote nue,
> Molt anpiriee et molt malmise;
> Arriere an la biere l'a mise
> Et desoz lo paile coverte.
> Et les dames vont lor desserte

> As trois mires doner et rendre;
> N'i vostrent mander ne atendre
> N' empereor ne seneschal;
> Par les fenestres contre val
> Les ont en mi la cort lanciez,
> Si que tuit troi ont peçoiez
> Cos, et costez, et braz, et james.
> Einz mialz nel firent nules dames. (5946–66)

[If they can get their hands on the doctors, they will not be kept waiting for their just deserts!

The ladies rushed into the great hall as one, and among the crowd was Thessala, who had no other thought than to reach her mistress. She found her naked over the fire, severely injured and greatly abused. She placed her back in the coffin and covered her with the shroud, while the ladies went to give the three doctors what they justly deserved. Without summoning or awaiting the emperor or his seneschal, they flung them out of the windows down into the courtyard, and all three had their necks, ribs, arms, and legs broken. No ladies ever did better!] (196–97)

The spectacular aspects of a *passio* are clearly echoed in this sequence, up to and including the irony of physical suffering being visited on persecutors who receive what they thought they would inflict on their victim. Again the action is described as a battle: the hurling, *lanciez*, of the physicians out of the window recalls the lances of a tournament (4878–81), and the idea of "might makes right" comes over in the bodily destruction of the doctors despite the fact that they are correct in their assumptions concerning Fénice's condition.

The rescuers are a feminine community: they act as one and take over political power as is plain in the narrator's mentioning of their flouting of the emperor's and seneschal's authority. The implication is that, while men might sanction such horrifying treatment of a woman's body, women would not, though the female courtiers are not necessarily advocating reverence for Fénice's qualities and abilities here. Presumably, these ladies believe her to be dead and are protesting the doctors' disrespectful treatment of her corpse. In any case, the body is miraculously healed by Thessala the herbalist (199–200) in obedience to Barthes' rules for the victims of sadism: "the body is instantaneously restored—for new expenditures."[13] Thus, with the revenge scene, Chrétien displaces the saintly ideal of a patience figure into a kind of feminine partisanship, a female religion, like the "secte" of Chaucer's Wife of Bath (*Clerk's Tale*, 1171). But one must not forget that the feigned death of Fénice amounts to the acknowledgment of a double standard concerning male and female heroism: *Cligés*, though tested, does not have to go through such helpless paralysis and an extreme and sadistic trial in order to become a hero.

Recent critics have been backpedaling from the idea that the empress represents an unambiguously profeminine figure. Joan Tasker Grimbert notes that "although Fenice firmly believes she is mistress of her own destiny, time and again she is proven wrong."[14] The ending of the romance includes the negative consequences of Fénice's independent actions in taking a lover: all future Byzantine empresses are cut off completely from the outside world (6642–61). She thus offers a very negative inheritance. Still, the empress is a patience figure who explicitly flouts an attempt to make her into something that she is not. True, she rejects being a saint or a totally passive sexual object merely in order to become another kind of male fantasy, and criticism of her morals is certainly possible; but such judgments pale in significance compared to her rejection of several dominant ideologies concerning the female patience figure. If her immovability and legacy for future empresses partake in counterfeit consciousness, the success of her sexual adventure and the extreme acts of her female courtiers suggest subversion of this idea at the same time.

CHAPTER 5

THE FEMALE PATIENCE FIGURE
AT AN EXTREME

> *The work, the opus, does not belong to the field, it is the transformer of the field.*
>
> —Jacques Derrida, "Before the Law," trans. Avital Rouall and Christine Roulston, in *Acts of Literature*, ed. Derek Attridge (New York: Routledge, 1992), p. 215

Secular Patience Literature: Chaucer's *Legend of Good Women*

The patience literature model applies to so many of Geoffrey Chaucer's works, including *The Clerk's Tale, The Man of Law's Tale, The Physician's Tale, The Second Nun's Tale, The Tale of Melibee,* and *The Book of the Duchess,* that he must be ranked among the most accomplished practitioners of the genre.[1] The most strategic use of this model by him occurs in *The Legend of Good Women* (c. 1386), where a panoply of female "martyrs of love" appears and where there is perhaps the most conspicuous marriage of secular and sacred hagiography in all of literature.[2] Not surprisingly, for a late patience work by a notoriously wily author, the mixing of these two traditions in *The Legend of Good Women* is highly self-conscious. The God of Love in the "Prologue" chastises Chaucer for depicting an unfaithful woman in *Troilus and Criseyde* and for translating *Le Roman de la Rose*, which contains much antifeminist material and reiterates many disparaging and cynical attitudes to love (F 325–35). Therefore, as "penance," the poet must

> The most partye of thy tyme spende
> In makyng of a glorious legende
> Of goode wymmen, maydenes and wyves,

That weren trewe in lovyng al hire lyves;
And telle of false men that hem bytraien.[3] (F 482–86)

The mere undertaking of such a task would clearly indicate that the author subscribes to, or at least is aware of, the idea of gendered patience literature.[4] The epithet "legende" implies hagiography, the first five protagonists in *The Legend of Good Women* are called "martyrs" in the Incipits to their lives (pp. 604, 606, 608, 614, 618), and the main subject-matter of the work is the sufferings of famous women, for example, Lucrece. She "was holden [at Rome] / A seynt, and ever hir day yhalwed dere / As in hir lawe," a turn of phrase that renders the work's debt to hagiography irrevocable (lines 1870–72).

Yet, one must not overemphasize the gendered patience properties of the content of *The Legend of Good Women*. There are really very few openly hagiographical aspects of the portraits of women, save for the narrative of Piramus and Tesbe. In the end, the pseudohagiography of this work comes over as mechanical. Part of the problem is the lack of any apparent ruling deity after the Prologue ends, while the Christian God can play only a minor part in action that is pre-Christian, and the legends all come from the classical age. Also the poet-persona's unexplained and rather childish devotion to love in the form of the daisy seems divorced from the dream-vision's personification of the imperious God of Love (F 314–18). Both of these representations of love come over as reductive, and neither of them (nor Alceste, Love's consort) seem to influence the rest of the poem's action. The suffering women seem to be reflections of the tendency in the more conventional hagiography of Chaucer's age to omit almost all elements save the protagonists' sufferings. His point might be that this adjustment toward suffering per se renders much hagiography affected and many pseudohagiographical works hollow. However, it is very difficult to discover *any* kind of ruling ideology in *The Legend of Good Women*, just as it is notoriously difficult to tease out clearly stated ideologies from most of Chaucer's other works. Once again he leaves readers with a vague yet nagging sense that he has torn to shreds certain ideologies that he has brought forward in his works, without even allowing readers the comfort of being able to prove his artful and thoroughgoing vandalism.

"Many a Tale Yfeyned": Duplication in *The Legend of Good Women*

A possible target for satire in *The Legend of Good Women* is the counterfeit consciousness that one sees in certain depictions of the Virgin in works like the *Legenda Aurea*. It is certainly possible to interpret the legendary part of this poem as a monotonous sequence of passive, "radically circumscribed," and unappealingly static women, defined only by similar-sounding suffering, as if *The Legend of Good Women* were trapped in a cycle of reduplication.[5] Yet Chaucer, unlike other writers, seems to recognize counterfeit consciousness's abilities to quash egalitarian principles and otherwise subjugate women. For instance, unlike the *Pearl*-poet's acceptance of the pattern of 144,000 virgins in heaven, Chaucer rejects the pattern of 20,000 possible subjects offered to him by Love in the Prologue (F 559–61). The sequence of legends leaves off after only nine have been related, and he even seems to express impatience with his material (614, 670, 953–55, 996–97, etc.). The task of writing the poem together with its self-consciously stated generic characteristics are perhaps too programmed for his liking.

Counterfete Cheere: Patience Literature and the Griselda Story

A discussion of the Griselda legend is inevitable in a study of patience literature because this narrative is the most prominent example of the genre in Western European literature outside of hagiography and because it includes possibly the most extreme patience material in all of literature. The version that has received the most critical attention by far is Chaucer's *Clerk's Tale* from the fourth fragment of *The Canterbury Tales*. Besides the examination of this most canonical of patience works, it also makes sense in the course of a feminist study of patience literature to examine Christine de Pizan's 1405 version of the same story in *Le Livre de la cité des dames* (*The Book of the City of Ladies*) in order to see what a woman writer and critic does with the patience genre in general, with its conventions, and with material that stretches the patience of a female character to a sadistic extreme. A comparison between Christine's account and Chaucer's *Clerk's Tale*, both of which work within the context of an extended history for patience literature and work with the fact that their subject-matter has often been told and retold, should indicate how two very experienced authors, one a woman and the other a man, treat the same story-tradition at roughly the same time of writing. These two versions of the story also invite comparison because, in so many ways save her sex, Christine is similar to Chaucer: a near-contemporary; a professional and well-known writer blessed with court patronage and social connections; learned in works that Chaucer knew and, like her, used as sources, for example, Giovanni Boccaccio and Francis Petrarch; prolific and popular, with works preserved in a number of manuscripts; inclined to depict herself engaging in intellectual pursuits; inclined to relate material within framing narratives.⁶ However, the conclusions that one may reach with regard to Christine and patience literature rather pale in comparison to the ways in which Chaucer overloads the conventions of the patience genre in his *Clerk's Tale*. The Griselda story is also significant for marking a point, near the end of the poem, where repetition syndrome becomes full-blown counterfeit consciousness.

In the case of *The Clerk's Tale*, one may judge the extremes of Grisilde's patient behavior as almost certainly a factor in his choice of subject-matter. Her fantastic patience stands her out in relief against the qualities of any of the other characters in Chaucer's works, including other patience figures such as Custance in *The Man of Law's Tale* and other female characters such as the Wife of Bath. This prominence suggests that the Clerk takes the tale-telling contest that Harry Bailey sets up as the driving force behind *The Canterbury Tales* seriously, senses advantages in narrating provocative events, and sees this narrative as a legitimate opportunity to surpass all of the other pilgrim's tales, all other versions of the Griselda story before it, all other portraits of wives in the marriage group, and all other portraits of women in *The Canterbury Tales* through his story-telling art. The Clerk can achieve these results by setting up a contest for "glory" among female "heroes" that is parallel to the contest among martial and athletic men in classical stories and also parallel to the contest among saints in the *Legenda Aurea* for the endurance of the bitterest sufferings (696–700, 935–38). The winner of the women's contest would be the supreme heroine of patience, "the ultimate in submission" (Shaw, "Body," 295), and Walter duly tries Grisilde "to the outtreste preeve of hir corage" (785–87). Under such story-telling circumstances, intensification of the heroine's torments might be justified, and the Clerk's descriptions of her certainly tend toward superlatives (713–14, 925–31, 979, 1018, 1045). One might even see Grisilde's warning to Walter that he not test his new wife in the way that he has tested Grisilde herself as not only a further sign of her charitable nature but also an acknowledgment that such torments might exceed her own and thus eclipse her reputation (1037–43).⁷

Patience is heavily feminized in the Griselda story. In the case of *The Clerk's Tale*, the gendering of patience is even more obvious than in the other versions of the legend because this version concentrates on the heroine's virtue of patience more narrowly than other versions, the narrator praises women as possessing greater abilities than men to be humble and true (935–38), singles out women as more interested in the extremes of Grisilde's "tests" than are the men in his audience (696–700), and addresses the "secte" of the Wife of Bath and "wyves" more generally at the end of his *Tale* (1170, 1183–84).⁸ Yet, every version of the Griselda story associates patience with being a woman. Her gender and class are not just important to the story. They are crucial for a narrative where matters of class and gender are inseparable. One need only observe that Griselda's relationship with her children is not just parental but specifically maternal; her relationship with her father is not just filial but domestic in a way that a son's in this era cannot be. Nevertheless, Griselda's total passivity marks a logical development in the greater concentration than previously on the sufferings of female saints that one may view in the *Legenda Aurea* and in the evolution of patience literature more generally.

Instead of relating the typical declarations of belief, public acknowledgment of belief at trial, tortures, and immobility (particularly for women), this narrative focuses on tortures and immovability almost exclusively, as if beliefs can be taken for granted. In the saints' lives, miracles of immovability nearly always occur at the end of the saint's career as signals of apotheosis, of a hardening of virtue into an ideal that recognizably belongs to the next world (*LA*, 31–32) Since the immovability motif applies mainly to female saints, it can become—in the way that Lot's wife can become—a step toward the establishment of a locus of male desire. On the one hand, while an immovable young virgin like Lucy can represent a defeat of male desire in that her immovability prevents her rape, on the other hand, she can represent a woman frozen at the moment of her greatest desirability. The Griselda story relates the career of just such a desirable figure, taking immovability as its starting point, not its endpoint, as if Lucy were to be reconfigured as a kind of golem, capable of (re)articulation solely by the Pygmalion-pronouncements of a man's sexual longing. Or, rather, Griselda represents a new distinction between the related ideas of immovability and stasis. Stasis seems to be inherent to her. Before marrying Grisilde in *The Clerk's Tale*, Walter scrutinizes her often, and, presumably is impressed not only by her "womanhood," virtue, and "chiere" ("expression," mentioned twice here) but also by the consistency of these attributes:

> Upon hir chiere he wolde hym ofte avyse,
>
>   Commendynge in his herte hir wommanhede,
> And eek hir vertu, passynge any wight
> Of so yong age, as wel in chiere as dede. (238–41)

She then agrees to a life of apparent emotional stasis simply because he asks this of her:

> "... be ye redy with good herte
> To al my lust, and that I frely may,

> As me best thynketh, do yow laughe or smerte,
> And nevere ye to grucche it, nyght ne day?
> And eek whan I sey 'ye,' ne sey nat 'nay,'
> Neither by word ne frownyng contenance?
> Swere this, and heere I swere oure alliance." (351–57)

This kind of facial stasis enables the articulation of male desire. Indeed, such stasis plays into the well-attested male fantasy that a love-object not change her appearance once a man has chosen her as his bride. Grisilde, obedient to the local marquis's "demandes" (348), moves from a life of poverty and toil to a life of luxury as the grandest lady in the province, then back again—and finally back to the grand life. But none of these relocations changes her, and her steadfastness is more than just a consequence of her virtue. People come from all over the land to the court of Saluces in order to confirm Walter's choice of spouse as simply an answer to his sexual wants, nothing more. Despite the marchioness's discretion, "heigh bountee," and brilliant abilities to bring quarrelling parties together, the people throng into the court in order to "biholde" her, whereupon "ech hire lovede that looked on hir face," emblematic above all of her static beauty (409, 420, 413). So why should they mind if Walter decides to replace his wife with a younger one (985–94)? And, significantly, the several "translations" of Grisilde's dress throughout the narrative make no mention of producing changes in her face, which never explicitly receives a veil or any other adornment.[9]

This change from the saints' immovability to idealized stasis is well on its way to prominence before the Griselda legend becomes popular. For instance, Chrétien's *Cligés* includes the adoption of saintly attributes by the female participant in a love-triangle. Then the Griselda story furthers this adoption into an even more extreme fantasy of male desire. Just as Fénice's body is available to the physicians in its immovable state, Griselda's body is available for sexual activity, and hence distinct from a saint's or martyr's. Unlike Fénice or Lucy, only Griselda's face is static, as opposed to her entire body—a displacement that features in the narrative (at least in part) because then her image as a whole can speak to her limited or partial saintly status. But, despite the connections of the Griselda legend to the romance genre, this heroine is at once more simple and more complicated than a mere love-object, and not only because her origins mean that she amounts to a repudiation of the courtly love ideal. Her husband may ask only that her "contenance" remain unmoved and therefore imply that he is interested merely in appearances, yet Grisilde swears that "nevere willyngly, / In werk ne thoght, I nyl yow disobeye" in *The Clerk's Tale* (362–63).[10] The fact that she mentions control over her thoughts and hence goes further than the marquis's "demandes" in her reply demonstrates her remarkable self-knowledge and self-regard. Essentially, she now insists that her qualities *are* inherent, as Walter observed before "in sad wyse" (237). She insists that there will be no inconsistency between her expressions and her true feelings, insists that she has a will of her own if she would choose to employ it ("willyngly"), and even includes a prudent admission that she knows that she could be forced (physically, presumably) to perform deeds against her will ("nevere willyngly"). A figure of immovable sincerity, she maintains that her marriage will be more than just a masquerade.

But she is also an image of how a male fantasist can both "have" (idealize) and "move" (marry) "his" martyr at the same time, can get the best of both worlds, the secular and the sacred: a woman whose body is available for his sexual pleasure and (perhaps even more importantly for him) available as a vessel for the production of his children, yet whose face can also signify the impassiveness of saintly perfection.[11] For Walter, Griselda is physically perfect. Her face is frozen into arguably a mirror-image of his own face, the public face of reputation, of ego, of a man's ability to have what he wants without guilt and without consideration of anyone else's desires. She shows no visible sign of his torture of her, so she retains her perfection throughout all the manifestations of his desire. In this regard, she would seem to recall a typical immovable martyr, like Lucy. But Griselda is instead a desirable female body with a paralyzed face that is her article of "wearable technology." She is the most artificial kind of hybrid. The "illegitimate offspring" of a man's specific instruction and of "patriarchal capitalism" more generally, the inexorable blankness of her facial expression symbolizes the obliteration of emotions from a sexual partner.[12] Again, this idea figures prominently in male fantasies of desirable women, and Griselda therefore is the medieval equivalent of an intelligent machine, a cyborg, as Donna Haraway describes it.[13] In sum, one may see in the development of patience literature from the passios to the Griselda story an evolution of the female patience figure from hero-martyr to marmoreal figure to sexual object sporting a marmoreal mask—an absurdly grotesque figure, surely ripe for the kind of satire Chaucer so often seems to find irresistible.[14]

Patience and the Griselda Story: Christine

An impulse toward satire is just one of the major differences between Chaucer and Christine, who tends to take her role as an advocate for women seriously, and tends to meet her male adversaries on their own turf. A related difference is that, while it is notoriously difficult to pin

Chaucer down with regard to his opinion concerning any virtue, vice, or ethical dilemma, and nowhere does Chaucer state exactly what he would seem to think about patience,[15] Christine often states her opinion concerning issues and virtues—particularly concerning patience. Indeed, her approbation of this virtue that appears at the end of her *Le Livre de la cité des dames*, where she compares male and female behavior generally, seems to approve the dominance of gendered patience literature, and to accede to the production of a genre that helps to manufacture gender roles by making sure that such roles gain an audience only once they have passed through the filters of male thought and narrative. Her attitudes here do not bode well for a revision of the sexism inherent in gendered patience literature:

> Et celles qui les ont divers, felons et reveches, mettent peine, tele en endurant que elles puissent convaincre leur felonnie et les ramener, se elle pevent, a vie raisonable et debonnaire. Et se yceulx sont tant obstinez que elles ne puissent, au moins y acquerront elles grant merite a leurs ames par la vertu de pacience, et tout le monde les beneistra et sera pour elles.
>
> Ainsi, mes Dames, soiés humbles et pacientes, et la grace de Dieu croistra en vous, et louange vous sera donnee et le regne des cieulx, car dit saint Gregoire que pacience est entree de Paradis et la voye de Jhesu Crist. (3.19.2–3)
>
> [And those women who have husbands who are cruel, mean, and savage should strive to endure them while trying to overcome their vices and lead them back, if they can, to a reasonable and seemly life. And if they are so obstinate that their wives are unable to do anything, at least they will acquire great merit for their souls through the virtue of patience. And everyone will bless them and support them.
>
> So, my ladies, be humble and patient, and God's grace will grow in you, and praise will be given to you as well as the Kingdom of Heaven. For Saint Gregory has said that patience is the entrance to Paradise and the way of Jesus Christ.][16]

In contrast to the distancing effects that appear at the end of *The Clerk's Tale* and the complicating interventions of dissonant voices into the narrative that disrupt it and seem to undercut the *Tale*'s professing of patience, Christine's understanding of patience seems much more naïve and accepting—even masochistic—when compared to Chaucer's.[17] She seems to see the endurance of life's injustices in general as the same as, or at least in the same vein as, the endurance of abuse from a sadistic husband, whereas Chaucer and Petrarch announce the distinction between the rule of God and that of a husband much more openly (*Clerk's Tale*, 1142–48; Petrarch, 288). Moreover, the narratives within Christine's *Book*, such as her version of the Griselda story, often seem to offer exempla for this author's precise (though discomforting) understanding of patience and humility: *ancores qui plus croist son grant loz est qu'elle estoit tres mal mariee* [The fact that (Mariannes) was unhappily married increased the praise for her even more] (2.42.1; 43.1); the wife of Bernabo goes into a foreign court in disguise rather than question her husband's arbitrary judgment against her (2.52.1). Yet, perhaps, Christine here, as she does elsewhere, also criticizes the male world of fame that is so important to the stories in Boccaccio's *Decameron*, the source of many of the feminine exempla in her *Book*, including the story of Bernabo's wife.[18] The husband's praise of this character, especially of her "chastity," causes the reckless wager of 5,000 florins by Bernabo that leads to her temporary disgrace and to his own penury (2.51.2), and, just previous to Christine's version of the Griselda story, Droitture ("Rectitude"), the allegorical narrator of the section of the *Book* concerning heroic (and often heroically patient) women, counters the notion that women cause evil in the world by rehearsing a long list of immoral men (2.47.2–2.49.5). The argument is *tu quoque* but, with the establishment of this significant context to Gliselidis's story, Christine suggests that Gualtier's torture of his wife comes from an unjust tradition of long standing, as Maureen Quilligan has noticed.[19] In addition, the seeming inadequacies of Gliselidis's character fade a bit when her story gets surrounded by so many others that feature heroines with many variant kinds of virtues. Christine thus comes over as a double-agent with regard to her sex-partisanship. Her attitudes often sharply contradict those of the profeminine side of the fourteenth-century debate concerning the abilities of women, while her pronouncements concerning such moral issues are relatively doctrinaire, not to mention transparent, compared to Chaucer's.[20]

Patience and the Griselda Story: Chaucer

Like Christine, Chaucer gives some evidence of being complicit in the polarization of women into "heroic suffering" roles. One of only two conventional saints' lives in *The Canterbury Tales*, *The Second Nun's Tale* describes a female martyr being tortured. *The Tale of Melibee* presents the beatings of two women as if these characters were merely conventional representations of a family's honor (971–72). Custance, the heroine of *The Man of Law's Tale*, is as clear an example of secular hagiography as one might imagine. She is passive to the point of omitting to reveal crucial information concerning her lineage that might help her in her career of one pathetic expulsion and exile after another (Fragment II, 972–73, 1055),[21] and most strikingly, any version of the Griselda legend seems uncomfortably complicit in the subjection of women by asking by implication a breathtakingly reductive question about domestic arrangements and class: is there any difference between a good wife and a good slave (696–700)?

The reduction of the female patience figure to the most juvenile kind of male power fantasy, a chimerical hybrid of slave and wife, a totally obedient woman unencumbered by any desires of her own or even any emotional expression—whom one might want to call "The Slave-Wife in the House" after the phantom identified by Virginia Woolf as "The Angel in the House"—represents an extreme yet logical conclusion to the history of patience literature as a genre and to the gendering of the patience figure.[22] The example of Fénice in *Cligés* has already confirmed the reduction of the female patience figure to a kind of passivity that the female martyrs never had, and also demonstrated that secularization of the patience figure means that its servility becomes more prominent as other aspects fade away. Where the martyrdom of Blandina would seem to suggest the overthrow of class differences through the exaltation of a serving woman over her mistress, the legend of Griselda proposes a reversal of such revolutionary egalitarianism. In the later story, a woman is rendered more and more impossibly servile. She is reduced to being a slave pure and simple when her husband repudiates her as his spouse. Who would marry the poverty-stricken, cast-off wife of a tyrannical and fickle ruler? Any chance at social mobility through marriage is gone for her. Then his request that she work as a domestic in his palace confirms her status as purely and only a slave: *his* slave.

Yet, Grisilde's partly marmoreal nature renders terms like "slave," or "wife-slave" inadequate to describe her, while in most ways Haraway's idea of a cyborg fits the bill. Grisilde's unquestioning obedience, her apparent lack of emotion, her ideal and unchanging erotic beauty, her "bisynesse," her almost superhuman domestic abilities (428–29, 974–80, 1015–22), her treatment as a kind of novelty—a changeling, even—by the narrative (due, in this case, to her origins in an unexpected social class), and her ability to put on a performance as Walter directs her are all attributes of the cyborg in Haraway's and others critics' conception of it. Grisilde's following of instructions to the letter once Walter has set out his marriage plan suggests that he has programmed her, and even Grisilde's connection to Christ in the text points to her cyborg credentials.[23] Thus, with the gender polarities of the Griselda legend in mind, and despite the fact that Chaucer and Woolf would hardly have recognized such a portmanteau phrase that pulls together ideas from such distant time-periods, Grisilde is best described as "The Cyberwoman in the House." The description also fits because readers' almost inevitable frustrations with

Grisilde's behavior are somewhat alleviated if one thinks of her as posthuman, as representing a revisionist kind of freedom, a contingent versus an independent body, an existence beyond the conventionally human.[24]

Chaucer is unique in the way that he ultimately treats the Cyberwoman in the House, and I am continually surprised at how little credit he gets for the clear partisanship that he expresses in *The Clerk's Tale* with regard to the profeminine and antifeminine debates of the fourteenth century. His Clerk refuses to put forward Grisilde as an example for human behavior, save as an example for endurance in the face of adversity in general, just as Petrarch declines to do so in the Latin source (Petrarch, 288). Then Chaucer is the only medieval teller of the Griselda story who has the courage to announce what his society needs to do with the Cyberwoman in the House. Like Woolf, Chaucer announces "I killed her": "Grisilde is deed, and eek hire pacience" (1177).[25] The rest of the Envoy at the end of *The Clerk's Tale* twists the knife in Grisilde's corpse by joking about Chichevache swallowing the reader and then by vividly describing a Griselda-antipode. Petrarch and Christine omit this kind of comment, though they have ample opportunity to provide it in their frame-narratives or in other places. True, Chaucer seems to replace Grisilde in the Envoy with merely another male fantasy, the scold (1183–212). True, he chooses to narrate the lengthy *Clerk's Tale* and to depict extremely passive women, such as Custance in *The Man of Law's Tale*, in other lengthy narratives that seem to offer no satire of the patience genre. True, one of these other narratives, *The Tale of Melibee*, appears later in the sequence of *The Canterbury Tales* than *The Clerk's Tale*, perhaps in order to supersede Chaucer's earlier thoughts concerning the role of the "ideal wife." True, my reading of the *Clerk's Tale* takes a particularly and perhaps dangerously serious and literalist attitude to its content and context. After all, the Clerk announces a turning in the narrative from "ernestful matere" to "song" (1174–75).[26] Nevertheless, the announced death of Grisilde occurs at the most emphatic juncture possible in *The Clerk's Tale*. The narrator's rhetoric just preceding the announcement draws attention to the song that will follow (1173–76). A new title, "Lenvoy," is then inserted into most of the manuscripts, and the stanza structure of the poetry changes. An envoy is often an opportunity to acclaim the import of what has come previously, and this particular Envoy stands out as a technical "tour de force," while its first line identifies precisely what the audience is invited to celebrate: the death of Grisilde; of a worn-out type, for Chaucer/the Clerk; of the Cyberwoman in the House, for modern audiences.[27]

The idea of death in *The Clerk's Tale* occurs so often that it must be a motif associated with Grisilde, and thus all of the poem's references to death prepare readers for the Clerk's killing of her (374, 502–04, 664–67,

1090–92, etc.). In other words, a helpful way of thinking about Grisilde is to attribute to her a "terminal identity" that is similar to that of the early saints. Terminal identity is a "doubled articulation in which we find both the end of the subject and a new subjectivity constructed."[28] Grisilde's new subjectivity is largely the miraculous patience that renders her so alien to the many readers of her story. Therefore, one reason that Chaucer or the Clerk can kill her is that she is already a phantom, the product of delusional thinking that tends to romanticize the past and try to force a "golden age" on a resisting world. Grisilde is evidence that the patience genre is growing tired, just as Chaucer possibly indicated already in *The Legend of Good Women*.

In any case, Chaucer portrays the Clerk as consigning the character of Grisilde, her virtue, and the patience genre to the grave (1177–78). Nor is nostalgia for her possible. Instead, one is invited to interpret the events in the Griselda story as an overloading of the conventions of the patience genre, and as an exposé of the ideals and assumptions concerning women that allow the genre of gendered patience literature to flourish. A careful look at *The Clerk's Tale* shows that the satire of the gendering of patience literature is both extreme and thoroughgoing in it.[29] Chaucer furthers satire of the patience genre by criticizing male institutions and beliefs, by satirizing the saintly woman figure familiar from patience literature through pushing her passivity to an extreme, and by allowing Grisilde's idealized image to retreat from audiences, readers, and pilgrims through distancing effects, such as the Envoy, at the end of the tale.[30]

Christine in her turn, rather surprisingly considering her stated approval of women's patient endurance of their husbands' reprehensible behavior, satirizes the patience genre in her version of the Griselda story by revising her sources and attacking conventions concerning women. In other words, both authors indulge in "re-contextualization, re-accentuation, and re-framing of previous texts or utterances," as William McClellan describes the process, in order to produce a kind of polemic: in order to assert that the genre has outlived its usefulness.[31] But only Chaucer swerves even further into what Harold Bloom calls "misprision," a reinterpretation of a preceding literary work through a deliberate and gross misunderstanding of that work; only Chaucer produces a remarkably thorough reductio ad absurdum of the patience genre that "expung[es]" the "other's sacred word" from that genre.[32]

Christine's Griselda Story: "Counterfete Cheere of Court"

The first and most obvious question that must come up during a comparison between Christine's and Chaucer's versions of the Griselda story is: do either of these authors revise, criticize, or satirize the patience literature conventions in order to demonstrate a profeminine stance? As one might expect in a composition that seems to be addressed to an audience of women with a view to educating them and justifying education for them, and that polemically defends women against antifeminist literature, a certain amount of women-positive attitudes come through in Christine's account of Gliselidis in *Le Livre de la cité des dames*, despite the fact that its author works within the traditional narrative patterns of saints' lives and patience stories.[33] Christine uses a female narrator, female allegorical figures, and a conception of feminine heroism in order to revise ideas fundamental to Boccaccio's version of the story and fundamental to patience literature in general, as one may see specifically in the way that she deals with her sources' depictions of acts of gazing. She takes Petrarch's *Epistolae seniles* 17.3 as her chief source and radically changes entire gazing situations—even gazing possibilities. For instance, she makes fewer references to the heroine's beauty than the versions with male narrators, though it is still there. Correspondingly, Christine omits most of the moral qualities that Valterius has in Petrarch's *Epistola*, yet she retains the observation that the marquis is *bel de corps* [handsome] (2.50.1; trans., 170). Christine's narrator introduces Gliselidis by her singularity, her age, and her service to her father through work (2.50.1), whereas Petrarch's account introduces her by her desirability: *unica illi ... Griseldis nomine, forma corporis satis egregia* (Petrarch, 260) [an only daughter ... called Griseldis, remarkable enough in physical beauty]. The Petrarchan narrator's discriminating eye for feminine beauty asserts his masculinity and assumes the cooperation of a male audience (who presumably would know how much beauty is enough).[34] Valterius then joins this community of masculine gazers when his assessment of Griseldis matches the narrator's in its superior attitude: he *In hanc virgunculam ... quandoque oculos non iuvenili lascivia sed senili gravitate defixerat* (260) [upon the girl ... had sometimes glanced with his eyes, not with the lust of youth, but with the more serious considerations of a mature man].[35] Christine reduces but does not eliminate the idea of seeing in the marquis's action when Gaultier comes into her version of the story perceiving, *avisé* firstly Gliselidis's [upright conduct and integrity,] *les bonnes meurs et l'onnesteté* (2.50.1; trans., 171) and secondly her beauty. As opposed to Petrarch, Christine mentions no gaze as the story begins; in fact, instances of gazing are so vastly reduced as to be almost nonexistent after the marquis's initial assessment of his future bride. In contrast, Petrarch's (and Chaucer's) versions use the separation between the narrator's, the public's, and Valterius's gaze as a major theme of the tale: the discriminating ability of the marquis overshadows the surface assessments of the populace (260), the testing of his wife takes place under his nearly constant scrutiny (276, 286), and the story's distinct gazing communities are at last reunited in the communal appreciation of the beauty of his children (284–86), who represent (among other things) a mingling of the public and private "virtues" of both parents.

Christine removes all of these references to sight, and, unlike Chaucer, lets many opportunities to expand on incidents of gazing slip by—until the reunion scene, when she seems to appropriate the gaze of men and give it to a woman. Before Gliselidis recognizes her children, *se tiroit voulentiers vers la pucelle et vers le filz que partir ne s'en povoit et regardoit ententivement leur beauté que elle moult louoit* (2.50.4) [she was drawn so strongly to the maiden and to her son that she could not leave and she carefully took note of their beauty which she greatly praised] (175). This attraction is not in the source (cf. Petrarch, 284), so the heroine's appreciation of the children's beauty in *Le Livre de la cité des dames* seems to originate in maternal emotion. Her powers of recognition persist despite the fact that her children are taken from her as infants, that years have passed, and that the children are reintroduced to her with concealed identities. One may contrast this treatment of Gliselidis's maternal feelings with those that Petrarch implies in his most conspicuous gaze-image. When Griseldis seems to be about to lose her son, she hands him over while *diuticule oculis inherens* (274) [clinging (to him) for a short time with (her) eyes]. The image is slightly downplayed in the anonymous French translation that Severs includes with Petrarch's *Epistola*: *un petit longuement le regarda* (275). Eyes get no mention. Christine, on the other hand, removes the motif of the motherly eye from its original spot altogether and places it just before the recognition scene, where it makes her heroine look almost prophetic. In addition, the removal of the one distinguishing feature from the abduction of Griseldis's male child makes Gliselidis's love for her children more equally distributed between the two sexes, because then the two abductions become virtually identical. Petrarch's gaze-image, in its situation, comes over as merely sentimental.[36] Through Christine's innovations, one may see that she reworks the gaze-theme in her version of the story so that the (revised) legend may support the attitudes on view in her *Le Livre de la cité des dames*: the virtues of women and their more abstract qualities, as opposed to those (such as appearance) that tend to work within male conceptions of idealized love-objects. There is further evidence of such support. In Christine, Gliselidis has more of an individual will than she does in Petrarch's, Chaucer's, or other versions. For instance, in the *Livre*, the heroine makes no vow to Gualtier (2.50.1), as she does in *The Clerk's Tale*. She thus appears to remain impassive of her own volition upon the abducting of her children and appears to have an inkling of what her husband might be planning. When she is cast out of

Gualtier's court, her father greets her without a tear, as if her stoicism were genetic (2.50.2). By including her father in Gliselidis's patience, Christine objectifies this virtue, making it not just the heroine's, but a fine thing for anyone to have, and thus diluting its association with primarily female characters. Also, as Thomas J. Farrell notices, there is no comment in the *Livre* on the unusual nature of Gliselidis's virtue as there is in Petrarch, who comments on her virtue being "manly."[37] In sum, the telling of a gendered patience story fails to overwhelm Christine's women-positive ideas completely, though these ideas sometimes appear to contradict the sadism of the story and her own views concerning patience that occur later in the *Livre*.

Occasionally, her new version of the Griselda legend transcends mere tension between female-positive and female-negative ideas and enters the realm of satire of the male-traditional position. For instance, she puts much more emphasis than Petrarch or Chaucer on the role of the court, which she seems to subtly criticize, while this extra emphasis plays up the satire of knightly adventure (a development of traditional male heroism) that is implicit in the journeys described in this tale. Such satire is also present in Chaucer's *Clerk's Tale*, and particularly where his and Christine's version agree completely concerning details of plot, but I concentrate on Christine's version here because her satire of courtliness is more pointed and more directly profeminine.

When Gualtier ventures out on his first wedding day, the narrator notes that the marquis *fist toute la route monter a cheval pour aler avec lui* (2.50.1) [had the entire company mount on horseback to accompany him] (171). This scene-setting (it amounts to an elaborate By Way) means that readers should expect exotic events. Gualtier loves the chase, and knightly romances often depict their protagonists encountering marvelous characters and events while out hunting. The movement of the entire court also implies adventure: a knight is usually solitary during his quest whereas a crowd is often present at the start in order to see him off and the climax of the typical adventure usually involves a sight worthy of spectacle.[38] But the "adventure" in the Gliselidis episode comes over as absurdly truncated when, after such great fanfare, with almost no suspense, and with no intervening incident, the company merely meets a peasant woman on the road. Far from being a marvel, Gliselidis comes from one of the (presumably many) working families in one of Gualtier's own villages near his castle. Courtiers must have seen her or women like her many times before. She is encountered while performing a perfectly ordinary domestic task: carrying a "jug" of water on her head.[39] Yet, Gualtier finds it necessary to include the entire court in this escapade, who then put queenly garments on the bride (2.50.1).

This first "translation" of Gliselidis into a new person through royal garb confirms that the first part of this tale, in any of its versions, is a deliberately foreshortened example of—and thus a parody of—the romance genre. In many romances, characters who have been in disguise or who have labored under the misapprehension that they were of humble origin are ordinarily revealed to be of noble or even royal birth. Typically, these revelations arrive through the examination of long-treasured tokens that prove the origins of the requisite characters. Also typically, these revelations arrive at the very end of a romance as part of a "happily ever after" scenario and are crucial factors in establishing the newly revealed characters' suitability for marriage.[40] These (re)discoveries thus represent an implicit (re)approval of social values conventional to the romance genre: noble birth is a prerequisite for "noble" qualities of character. In parallel fashion, most of the popular female martyrs come from noble Roman families. But the Griselda story upends these social values. Certainly Gliselidis in the *Livre* is revealed to be (before her wedding day, anyway) as far removed from royalty as is possible. Thus, just like the revelation of Gualtier's bride, Gliselidis's first transformation occurs strangely early in the narrative for a romance, and consequently seems to question the typical happily ever after scenario of this genre by beginning the story with a wedding instead of ending it with one. Such reordering suggests that this marriage will actually *be* the adventure of the story—a process (in fact, a sadomasochistic charade) as opposed to a logical culmination. This kind of satire of knightly romance occurs in Chaucer's *Clerk's Tale* as well. At Grisilde's wedding, Walter puts her on a snow-white horse, as if marrying him were a knightly act by her (387–89). Her vow not to complain is like a knightly vow (362–64). By showing Grisilde as a hero of patience in the way that a man is a military hero or a courtly lover, Chaucer highlights the limits of the traditional ideals of heroes and heroines and satirizes, as Christine does, both the manly adventure narrative and the patience genre.[41]

Christine produces further examples of such satire, and her satire remains focused on courtly ideas. When Gliselidis works as a serving woman in the palace just before Gaultier's supposed second wedding, her quality shines through despite her ragged dress and her servile situation (2.50.3). The courtiers recognize that she is of much greater worth than her current position indicates, as if she were one of the noble knights who goes into disguise, usually as a cook or other kind of servant, at the king's court in one of the Arthurian romances, in order to be discovered at an opportune time.[42] Ironically, here, virtue as opposed to nobility shines through as if the two ideas were unconnected, in opposition to the advocacy for—and visible manifestations of—nobility in the romances. Meanwhile Gliselidis's virtue has been associated with her sex by Christine. In contrast, Chaucer depicts the court admiring the "prudence" of the heroine (*Clerk's Tale*, line 1022); the idea of a person displaced from accustomed social position is not as clear as it is in Christine's account. Then, at Gliselidis's casting out scene in the *Livre*, her relationship to the court is stressed again. Just as in *The Clerk's Tale*, she strips before the multitude, but she also *fu montee a cheval et, accompaignee des barons, chevaliers et dames qui tous et toutes plouroient, maudissant le marquis et regraitant la bonté de la dame* (2.50.3) [mounted a horse and rode out, accompanied by the barons, knights, and ladies, who all wept, cursing the marquis and mourning the lady's goodness] (173–74). Only in Christine does the heroine gain the sympathy of such an explicitly courtly audience. Again, the scene echoes romance convention by imitating the typical romance hero's knightly departure, often to the accompaniment of much weeping, upon a particularly dangerous quest. Rarely in literature is a woman's assumption of such a knightly position on horseback so emphasized, a position that not only demonstrates the most explicit criticism yet of the man's world of fame (because Gliselidis leaves the court with her virtue and integrity intact unlike the fickle court with its fickle ruler), but also a position that shows that she has replaced Gaultier her husband in fame, status, and social influence. Once again the destination of this "courtly" journey, the poorest house in the village, suggests parody of knightly adventure and of male activities in general. And at the end of Christine's version, Gliselidis usurps male fame altogether: *tous tenoient grant parolle de la louange de celle dame* (2.50.5) [All spoke in praise of this lady] (176). Unlike Chaucer, Christine mentions the fame of no-one else. Despite the fact that she appears to support the idea of patience, even if it means women's subservience to men, her version of the Griselda story strongly criticizes important literary conventions that stem from male-traditional attitudes.

Chaucer's Intensified Satire of the Griselda Story

Like the discussion of Christine's satire of patience literature in her version of the Griselda story, a discussion of Chaucer's similar satire begins aptly with observations concerning the characters' gazing habits.[43] Most obviously, he builds on Petrarch's sight-theme by interposing, between the story and the audience of the poem, a narrator who possesses a gaze, and who comments upon the gazing of others. At first, the Clerk's commentary seems to be completely unlike Christine's (or Droitture's) in that it is overtly masculine. He seems to identify with his "hero." He and Walter together perceive Grisilde's virtues in a stanza that contains five verbs of seeing (232–38), and the narrative largely follows the earlier ones of the story as Walter's glance supposedly demonstrates discernment and intelligence. Apparently, this marquis can see into the heart of Grisilde with a kind of Augustinian x-ray vision, and his heightened insight receives emphasis from his higher vantage point on horseback, which implies that his ability to see what the public cannot comes from social superiority. However, the reader gets more and more uncomfortable with the marquis's acts of gazing, as the testing of the heroine becomes more and more outrageous: as the hiding of information from Grisilde and the public becomes more and more paranoid (while less and less credible).[44] Grisilde's triumph at the end of the tale and the Clerk's condemnation of her ordeals prove that Walter's gaze is merely one more expression of (and implement of) the sadism at the heart of this legend (237–38, 256–57), and Grisilde's victory strongly implies that her social rise contradicts the "characteristic" powers of the nobility that the marquis likely represents: he is much less virtuous than she is despite her lowly origins. These disparities make Chaucer appear to subject the very notion of social "betters" to searching criticism.[45] The Clerk's criticism of Walter is criticism of the traditional male authority figure, clear from the word "shapen" (275) that makes the marquis the creator of Grisilde's marriage feast and which connects him to God. The hierarchies conventional to late patience literature are therefore under attack as well.

Yet, it is easy to take a reading of the Clerk's condemnation of Walter too far. For instance, in an effort to try to resolve the contradictions at the heart of Chaucer's *Clerk's Tale* by trying to absolve Grisilde from total passivity, critics sometimes, in making a case for her assertiveness, downplay the emphatically male viewpoint of the poem, one of its very few consistencies. This gaze begins the poem, continues through it, and even persists through the various endings, because the narrator of this particular Griselda story cannot help but be a gazer himself, even as he criticizes the marquis. For the Clerk, Grisilde is "fair ynogh to sighte" (209). He mentions her beauty before he mentions her name and says that she has "vertuous beautee" (211) and is "faireste under sonne" (212). He assumes that the public's gaze is male (988–91). Chaucer therefore seems to uphold a community of masculine gazers, thinkers, and readers through the opinions of his Clerk.[46] Not only does the narrator address a male audience in general, but he also has a particular kind of masculine audience in mind. As Carolyn Dinshaw and Seth Lerer notice, when the Clerk seems to appreciate the story's landscape through Petrarch's eyes during the prologue to the tale (43–56), he expresses a desire to place his audience in "a brotherhood of literate men of all times and all places," a brotherhood that excludes women and the unlearned, and thus refashions his audience into a group of learned and literary male tourists, with Petrarch, who was familiar with this countryside by sight, as their particularly authoritative literary colleague and "companion" for the escapade.[47] A passage like "Houses of office stuffed with plentee / Ther maystow seen, of deyntevous vitaille / That may be founde as fer as last Ytaille" (264–66), with its direct address to the audience and with its emphasis on seeing (Chaucer's addition [cf. Petrarch, 145]), keeps the Clerk's travelogue running throughout the *Tale*, so that the travelers seem to cooperate in the legend's telling. Even when the narrator addresses the women in his audience (696–97), asking them to judge if Walter's trials have gone far enough, he hives them off from the brotherhood of men by provoking debate between the sexes, and he puts them in Grisilde's place by challenging them to endure the story's extremes without complaint. The male view dominates.

I realize that here I part company with some of the poem's critics. For instance, I agree with Dinshaw that the Clerk demonstrates sympathy for Grisilde, that he sometimes connects with the heroine, and that he "breaks th[e] man-to-man structure of clerkly *translatio* with his 'But' turned toward women" at the end of the tale, so that the discourse rides off into "contradictions in suspension"; but not before this narrator establishes an overwhelming male tradition. His "identification with the female" is far less prevalent.[48] For instance, lines 1086–87, "a pitous thyng it was to se / Hir swownyng," imply that the Clerk witnesses Grisilde's great emotion himself, just as he witnesses the countryside in his traveler persona, which reappears at strategic points in the narrative and reestablishes the male perspective (1112). The most strategic of these points comes near the end of the tale: "But o word, lordynges, herkneth er I go" (1163). Go where? The Clerk/guide seems to disengage from his topic, from the "sight" (Grisilde) that has dominated attention so far, and to hint at a restarting of the Canterbury pilgrimage. Such turning to fresh material suggests that, for the duration of the Griselda legend, the pilgrims have been engaged in looking at a pretty picture that must be left behind in order for the journey to progress. The traveler voice then continues with "It were ful hard to fynde now-a-dayes / In al a toun Grisildis thre or two" (1164–65). The visual image of a cluster of Griseldas in a town is bizarre to contemplate; but the Grisilde-countryside-journey connection recalls a motif established earlier by the Clerk through the use of identical rhymes. Both couplets are parts of scene-setting prologues (at the start of the tale and at the start of Part Two). The first prologue leads into the story's setting, "And many another delitable sighte, / And Saluces this noble contree highte" (62–63); the second leads into the description of Grisilde, "A doghter hadde he, fair ynogh to sighte, / And Grisildis this yonge mayden highte" (209–10). The *Tale* thus establishes her as a wonderful "sight" that the people of Saluces and the audience of the poem might be amazed at, and then underlines this connection (332–34, 419–20, 894–96). But satire of the patience genre appears most explicitly when the Clerk virtually destroys any individuality that his legendary heroine might have with the vast understatement of the "Grisildis two or thre" image that makes her so common as to resemble women in any of the towns between London and Canterbury, an ironic "teach[ing of] us how to multiply Griselda's pattern in our own lives" that again hints at the cyborg.[49] Although only a few lines earlier the narrator seemingly denies the usefulness of type-characters (1142–48), in an abrupt misprision he now supercharges his Grisilde with typeness. The suggested mini-pilgrimage to look for two or three Griseldas in town even hints at sexual tourism.

However, despite the fact that male narrators and audiences dominate through most of the poem, one may not dismiss Chaucer as antifeminist and firmly on the side of misogynist medieval writers. The dominating gaze receives implied criticism from the Clerk. At many junctures, his bombastic attacks upon the public gaze as capricious implicate the brotherhood of travelers as well. Further implied criticism of the prevailing gaze occurs with the Earl of Panyk's appeal to the sense of sight upon his arrival in Saluces: "nevere was ther seyn with mannes ye / So noble array in al West Lumbardye" (944–45). The passage strikes the reader as a superfluous By Way—this kind of detail would be unthinkable in one of the early passios—and ironic because these pleasures for the eye amount to merely one of Walter's many deceptions. Moreover, as critics notice, Grisilde is less passive than she might appear and her subversive challenges to authority involve the use of her gaze. She starts out as an object of masculine attention, but soon the tables are turned: "She wolde fayn han seyn som of that sighte" of the marquis's purported bride, not knowing that she thus desires sight of herself (280). She then gazes at Walter intently (334–40). Later the heroine's assertiveness goes so far that she defeats Walter's gaze completely: "whan this markys say / The constance of his wyf, he caste adoun / His eyen two" (667–70). Only Chaucer describes Grisilde as effecting the eyes of her tormentor specifically at this juncture. Petrarch has Valterius averting his face rather than his eyes, and, in one version of Petrarch's text, a similar aversion marks the height of Valterius's control over his wife's will and of his attempt for control over her emotions: when Griseldis greets the bridal party, she shows her servant-status with *vultuque demisso reverenter atque humiliter* [(her) face respectfully and humbly lowered] (Petrarch, 284, n. 25). Perhaps Chaucer deliberately transfers this aversion image from a female to a male character in order to strengthen her and weaken him.[50]

At the casting out, Grisilde's walk to her former home in only a shift would seem to be a blatant example of spectacle, but, as critics observe about her during this episode, her speeches to Walter are forceful deeds that belie an interpretation of her as a mere passive receiver of gazes and misfortune, and in fact this scene shows Grisilde becoming the agent of almost *all* of the activity, and visual activity in particular.[51] She uses the passive voice, "Be seyn," in her request for a garment, and thus reverses the action of gazing so that being looked at seems more "active" than looking. The same passage features many verbs that describe Grisilde's movement: "turne," "wente," "walkyng," "go" (872–80). The poem does not describe anyone looking at her during the return. The people weep and "hire folwe" while Grisilde "fro wepyng kepte hire *eyen* dreye" (897–99; my emphasis), and the reversal of gazing roles continues as the poem uses "Ne shewed she" to define (negatively, through a process of elimination) her steadfastness (922).[52] Grisilde's passivity seems to emit from her like a halo, so that her father cannot even put her old coat on her (915–17), while the lookers are reduced to utter passivity and to the futile emotions of childishness. At the same time, Walter's gaze has been utterly defeated. By causing him to avert his eyes, Grisilde defeats the gaze that is the maintainer of social hierarchy, that fixes a woman or other servile figure in discourse and in society. From the moment of her stripping, the narrative does not describe him using his powerful gaze until the poem's climax: "And whan this Walter saugh hire pacience" (1044), as if Grisilde has gained a visible manifestation of the virtue, like a "crown" of patience for a female martyr.[53]

Besides her husband's, she also defeats the gaze that may be allegorized as the audience of pilgrims and the reading audience of the *Canterbury Tales* by becoming increasingly distant from these audiences' sensibilities during the course of the narrative. She lacks realism almost completely by the end of the story when the shifting points of view and shifting attitudes (1139–212) distance her even further, with such phrases as "Al putte he [Grisilde's son] nat his wyf in greet assay. / This world is nat so strong," which imply that Grisilde is a "world" unto herself (1138–39). These shifts are "a test that Chaucer performs upon the sharpness of the pitying eye; the eye of the reader is asked to penetrate through the meretricious attractions of theatrical events and exercise itself upon the still but ever-receding point of Grisilde's person."[54] The result of such tension is that Grisilde becomes so "linked up with the peculiarities of adventure-time and abstract space" that she becomes "invisible," "a kind of relic whose truth can only be taken on faith … a sign."[55] Her capacity to defeat knows no bounds. Yet, readers are then left wondering if this heroine can have any purpose. After all, the Clerk's disqualification of

Walter as the *Tale*'s hero leaves no alternative but her. Also, this narrator specifically identifies "purpos" and "entencion" as the "stake" to which ironic martyrs such as Walter are bound, as if the Clerk understands that patience is an act of the will, and that very little about any exhibition of this virtue—perhaps of any abstract idea—is provable (701–07). The analysis of patience in this *Tale* is amazingly sophisticated, probing, and thoughtful.[56]

Grisilde's Exemplarity

I realize that my reading of *The Clerk's Tale* goes against that of critics who hold that Griselda's career in literary history demonstrates that her legend's primary role is to provide a "patient wife" exemplar.[57] Certainly, one may find a blizzard of continental and later English analogues to the *Tale* that offer up the "moral" of Griselda's exemplarity.[58] But the Clerk seems to repudiate this moral: "This storie is seyd nat for that wyves sholde / Folwen Grisilde as in humylitee, / For it were inportable, though they wolde" (1142–44), while a reading of Walter as analogous to God is hard to stomach, and the *Tale*'s Envoy culminates in a Grisilde-exploding exhortation to wives to rail at their husbands and assert their power over them.[59]

In addition, Walter's habits of counterfeiting and the several images of counterfeit Grisildes that the Clerk employs at the end of the *Tale* seem to confirm that the poem treats the idea of the imitation of Grisilde in an ironic fashion (736–49, 1165, 1168), as if Chaucer understands that the duplication of the events in her legend, with its otherwise unexampled passivity, marks a significant "endpoint" to the patience genre.[60] In fact, the contradictory aspects of the Griselda story herald the arrival of full-blown counterfeit consciousness within this genre, as the Clerk's images of two or three Grisildes and of a brass coin suggest. Whereas saints' lives by the time of the *Legenda Aurea* often demonstrated a trade in narrative materials back and forth from one martyr to another, the Griselda narrative actively courts only duplication, not mimicry, of its patience figure. True, her story is very popular, and many versions of it exist. But, if it is such an important exemplar for Christians, men and more particularly women, then why is it never once expropriated *into* hagiography or mined for its obviously hagiographical material? Instead, the story becomes branded as hers alone, and Griselda becomes the proverbial patient figure.[61] In sum, once patience literature is fully gendered and is taken to its furthest extreme with the Griselda legend, repetition is fully revealed as counterfeit consciousness.

The comprehensive satire that characterizes *The Clerk's Tale* then is plain. Patience literature in it is reduced to a highly schematic battle of wills between two characters: a patience figure (Grisilde) and a pseudo-patience figure (Walter) who is essentially, as a mirror for Grisilde, the traditional patience figure with—paradoxically—the suffering taken out. His lack of apparent emotion and his stubbornness make him an exemplar of patience, but in an unworthy (i.e., worldly) cause. And here the "cause" for patience is marriage, so that the two genders are crucial (and utterly polarizing) within the action of this *Tale*, which cannot help but reflect the arbitrary nature and essential injustice of placing one gender in a superior position to the other when extreme suffering results from a "test" imposed by a husband.

In other words, just like the story of Blandina, Chaucer's *Clerk's Tale* wrestles with the issues of egalitarianism, but in a new way. The later work is ironic in temperament, but it nevertheless follows the pattern of patience literature very closely. It even deals with the idea of inheritance, just as the lives of the female saints Felicity, Lucy, Paula, Cecilia (Chaucer, *The Second Nun's Tale*, VIII 540–46), and others do. Where these women pass on their learning or leave behind a house to be consecrated as a church, the inheritance in *The Clerk's Tale* is a particularly feminine yet harsh kind of language and knowledge: the piercing speech of the scold in the Envoy.[62] The exact terms of this inheritance are that a woman should "sharply" take for herself "the governaille." The poem enjoins women to "Emprenteth wel this lessoun in youre mynde" (1192–93). Moreover, going even further than the Wife of Bath, such dominance of a wife over her husband according to the Envoy furthers the "commune profit," that is, presumably the welfare of both sexes (1193–94), and the imprinting power of the scold's language is impressive. Significantly, in the light of the extreme artificiality of Grisilde as a hybrid and as the wearer of a marmoreal mask (as if her face were a kind of technology) this language can get through a husband's armor, when an armed knight must represent the height of male-instituted medieval technology (1202–04). The scold's message is a kind of feminine inheritance, but it is hardly an inheritance from Grisilde. Or is it? Is Chaucer proposing that the example of Grisilde inevitably leads to extreme and cynical attitudes toward women, personified in the strident figure of a scold?[63]

Grisilde as an Art Object

One cannot know. Ultimately, Grisilde's face and any conception of her virtue defeats the gaze of her husband and of the populace because she exists ultimately for the legend's audience alone, the only possible witnesses to the total and unrealistic consistency of this face/character. Through allusions to Petrarch, travel, learning, and female attractiveness, the Clerk has already established the kind of audience that he has in mind, so this heroine is utterly different from Christine's Gliselidis in one significant respect: she is completely and only a work of art created by men, who fix her in their knowing gaze and admire her Mona Lisa–like inscrutability along with her statue-like beauty, who chisel her out of the cold stone of their attitudes to women.[64] Of course, such works of art are by their natures nonhuman and incredible. For instance, the artist demands absolute stillness from his model, and Grisilde supplies it with her wall-like facial expression. If one visualizes many of her actions throughout the tale, they come over as set-pieces, thoroughly modeled: a young woman goes out to fetch water from the well (274–77), enacts the pietà when she gives her children up, and walks home in her underclothes.[65] The idealism and the power that she almost seems to radiate are also typical artist's subjects (240, 413, 440). One need only examine the auras and halos in medieval depictions of saints for examples. Although the tears and melodramatic emotions at the discovery scene (1047) would seem to be a repudiation of her previous "mystic blankness,"[66] these emotions are also highly artificial in that they are typical of sentimental reunion scenes with mothers. Ironically, then, if the Petrarchan brotherhood is defeated by Grisilde, defeat comes at the hands of a product (a work of art) that the brotherhood created out of its desires.

Walter's longing for this kind of artist's fantasy is confirmed when he at last reveals his intentions to Grisilde. He claims that the purpose in hiding his children was "for to kepe hem pryvely and stille, / Til I thy [Grisilde's] purpos knewe and al thy wille" (1077–78). He can never know all of her will and therefore seems doomed to a life of peculiar fantasies.[67] And Chaucer shows this masculine delusion about women for what it is when Harry Bailey wishes at the end of the *Tale* that his wife had heard the Griselda legend once (1212d), and then comments, "As to my purpos, wiste ye my wille; / But thyng that wol nat be, lat it be stille" (1212f–12g). Grisilde, as a personification of the "stillness" that Harry mentions, is an art object, a "thyng that wol nat be," in this final (according to most manuscripts of Fragment IV) and rueful comment on the *Tale*. Harry's paradoxical mood of desire for an ideal object, mixed with resignation to its unattainability, comes through as well in the tension between stillness and action that exists in Walter's orders concerning Grisilde's smock when she is cast out: "Lat it be stille, and bere it forth with thee" (891).[68]

Grisilde as More Than an Art Object

Yet, at one point Chaucer seems to allow Grisilde to escape from the male fantasy of art and stillness, but only in a very abstract fashion. During the casting out episode, she disqualifies herself from being the lady of Walter's house, "The heighe God take I for my witnesse." Instead, she is "But humble servant to youre worthynesse; / And evere shal, whil that my lyf may dure, / Aboven every worldly creature" (821–26). "Heighe" is Chaucer's addition, as is "Aboven ... creature." These terms allow Grisilde to assign God the most exalted gaze and viewpoint, and they perhaps recall the description of death, "But as it were a twynkling of an ye" (if anyone's, God's eye), from line 37.[69] She therefore seems to put herself in God's position, "heighe," with the last line in the stanza, for "Aboven" (parallel to "heighe") could refer to her life as readily as it does to Walter in the structure of the sentence "whil that my lyf may dure ... / Aboven every worldly creature." With this meaning, the phrase puts her above the action in "heigh style": in the place an author or narrator occupies while addressing kings (18) or composing highly literate, travelogue-like prefaces (41); in the place of the Clerk, Chaucer, Christine, or Petrarch; in the place of a votive image, gazing out from a point above eye-level in a church.

The "twynkling" at line 37, the height that Grisilde reaches, and the height that she assigns to God raise the possibility of God's gaze as dominant in this story. Despite allegorical readings of the *Tale* that bring in Old Testament typology, secular hagiography, lay piety, Mariology, and the like, Grisilde's endurance of unjust suffering connects her most obviously with Christ, and this interpretation is the only allegorical connection that the narrator seems to invite explicitly with his references to an ox's stall (291, 395–99).[70] The ideas that would spring up from pondering this connection, such as God as impossible to like and distant—a woman, masochist, victim, slave, monster, wall, and void—are I believe meant to be disturbing and meant to provoke an audience into thinking about the roles and actions of God in the world and in such a legend. Thus, in some ways, the problems of the Griselda story, its relationships to saints' lives, its ambiguous promotion of patience, its suggestions concerning relations between the sexes, and its contradictory gazes are long-standing philosophical problems. People often find the ideas of the reversal of sex-roles, the reversal of social roles, the existence of suffering, the existence of God on earth, the existence of a presence that watches one's every move, and the existence of evil (particularly unpunished evil) difficult to accept. I think that Petrarch, Christine, and Chaucer all knew how provocative they were being in retelling this legend: Petrarch with his acknowledgment that the story divides its audiences, Christine with her participation in feminist debate, and Chaucer with his complex and contradictory treatment of the legend as an example of patience literature, a treatment that continues through the complex and contradictory conclusion to the *Tale*. The Clerk insists upon the artificiality of his heroine when he dismisses her as "deed" (1177) and restores her to object status by describing her virtue as gold compared to brass (1166–67; 1117). A golden image of the saintlike Grisilde suggests a keepsake, a statue, perhaps a commemorative medal of her and of this part of the pilgrimage, which a gazer could look at whenever he wants. But the *Tale*'s conclusion is no simple retrenchment of male gazes. It cannot be when it is directed to the Wife of Bath (1172), and when women maintain the "heigh" vantage point that Grisilde achieves earlier in the narrative throughout the *Tale*'s multiple endings: the Clerk asks God to maintain the "secte" of the Wife of Bath in "heigh maistrie" (1172–73; 1183).

Chaucer's version of the Griselda story as patience literature thus consistently displays a masculine gaze, but occasionally and briefly acknowledges the existence of a competitive female one during examples of the glimpses into a profeminine "tradition" that Castelli observes in some medieval works.[71] These acknowledgments and *The Clerk's Tale*'s satire of patience literature force male perspectives (and perhaps all perspectives) into a state of unresolved tension: the prevailing mood of *The Canterbury Tales*.

CHAPTER 6

THE FEMALE PATIENCE FIGURE AS SHRINE

> *How blest you are, when you suffer insults and persecution and every kind of calumny for my sake. Accept it with gladness and exultation, for you have a rich reward in heaven.*
>
> —Matthew 5:11–12
>
> *Social and political events gain meaning in [a literary work] only thanks to their connection with private life.*
>
> —M. M. Bakhtin, *The Dialogic Imagination*, p. 109

The Book of Margery Kempe as Late Medieval Patience Literature

The genre of patience literature is particularly helpful with regard to the study of *The Book of Margery Kempe* (c. 1438), which has recently attracted much critical attention.[1] Many events in Margery's spiritual autobiography on the surface seem bizarre to modern audiences, even when readers are familiar with other medieval works because many such readers (and particularly literary critics) want the conventions of mysticism, hagiography, or "real life" to prevail within such a composition, but not all three at once, intermittently upstaging—sometimes fracturing—one another almost without notice.[2] Hagiographical motifs such as prison (12, 134–35), self-denial (12, 61), mortification of the flesh (11–12), dangerous mobs (28, 33), and trials before authority-figures (28, 37, 129–33) jostle in the *Book* with disconcerting fits of tears and wailing (68, 182, 184), outrageously cutting criticism (120, 125), childishly mean personal insults (62), and vicious threats (14, 113). But this jarring mixture of events and, in more general terms, the tortured conflict between life on earth and spiritual ideals that runs through much of *The Book of Margery Kempe* seem less unusual and alienating if one looks at her career through the lens of patience literature as opposed to that of (perhaps comically) unsuccessful auto-hagiography.[3]

Recently scholars have shown more sensitivity than previously to the *Book*'s generic contexts and have begun to analyze this text with other patience narratives in mind.[4] Such treatment allows the blurring of mystical, hagiographical, and historical genres so that Margery's attempts to reconcile her religious life with her visions, desires, and her worldly existence seem more reasonable. The author and compilers of Margery's *Book* may not have organized their material according to typical hagiographical traditions or prevailing modern literary expectations, but I believe that they knew that the protagonist of the work must suffer, and in a way that must highlight her gender. Nor, due to her marital status, her familial relationships, and the developments in the history of patience literature, can her trials take the same form as a conventional martyr's. Margery says, "'I suffir not so mech sorwe as I wolde do for owr Lordys lofe, for I suffir but schrewyd wordys, & owr merciful Lord Crist Ihesu, worshepyd be hys name, suffyrd hard strokys, bittyr scorgyngys, & schamful deth'" (129–30).

The ideologies of later medieval patience literature mean that some of the *Book*'s events, such as Christ's often vacillating instructions to Margery that seem designed to rain accusations of hypocrisy down upon her head (32), the frequent humiliations visited upon her, for instance, loss of bodily control (so different from the typical dignity of the martyr even under the most trying circumstances) (68), the irony of a wealthy woman rendered destitute and dependent so often during her pilgrimages in Italy, the Holy Land, and Germany (92, 102, 232, 238), and her obligation to deal with the consequences of her husband's senility and incontinence often seem capricious, even sadistic (181). The most obvious examples of seemingly random sadism are the "schrewyd wordys" that her detractors hurl at her: "The munke seyd, 'I wold þow wer closyd in an hows of ston þat þer schuld no man speke wyth þe'" (27); "it is pety þat þow leuyst" (36); "sum wolde sche had ben in þe se in a bottumles boyt" (69); "folke spitted at hir ... sum scornyd hir and seyd þat sche howlyd as it had ben a dogge" (105).[5] Yet, in late medieval patience literature, such extremes of sadism and caprice may well be what audiences would expect—witness the popularity of the Griselda-legend—and these expectations explain why Margery's struggles must be so many and so unrelenting: against fear (77, 124, 231), abandonment (75), alienation (80, 95), ostracization (45, 75–76), illiteracy (4), sexual desire (14–15), sexual threats (14, 113), treatment as a sexual object (12), civil authorities (112, 116, 129, 135), church authorities (28, 35–37, 40, 129–33), privation while traveling (80, 92, 106, 232, 238), theft of her belongings (64, 67) embarrassingly intrusive questioning (36, 116, 120, 122, 124), false accusations (29, 32, 243), character assassination (33, 62), antifeminist declarations (116, 123), and mobs who want to burn her as a heretic (28, 33, 36, 129). These generic demands also explain why her struggles and frequent humiliations are so often, like the martyrs', "conspicuously public."[6] Even her failure at beer-making is simply due to the generic requirements of late patience literature: she must suffer, and an unsuccessful business venture provides an opportunity (9). In any case, the text makes it explicit that Margery's trials are not randomly construed, but instead part of a general theme of her *Book*. Jesus tells her "þe mor schame, despite, & reprefe þat þu sufferyst for my lofe, þe bettyr I lofe þe" (81, 85, 131). He later explains that the piercing words that acquaintances use against her are like the sufferings He endured at the Crucifixion, an analogy that she also mentions (107, 123, 130). Christ adds that He will see to it that she suffers by words alone (85).

Women and the Shrine

At the same time that women, even late medieval women like Margery, become more and more associated with (and duplicated with) a kind of heroic patience, while men maintain the so-called heroic masculine virtues together with the many variations of what one might call contemplative or intellectual heroism, women become more and more associated, much more than men are, with an abstract idea of space that is best called "The Shrine." The Shrine arrives from the marking out of space by heroically patient women and other figures such as Lot's wife, through domestic spaces and the miraculous immovability and stasis of figures such as Lucy, Fénice, and Griselda, to a (re)characterization of the space surrounding such patience figures as sacred space. Lot's wife represents a nascent shrine, Lucy a more established one, and Fénice and Griselda represent highly literary ones. This development is not solely a product of the Middle Ages. The recent explosion of critical material concerning space and medieval women, by, for instance, Kristeva, who sees the mother-figure in examples of Western medieval art as "within an 'enceinte' separating her from the world of everyone else"; by Cynthia Hahn, whose work concerns the relationship between public acts of seeing and of "belief" at early medieval saints' shrines; by Sarah Stanbury, whose work deals with issues of space in late medieval art and English writing, including Chaucer and Margery; and by others, has contributed to the development of this concept.[7]

Recent theories regarding pilgrims' shrines in the medieval era become remarkably promising as strategies for reexamining female figures of patience. Before the onset of this kind of criticism, as Stanbury has noticed, analysis of medieval literature and artworks had focused on "the textual body," when the medieval understanding of the body was more that of a "cultural body, regulated and exposed by lines of sight that are tightly bound to schema for representing the painted or the plastic body in contemporary manuscript illumination, panel painting, or statuary."[8] The most important example of the Shrine in English history would be the shrine to the Virgin at Walsingham. This shrine featured the Holy House of Nazareth, said to have been built at Mary's command. The house first appeared in 1061.[9]

One cannot now examine the schema or dynamics of space at Walsingham because the buildings there have not survived in their medieval forms (there is an analogous shrine at Loreto in Italy), but even a cursory examination of relatively few surviving churches in Europe demonstrates that, like texts, many medieval spaces assume an "'eye of piety' (*oculis pietatis*) that fractures distance, fusing self with the objects of devotional desire in a hybridized mix of maternal, infantile, and erotic impulses," in "a series of visual moves that brings the viewer into … tactile intimacy" with aspects of this space, as Stanbury describes such dynamics.[10] One would be oversimplifying, therefore, if one were to infer that the more direct gazes of earlier as opposed to later medieval images of female saints are due to a kind of feminine mediating power or feminine language through female inheritance, though the pattern of such development in imagery is often striking enough to reveal a major change in representations of gazing. Fundamental differences between the twelfth- and thirteenth-century artworks of the church of Saint Maria in Trastevere in Rome, for instance, are hard to miss.[11] In the apse mosaic from the twelfth century, Mary looks out at the viewer from a point well above eye-level. She is depicted enthroned with Jesus. Just below these artworks are a series of thirteenth-century mosaics that present scenes from the Virgin's life where Mary's eyes always look away from the viewer. In fact, female figures with averted eyes are so ubiquitous in Western artworks that I hardly need to provide examples, while portrayals of saints from earlier than the twelfth century often feature very large eyes that stare directly out with arresting gazes, as one may see in images of mosaics from the churches of Saint Prassede and Saints Valerian and Cecilia in Rome (See Figures 6.1 and 6.2).

There are images in many other Roman churches, for example, those of Saints Clemente, Pudenziana, Suzannah, and Maria in Domnica, where one meets with similarly staring gazes from early medieval depictions of women. In some of these locations, the effects of these gazes on the viewer are magnified by the tightness of the spaces surrounding the images, for example, in the grotto in Saint Clemente and the chapel of Saint Zenobia in Saint Prassede. In contrast, from roughly the thirteenth century on in the churches of Rome (and of course there are exceptions),

Figure 6.1 Mosaic of saints in Santa Prassede, Rome. © Holly Hayes/Art History Images.

Figure 6.2 Mosaic of saints in Santa Cecilia in Trastevere, Rome. © Holly Hayes/Art History Images.

artworks tend to depict female figures with averted eyes, a development in art history that foreshadows the arguments of Mulvey from the 1970s concerning the presentation of female characters in popular cinema.[12]

Women and the Shrine in Chaucer's Works

As these arresting gazes of women intimate and as Stanbury rightly proposes, the Oedipal and fetishized gaze that Mulvey describes—and that affects current attitudes toward the female body so strongly—does not apply consistently to the artworks of the Middle Ages. Instead, these artworks suggest a "fluidity of visual relations that surround the body" and "upset any fixed gender binary."[13] Certainly, it is difficult to argue for a fixed gender binary in Chaucer's work when, for instance, the dreamer in *The Legend of Good Women* gets as low as he possibly can to the ground in order to engage with a votive object, the daisy, which seems to be able to return his gaze: the narrator identifies the flower as the "day's eye" (F 178–84).[14] Furthermore, the specific examinations of space by Stanbury and others in texts such as Margery's *Book* would seem to match some of the action in Chaucer's *Clerk's Tale*. Most significant for my argument is that the behavior of the people under Walter's rule in this *Tale* imitates the behavior of pilgrims at shrines in contemporary historical and literary accounts.[15] These people arrive at Grisilde's lowly dwelling as if it were a shrine, and, "pilgrims" that they are, examine the outside of the hovel/shrine for manifestations of the "saint's" acts: "The people cam unto the hous withoute, / And wondred hem in how honest manere / And tentifly she kepte hir fader deere" (332–34). Their "wondering" suggests the witnessing of miraculous events. In this case, these are the honest and dutiful fashion in which Grisilde tends to her father—an unusual miracle by the standards of the day, brought upon apparently by Walter's unusual choice of bride (as opposed to a more conventional spiritual revelation). Ironically, while these pilgrims watch their newfound shrine, negotiations are taking place inside it for the removal of its cult object: Grisilde herself.[16]

Yet, even as an object, Grisilde, like the daisy in *The Legend of Good Women*, is not as passive as she might appear. She reverses the gender polarity of typical gazing activity when the local marquis steps into her house, whereupon her powers of sight are stressed three times within five lines:

> … nevere erst ne saugh she swich a sighte.
> … she were astoned
> To seen so greet a gest come in that place;
> ……………………………………
> For which she looked with ful pale face. (336–40)

These references to gazing are Chaucer's additions to the previous accounts of the story.[17] Grisilde's looks here suggest desire. They clearly depict her turning Walter into an object. Unlike the careful distinction between lustful and mature seeing that appears in all versions of this tale as a description of Walter's glance at his future bride (232–38), one has to *assume*, if one wishes to take such a view of the heroine, that she has no lust for her future husband when she looks at him. Her ascetic disposition might lead one to think so (214, 228), but the narrator does not mention any lack of "likerous lust" here. He instead relates that Grisilde is astonished "to seen so greet a gest" as Walter in her house (337–38). This emotion seems unlike lust, but does not preclude it, and her marriage might well allow her a chance at erotic adventure as well as a release from her life of poverty. In other words, she does not escape the gaze of men as she seems to do in Christine's version of the Griselda story, but she gives as good as she gets.[18]

As the admiration of the people of Saluces for Grisilde's care of her father and house makes clear, the Shrine in its role as a space associated with women has strong connections to domestic life. Another example occurs in *The Book of Margery Kempe*, where, in one of the protagonist's most extensive visions, she seems to fantasize about occupying the Holy House of Nazareth. Margery sees herself in this vision as a kind of domestic servant to the women of the holy family (18). Later in this vision, after she witnesses the nativity, she continues an unabashedly domestic role when she purveys lodging for Mary, and Margery seems to take much emotional satisfaction from her adoption of this role and for the praise she gets for it from the Virgin (19). This treatment contrasts with Margery's undeniably complicated relationship with domestic functions in earthly as opposed to visionary experience (8, 38).[19] Sacred domesticity seems much more palatable to her than secular. Thus, in their very different ways, the examples of Margery and Griselda announce that the nascent shrines that begin with By Ways and the petrification of Lot's wife have evolved into domestic shrines by the time of late medieval patience literature.[20]

One may observe many other instances of how Shrine theory in its sacred mode links with more secular, domestic roles for women. An example that reveals similarities to Margery's visionary experience is Chaucer's *Second Nun's Tale*, based on the passion of Saint Cecilia.[21] Chaucer's version begins in remarkably undefined space: neither the homes of Saint Cecilie and Valerian, her not-yet-Christian fiancé, nor the church where she secretly gives voice to the emotions in her heart to the accompaniment of the organ receive any identification or description, so that one has to assume, for instance, that the couple's wedding night occurs at Valerian's house. Cecilie then sends Valerian to the Appian Way and to the poor people who dwell there (172–74). The road is less a place than a conduit for his conscience, emblematic of the process of his conversion to Christianity. Then, as soon as Valerian finds Pope Urban, the location suddenly receives definition: "the place" (183), "Among the seintes buryeles lotynge" (186); "Pope Urban hym cristned *right there*" (217; my emphasis). This treatment of By Ways is very different from other versions of this story. The sudden appearance of defined space, here a burial ground for martyrs, indicates the destination of Valerian's spiritual journey as well as the object of the entire narrative, which ends with the martyrdoms of all the major characters. Now that he has received baptism, Valerian's "hoom" and "his chambre" can become more definite spaces (and notably domestic ones) for the spiritual marriage that now takes place between him and Cecilie.[22] Appropriately, then, images of heaven as a specific place now crowd into the narrative: "paradys" (227), "blisse above" (281), "yhid in hevene pryvely" (317)—a place openly contrasted to the everyday world, which is dismissed as only a dream (262–64).

Then, as the spiritual states of the three future martyrs become further consolidated, Chaucer's treatment of place becomes closer to the other version's of this martyr's life, as the dwelling place seems to shift into Cecilie's ownership. The imposition into the text of commentary from a "preface" by Ambrose hints at this event when the quotation says of the saint: "'The world and eek hire chambre gan she weyve'" (271, 276), and the situating of this line just before she preaches against idolatry to Valerian's brother, Tiburce, implies that Valerian's chamber has become hers. Finally, her martyrdom takes place in her house, as the text not only mentions but emphasizes through repetition. The judge "bad men sholde hir lede / Hom til hir hous, and 'In hire hous,'" he declares that she should be burned in a bath (513–15).[23] The interior space and parody of bodily care are noteworthy because the early martyrdoms stress instead the public locations of the executions and tortures of the martyrs, if they mention places of execution at all. Only traditions later than the passios come to associate female martyrs particularly with domestic spaces, as the attributions and histories of several churches in Rome indicate. Saint Maria in Domnica was built over the house of a female Roman martyr, Saint Cyriaca. At Saint Suzannah's, the shrine is supposedly the dining room of the martyr's residence. The church of Santa Croce is supposedly on the site of Saint Helena's fourth-century palace. Saint Pudenziana made her house into a church, according to tradition, though the building ascribed to her is actually over a Roman bathhouse.

Even more significant in the case of Chaucer's Cecilie is that her family is removed from the property ownership, which seems to come to her as a kind of inheritance. Certainly, she disposes of it as she sees fit and the text stresses her ownership of the house, as if suddenly no male family members existed. She says: "and that I myghte do werche / Heere of myn hous perpetuelly a cherche" (545–46). The church persists to this day, according to the poem, and "Hir hous the chirche of Seint Cecilie highte" (550).

Other shrines in Chaucer's works are associated with the female body and depicted as women's property and inheritance. Grisilde's role as a female domestic linked with particular spaces has probably attracted the most attention of any of his characters with regard to this kind of analysis.[24] For instance, when the people of Saluces accompany Walter on his wedding day in order to view her dwelling place, they seem to presume that this space is hers. Grisilde is the poorest person in her village, yet she cultivates a space of her own, something that is wonderful to examine. Her good (and growing) reputation among the people begins in their assessment of her house and of her care for her father, expressed in the poem almost as ownership over him (*Clerk's Tale*, 332–36). Walter acknowledges this space as hers when he speaks to Grisilde of "youre village" (496). Hence Stanbury considers Grisilde to be "a complex object/sign and symptom of domestic ordering."[25] Meanwhile Walter wants Grisilde's feminine space and this desire fits with the way men try to counter verbal competition by attacking perceived speech organs inside their competitors.[26] That is why Walter tests Grisilde's patience and "womanhood"—these are inside her: "in the brest of hire virginitee / Ther was enclosed rype and sad corage" (219–20). He tries to invade and possess this space.[27]

Obviously Walter's desire for Grisilde's space fits into male habits of objectifying women, reducing them to body parts: the kinds of attitudes that appear in the waterpot imagery in the *Tale* (276, 290), in Christine's version of the story, and in the analogous bible story. A woman carrying a vessel of water displays her function as a mere vessel for containing, bearing, and nurturing a man's children. But the *Tale* goes beyond objectification. Wolfgang Rudat further examines the feminine space in the poem by demonstrating Walter's sexual jealousy of his own children and his attempt to (re)propagate them by hiding them and reintroducing them to his community. Rudat and others have concluded that Walter has a pathological womb-envy.[28] Sex with his wife (perhaps a kind of institutionalized rape, although readers do not find out what Grisilde thinks of sex, and she declares her love for Walter [972–73]) is an attempt to invade her enclosed space. But the result is children, who are, among other things, a language that no man can speak. His abduction of them is then, as Patricia Cramer says, "the father's co-optation of origin," a man's envious counterblow to "the mother's ability to give birth."[29] Still, Walter wants to co-opt further kinds of feminine space that Grisilde possesses.

He removes the children from her, from public sight, and (secretly) to his exclusive purview, because—not content with his patriarchal control over her inheritance—he must exercise control over any phantom inheritance as well; because motherhood, or, more accurately, the provision of legitimate heirs for her husband, is the sole aspect of her role that might distinguish her from being a slave. Removing these reestablishes Grisilde's role as one of unquestioning allegiance to him alone. When the two abducted children are returned to Saluces, Walter says: "Thou bare hym in thy body trewely. / At Boloigne have I kept hem prively" (1068–69). The connection between this secret location and Grisilde's body is so obvious that Allyson Newton proposes that this sequence of events enacts a patriarchal "occlusion of Griselda's maternity" after the pattern of the views of the church fathers and of the Old Testament patriarchs.[30]

But Grisilde rises above such a pattern. The most obvious indication of her continued ownership over her feminine/feminized space, her "sadness," is the famous scene when Walter repudiates her as his wife and she says "'Naked out of my fadres hous ... I cam, and naked moot I turne agayn,'" a direct quotation from Job, except that Job says "mother's womb," not "father's house" (871–72; cf. Job 1:21). Therefore, in the *Tale* the home Grisilde comes from is a kind of womb that she has made for herself. Parallel to her internal virtue is this externalization of the space and the powers of creativity that Walter wants to possess so much. He takes his children away from Grisilde and has his sister raise them in order "to consolidate paternal influence while diminishing maternal."[31] But no man can take this space, not even him, as the poem makes plain. Grisilde demonstrates her total ownership with "'Ye koude nat doon so dishonest a thyng, / That thilke wombe in which youre children leye / Sholde biforn the peple, in my walkyng, / Be seyn al bare; wherfore I yow preye, / Lat me nat lyk a worm go by the weye'" (876–80). Having gained a reputation as almost an abstract representation of service to others' bodies— her father's, Walter's, his subjects', her childrens'—she here expresses ownership and possession of her body and/as her virtue, evaluates the crowd's impression of her, and promotes her own views concerning right and wrong: a turning point in the *Tale* as many critics have perceived.[32] Grisilde recognizes that Walter equates her only with her womb. She says of the smok "That I therwith may wrye the wombe of here / That was youre wyf." The sentence construction allows for a meaning that indicates Walter's ludicrously reductive identification of her (887–88): "the womb ... that was your wife." Moreover the womb-imagery continues to the end of the poem. In the Envoy, the traditional competitive male figure is punctured in the way that Walter would like to invade Grisilde: "For though thyn housbonde armed be in maille, / The arwes of thy crabbed eloquence / Shal perce his brest" (1202–04). Nevertheless, the marquis (indefatigably obsessed) wants to co-opt *all* kinds of feminine space that Grisilde controls, for instance, her "powerful influence during early infancy," the "maternal space" that Kristeva identifies in *Desire in Language* and describes most fully in *Tales of Love*. In trying to take away this space, Walter tries to intervene into processes of language acquisition and identity politics that must be exclusively maternal.[33] Again Grisilde's eventual victory thwarts his attempt, though not his desires.

Troilus and Criseyde

Grisilde's victory over her husband demonstrates that extremely fatalistic understandings of the roles of women in the Middle Ages and, for instance, Stanbury's concentration on the "hybridizing" of gendered gazes in medieval works and at medieval shrines sometimes lead to downplaying of how powerful the effects and gazes of patient women can be. A particularly extreme power of this kind appears in Chaucer's *Troilus and Criseyde* when Troilus gazes upon the empty shrine of "Criseydes hous" (5.528).[34] Clearly identified as an object of her possession (and as an image of the interior of the female body that Troilus can no longer penetrate), this palace has previously been associated in the poem with a very exclusive feminine community—in fact almost entirely female, where Criseyde has been sequestered away from Trojan society (2.813–924). Troilus's later meditation upon her closed-up house and the other sites important to his love-affair is full of religious terms, such as "blisful," "grace," "temple," and images of light (5.566, 570, 580, 581, 543–48). He calls the house a "shryne, of which the seynt is oute" (5.553). Then his obsession with gazing on the "holy places" of his past even causes a sort of obliteration of his own identity:

> Therwith, whan he was war and gan biholde
> How shet was every wyndow of the place,
> As frost, hym thoughte, his herte gan to colde;
> For which with chaunged dedlich pale face,
> Withouten word, he forthby gan to pace,
> And as God wolde, he gan so faste ride
> That no wight of his contenance espide. (533–39)

It is almost as if the absence of Criseyde blows back at him into his own face, producing an absence there too. Some would argue that Troilus has little identity to destroy,[35] but here the separation of a female character from the Shrine hints at the freedom that Criseyde seems to project through her stance and expression when she stands in the temple near the start of the poem and appears to challenge any spectators with the demand "'What, may I nat stonden here?'"—or anywhere (1.292). This separation further suggests that the commodification of women (into buildings, flowers, statues, etc.) by men helps to destroy not just women but men as well.

Women and the Shrine in *The Book of Margery Kempe*

The idea of criticizing the usual depictions of women within the context of shrines brings me again to Margery Kempe. Certainly, she disrupts the conventional attitudes concerning the typical object of the male gaze, as many critics would agree. Lisa Manter, for instance, makes the most specific argument to this effect, saying that Margery's visions of the "manhood" of Jesus allow Margery to reconcile her erotic appreciation of Christ's body to her identification with Him. Margery's gazing at her Savior thus frees her from the trap of Mulvey's screen theory.[36] I think that I can provide a counterpart to Manter's argument by changing the viewpoint from Margery's gaze to how Margery defeats the male gaze, a process that is easy to map in general terms. We never hear what she looks like. Her constant changes of clothes, from pilgrim garb, to sawed off skirt, to white clothes, to more conventional garb, to white clothes, to black clothes, and so on (32, 62, 84–85, 91–92)—although these changes have obvious connections with her spiritual career—have the effect of making it very difficult to settle upon a focused and detailed visualization of her.[37] In fact, the scrambled chronology of the *Book* makes it very difficult even to decide upon a visualization of her using the criteria that readers would typically employ in order to picture literary characters, for instance, how old she might be (6, 234).

Yet, we learn enough about her to interpret her as the self-identified shrine of her *Book*. Indeed, she writes so much about herself in this regard that critics have taken her to task in the past for omitting description of the presumably fascinating sites she visits.[38] Most tellingly, Margery seems to think of herself as a kind of shrine when she desires the "worshep" of the people early in her *Book*. At this juncture, the text accuses her of vainglory (9), but eventually God gives her exactly what she wants in terms of "worship," with one simple but important change: He promises to "makyn al þe werld to wondryn of þe, & many man & many woman xal spekyn of me for lofe of þe & worshepyn *me in* þe" (73; my emphasis).[39] However, if she represents a final development in the processes of adding By Ways to patience narratives and of the petrification of female patience figures by becoming in herself a shrine, readers would be justified in calling her an empty shrine, because that is how God describes her. Late in the *Book*, He says that the saints, and He names in particular Katherine, Margaret, and all the holy virgins, "xulde arayn þe chawmbre of þi [Margery's] sowle wyth many fayr flowerys & wyth many swete spicys þat I myth restyn þerin" (210). He describes Margery as empty physical space, as if she is able to forego any (male) attempts to build up a shrine around her or otherwise contain her in it. Instead, she is able to internalize the Shrine, as she has already suggested by mentioning the city of her soul (68). In the same "chamber of the soul" passage, God goes on to say "þu thynkist sumtyme, dowtyr, as þow þu haddist a cuschyn of gold, an-oþer of red veluet, þe thryd of white sylke in thy sowle" (210). He here describes her as a kind of reliquary that could contain the three persons of God, but lacks these at the moment. Jesus also chooses a more down-to-earth image for Margery as an empty shrine: a mirror in which other people might see the sorrow of their sins, and so repent (186). He imagines her as a devotional object par excellence for the everyday medieval and postmodern worlds: one in which any identity might appear, regardless of any individualizing attributes such as gender.[40]

But Margery does more than just transcend and internalize the Shrine. She also fragments the space-patterns of it and of conventional activities at shrines more generally so that the usual pathways of the male gaze are constantly disrupted in (and through) the text of her *Book*. For instance, one of the effects of the various shrines that dot the medieval landscape and that are typically dedicated to individual saints is to tighten the devotional focus of believers onto approved objects such as statue, reliquaries, and other representations. At pilgrimage sites and other shrines, devotions can be controlled. Established for certain feast days, contemplative acts are typically carried out by specific, identified clerical groups who often regulate access to shrines and votive objects.[41] The text constantly describes Margery, on the other hand, as experiencing uncontrollable weeping and loud vocalizations that she specifically associates with the passion of Christ when these events can and do occur at completely unpredictable moments. Admittedly, Margery's wailing and weeping episodes as described in the *Book* often visit her during church services (84, 184), but the text also indicates that sometimes the onset of her outcries would seem to be random. Weeping and vocalization would occur, "yf sche herd of owyr Lordys Passyon. & sumtyme, whan sche saw þe Crucyfyx, er yf sche sey a man had a wownde er a best wheþyr it wer, er ʒyf a man bett a childe be-for hir er smet an hors er an-oþer best wyth a whippe, ʒyf sche myth sen it er heryn it, hir thowt sche saw owyr Lord be betyn er wowndyd … as wel in þe feld as in þe town, & be hir-selfe alone as wel as a-mong þe pepyl" (68–69). So, if Margery is a kind of shrine or reliquary, she is a living and fully movable one, as opposed to the static ones like statues, Loth's wife in *Genesis A*, and Grisilde in Chaucer's *Clerk's Tale*. Like her narrative, she "conflates interior spiritual authority with external place-oriented mobility," as Ruth Summar McIntyre puts it.[42] Margery counters the idea of regulated contemplation by always threatening to break out into a devotional moment at any time, even in the fields or by herself—away from the typically male powers-that-be. She makes this threat into an emblem herself when she carries the "measure of Christ's grave" around with her, a way of rendering sacred space portable (78). In other words, her desire for holy places is too strong for the male powers-that-be, as McIntyre says. Moreover, Virginia Chieffo Raguin observes that Margery often invaded sacred spaces that were usually restricted to clerics.[43]

By disrupting the patterns of gazing at shrines she even goes so far as to usurp (at least momentarily) the places of the votive objects in the famous shrines that she attends on her pilgrimages, and thus reverses, like Grisilde, the gazing actions that would normally take place at these locations. A very common reaction to Margery's noisy devotions are that people were "astoynd" by them, and particularly if these witnesses had experienced them for the first time (68). Conventionally, this language of awe is applied to miracles and particularly to miracles and renewals of faith caused by votive objects (66, 124–25, 140, 147; cf. *LA*, 173, etc.).[44] The constantly reiterated astonishment at her roars and weeping, then, suggests that she would often draw attention away from the more usual focal points of these holy places and put it upon herself. As McIntyre notes, one may contrast this attracting of attention to the expressed desire by some men in England that Margery return to her house and engage in domestic tasks (*Book of Margery Kempe*, 129). But in Jerusalem Margery can be "the author and central character of the scenes, a point of worship, and for the sake of her audience, a centerpiece for meditating on God."[45] In fact, in two places in the narrative, a specific displacement of a votive object by Margery takes place: once when she reacts to a Christ-doll taken out of a chest by a group of pilgrims (77–78), and once when she reacts to an image of the pietà (148). Raguin proposes that Margery actively engineered such displacements even when she went to church in her home town "through her strategy of placement on eye line with the inhabitants of Lynn": she got in the way of the congregation's view of the altar. Further evidence of Margery actually turning into a version of the object that she sees is clear in that critics have often remarked upon how her uncontrollable physical reaction to accounts of Christ's passion imitate the crucifixion. She spreads her arms wide and writhes as if she is being tortured (68).[46] Such actions break the conventions of the reduplication of devotional images that the Christ-doll and the pietà represent. Margery's insistence on inserting herself into important Christian iconographies and the highly individual character of her sufferings amount to radical subversions of imitation and thus of counterfeit consciousness.

But in some ways explicit connections between Margery and votive objects are redundant, because her protracted bouts of weeping already make her into a kind of generalized and conventional woman of sorrows, like Lot's wife, as witnesses to Margery's behaviors demonstrate when they (quite reasonably) try to place her within familiar traditions: "owyr Lady cryed neuyr so ne no seynt in Heuyn" (69). The comparison to the Virgin is apt, because in Margery's era the sorrow of Mary is often described as a language that is so extreme that it must be learned, and typically it would be learned by women from other women (191–95). In medieval dramas and lyrics, Mary often says or sings, "Who þat cann not wepe, at me may lere."[17] What Margery does then with her crying, weeping, and roaring is to appropriate this language of sorrow: "þe mende of owr Ladijs sorwys whech sche suffryd whan sche behelde hys precyows body hangyng on þe Crosse & sithyn berijd be-for hir syght sodeynly ocupijd þe hert of þis creatur" (140). Later the *Book* describes her as "perfeccyon of wepyng," as if she has successfully mimicked the Virgin by adopting Mary's language of suffering; as if Margery has become a work of art (162). One might argue that Margery takes Marian sorrow to a new extreme of expression through her vocalizations.[48] She certainly draws attention to herself as an increasingly complicated kind of "reproduction" and votive object.

A New Kind of Shrine in Margery's *Book*

Shortly after the most important connection between Margery and Mary occurs in the *Book* (18–19), a significant interplay between votive objects takes place. On the road from York to Bridlington, Margery and her husband John argue about her role in their marriage (23). Her husband eventually sits down underneath a cross beside the road, and asks that she renew sexual relations with him, pay his debts, and eat and drink with him on Fridays as she used to do (24). The frequent mentioning of Friday throughout the chapter further emphasizes the role of the cross in the proceedings.

In the past, readers have come away disappointed with the compromise that is reached between the couple: Margery prays tearfully to God for guidance whereupon Jesus comes to her and tells her to agree to pay off her husband's debts and break her Friday fast (25). She puts this proposal to John, who agrees to refrain from demanding sex from her if she concedes these other two points. The divine intervention comes over to many readers as very convenient for Margery's immediate needs, while a willingness to water down His demands casts God into an unfamiliar role.[49] However, from the perspective of late medieval patience literature and what one might call the iconography of the scene, the events make much more sense and fit the pattern of the narrative as a whole. Since Margery is the central patience figure of the text and her suffering is in many ways the glue that holds the narrative of her *Book* together, she is not likely to get exactly what she wants all of a sudden, nor does she here. Moreover, the episode sets up the ensuing motif of Margery's later poverty and privation during her extensive travels, and it amounts to a mini-pilgrimage in itself.

A renewal of Margery's and John's marriage upon different terms from before is implied near the end of the scene when the two kneel under the roadside cross that they have encountered (25). Since Margery is associated with Mary and Margery's husband is named John, the placing of these two figures under a cross recalls the words of Jesus to His Mother at the crucifixion: "woman, behold thy son" and to the disciple, "behold thy mother" (John 19:26–27). Thus, a brief instance of spontaneous iconography appears: an interplay between a Marian image, a cross, and a vision of Christ. In a field near Bridlington, a new kind of votive object is momentarily created, one that vindicates the personal needs that have been at the heart of Margery's discussion with her husband—one that only readers of Margery's *Book* can access. Here is only one example of this text's ability to recreate not only votive objects but also other manifestations of Margery's life of spiritual conflict and negotiation: that is, to make shrines appear more or less whenever and wherever her emotional contemplations would occur.

Margery Kempe is a votive object that knows she is a votive object—indeed is told that she is one by God—but a votive object that has no need for the conventions of perception that require that an object have an interior and an exterior. This "reliquary" has no relics inside it save God Himself, not yet arrived when Christ describes Margery as a reliquary in the *Book*; this "statue" has no shrine to enclose what she is doing and thus give it context or make it subject to the restrictions of tradition. Instead, she fragments the patterns of gazing at typical pilgrim's shrines, continually tries to create her own elusive shrine around and in herself, and obsessively goes in search of a shrine that might suit her experience. But the internal divisions that rock late medieval Christianity, the difficulties that she has defining herself within an unsympathetically male-centered society, and the more general social conflicts of her time make Margery's creative efforts and her searches extremely fraught and taxing. In the end,

Margery's *Book* is patience literature at the very limits of that genre, with her fevered demonstrations of sorrow at Christ's suffering amounting to a kind of parody of patience.

Yet, surprisingly, she embodies an apt synthesis for the conclusion of my study of patience literature. With the disconcertingly negative and outrageously partisan reactions to her relentless patience career so baldly stated in her *Book*, Margery in many ways represents the gradual feminization of suffering throughout the Middle Ages better than any other figure, and she even has a tantalizing connection with Lot's wife. When an unsympathetic monk says to Margery, "'I wold þow wer closyd in an hows of ston þat þer schuld no man speke wyth þe'" (27), he not only expresses a wish that she were an anchoress and therefore presumably an easier figure for him to understand and relate to, but he also associates her with the cold stone and silence of a woman under the control of a kind of visionary paralysis that Lot's wife, Lucy, Fénice, and Griselda, in their different ways, represent.[50] At the end of the same chapter in which the monk's insult appears, Christ calls Margery, "a peler of Holy Cherch," whereupon a drawing of a pillar appears in the left margin of the manuscript (29, see also n. 6). The text and image recall references in the early Christian apologetic works to martyrs as pillars of the church and also recall the "pillar of salt" tradition of Lot's wife—in any case, a stone pillar is a perfectly justifiable artistic representation of patience. But Margery works less like Griselda and more like a reanimated version of Lot's wife. With her insistence on attention and her reinvention of gazing strategies at shrines, Margery acts as if she has exploded out of a pillar-like, paralyzed state. As such, her work and career represent one of the more significant and polarizing moments of reengagement with the revolutionary egalitarian ideas that are so remarkable a feature of the early passios.

NOTES

Introduction: *clarissimum in feminis*

1. Geoffrey Chaucer, *The Clerk's Tale*, lines 932–38. For Chaucer's works I use Geoffrey Chaucer, *The Riverside Chaucer*, ed. Larry D. Benson, 3rd ed. (Boston: Houghton Mifflin, 1987). Subsequent references to Chaucer's works will be from this edition and will appear parenthetically in the text.
2. Lars Engle, "Chaucer, Bakhtin, and Griselda," *Exemplaria* 1 (1989): 448.
3. See J. Burke Severs, *The Literary Relationships of Chaucer's "Clerkes Tale"* (New Haven: Yale University Press, 1942), pp. 3–37.
4. See J. Allan Mitchell, "Chaucer's *Clerk's Tale* and the Question of Ethical Monstrosity," *Studies in Phililogy* 102 (2005): 1–26.
5. M. M. Bakhtin, *The Dialogic Imagination: Four Essays*, ed. Michael Holquist, trans. Caryl Emerson and Holquist (Austin: University of Texas Press, 1981), p. 106.
6. See Laurel Braswell, "Chaucer and the Art of Hagiography," in *Chaucer in the Eighties*, ed. Julian Wasserman and Robert J. Blanch (Syracuse, NY: Syracuse University Press, 1986), pp. 209–21; Valerie Edden, "Sacred and Secular in *The Clerk's Tale*," *Chaucer Review* 26 (1992): 369–76; Kathryn McKinley, "The *Clerk's Tale*: Hagiography and the Problematics of Lay Sanctity," *Chaucer Review* 33 (1998): 92; Diana T. Childress, "'Secular Hagiography' in Middle English Literature," *Philological Quarterly* 57 (1978): 311–22; Margaret Hurley, "Saints' Legends and Romance Again," *Genre* 8 (1975): 6–73; Jocelyn Wogan-Browne, "Saints' Lives and the Female Reader," *Forum for Modern Language Studies* 27 (1991): 314–32; Saul Nathaniel Brody, "Chaucer's Rhyme Royal Tales and the Secularization of the Saint," *Chaucer Review* 20 (1985): 128; and Jo Ann McNamara, "The Need to Give: Suffering and Female Sanctity in the Middle Ages," in *Images of Sainthood in Medieval Europe*, ed. Renate Blumenfeld-Kosinski and Timea Szell (Ithaca, NY: Cornell University Press, 1991), pp. 199–221.
7. See, for example, Catherine Sanok, "Reading Hagiographically: *The Legend of Good Women* and Its Feminine Audience," *Exemplaria* 13 (2001): 339–54.
8. Bakhtin, *The Dialogic Imagination*, p. 107.
9. See Amy W. Goodwin, "The Griselda Game," *Chaucer Review* 39 (2004): 53.

10. See Ralph Hanna III, "Some Commonplaces of Late Medieval Patience Discussions: An Introduction," in *The Triumph of Patience: Medieval and Renaissance Studies*, ed. Gerald J. Schiffhorst (Orlando: University Presses of Florida, 1978), p. 77; and Prudentius, *Psychomachia*, in *Prudentius*, ed. H. J. Thomson, 2 vols. (Cambridge, MA: Harvard University Press, 1969) 1:274–343, lines 125–30.
11. See Hanna, "Some Commonplaces," p. 68.
12. See Elizabeth D. Kirk, "'Who Suffreth More Than God?': Narrative Redefinition of Patience in *Patience* and *Piers Plowman*," in *The Triumph of Patience*, p. 91.
13. See Goodwin, "The Griselda Game," p. 54.
14. See Augustine, *de Patientia*, chapters 17, 23, 29, ed. Joseph Zycha CSEL 41 (Vienna: Tempsky, 1900), pp. 665–91; Galatians 5:22 and Ephesians 4:2. I use *The Catholic Bible: Douay-Rheims Version* (Charlotte, NC: Saint Benedict Press, 2009). See William Langland, *Piers Plowman: An Edition of the C-Text*, ed. Derek Pearsall (Berkeley: University of California Press, 1978), Passus 12, lines 170–76; Passus 15, lines 274–78.
15. Jacques Derrida, *Ulysses Gramophone*, in *Acts of Literature*, ed. Derek Attridge (New York: Routledge, 1992), p. 291; *Margins of Philosophy*, trans. Alan Bass (Chicago: University of Chicago Press, 1982), p. 9.
16. See Herbert Musurillo, ed. and trans., *The Acts of the Christian Martyrs* (Oxford: Clarendon Press, 1972), pp. 79–81, and 25, 69, 129. Subsequent references to the acts of martyrs will be to this edition, using parenthetical page references in the text. I also use Musurillo's facing page translations.
17. Impatience is wrong because it "reduplicates Adam's primal sin, ... substitutes man's judgment for God's," and expresses doubts concerning God's plans. Hanna, "Some Commonplaces," p. 73; Tertullian, *de Patientia*, ed. E. Dekkers, in Tertullian, *Opera*, 2 vols., CCSL 1 and 2 (Turnhout: Brepols, 1954), 1:4.4. All my references to Tertullian's works are taken from these two volumes. All subsequent references will appear in the text.
18. See Peter Cantor, *Verbum Abbreviatum CXIV. PL* 205:300–301. Peter Cantor writes c. 1186.
19. Julianus Pomerius, *De vita contemplativa* 3.20.2, *PL* 59:504; Tertullian, *de Patientia*, 1.3, 3.11.
20. Gregory the Great, *Dialogi* 1.2, *PL* 77:161.
21. Basil, *Homilia in Psalmum LXI*, *PG* 29:469–84, Cyprian, *de bono patientiae*, in *A Donat et la Vertu de Patience*, ed. Jean Molanger, SC 291 (Paris: Éditions du Cerf, 1982).
22. Jacques Derrida, *Dissemination*, trans. Barbara Johnson (Chicago: Chicago University Press, 1981), p. 221.
23. Tertullian, *de Patientia*, 2, 3.
24. The Penguin translation gives a better sense of this extreme emotion: Vettius Epagathus "boil[ed] with indignation." Eusebius, *The History of the Church from Christ to Constantine*, trans. G. A. Williamson (Harmondsworth: Penguin, 1965), p. 194.

25. Brent D. Shaw, "Body/Power/Identity: Passions of the Martyrs," *Journal of Early Christian Studies* 4 (1996): 279, 278. Subsequent references to this article will occur parenthetically in the text. See also Daniel Boyarin, *Dying for God: Martyrdom and the Making of Christianity and Judaism* (Stanford, CA: Stanford University Press, 1999), pp. 1–41.
26. Judith Perkins, "Space, Place, Voice in the *Acts* of the Martyrs and the Greek Romance," in *Mimesis and Intertextuality in Antiquity and Christianity*, ed. Dennis Ronald MacDonald (Harrisburg, PA: Trinity Press International, 2001), p. 117.
27. See Derrida, *Margins of Philosophy*, p. 5.
28. See Derrida, *Of Grammatology*, trans. Gayatri Chakravorty Spivak (Baltimore: Johns Hopkins University Press, 1976), pp. 112–13; and Julia Kristeva, *Desire in Language: A Semiotic Approach to Literature and Art*, ed. Leon S. Roudiez, trans. Thomas Gora, Alice Jardine, and Roudiez (New York: Columbia University Press, 1980), pp.133–46.
29. Perkins, "Space, Place, Voice," p. 117; *The Suffering Self: Pain and Narrative Representation in the Early Christian Era* (London: Routledge, 1995), p. 246.
30. Brent D. Shaw, "The Passion of Perpetua," *Past and Present* 139 (1993): 15.
31. Jacobus de Voragine, *Legenda Aurea*, ed. Th. Graesse, 3rd ed. (1890; repr. Osnabrück: Otto Zeller, 1965). Subsequent references to this work will be to *LA*, by page numbers.
32. See Sanok, "Reading Hagiographically," p. 330.
33. Maud Burnett McInerney, *Eloquent Virgins: From Thecla to Joan of Arc* (New York: Palgrave Macmillan, 2003), p. 49.
34. Gregory the Great, *Homeliae in Evangelia*, ed. Raymond Étaix. CCSL 141 (Turnhout: Brepols, 1999), 2.35.4; Hanna, "Some Commonplaces," p. 68. See Gregory the Great, *Dialogi* 3.26.
35. I use Hanna's translations of the passages that he quotes. See Augustine, *de Patientia*, 2, and Hanna, "Some Commonplaces," p. 68.
36. Lynda L. Coon, *Sacred Fictions: Holy Women and Hagiography in Late Antiquity* (Philadelphia: University of Pennsylvania Press, 1997), p. 8. See also Gregory the Great, *Moralia in Job*, ed. M. Adriaen, CCSL 143. 3 vols. (Turnhout: Brepols, 1979–85), chap. 30.
37. See Catherine Sanok, *Her Life Historical: Exemplarity and Female Saints' Lives in Late Medieval England* (Philadelphia: University of Pennsylvania Press, 2007), pp. xi, 27 (and n. 13), 34–49.
38. Clement of Rome, *First Epistle to the Corinthians*, in *A New Eusebius: Documents Illustrative of the History of the Church to A.D. 337*, ed. J. Stevenson (London: SPCK, 1960), p. 4. I do not mean to imply that any religion is more inherently sexist than any other.
39. Tertullian, *Ad Scapulam*, ed. E. Dekkers, *Opera* 2:1132 (translation: Rudolph Arbesmann, in *Tertullian: Apologetical Works and Minucius Felix: Octavius*. FC 10 [Washington, DC: Catholic University of America Press, 1950], p. 160); Shaw, "Passion of Perpetua," p. 13.
40. Minucius Felix, Octavius, ed. W. C. A. Kerr, trans. Gerald H. Rendall (London: William Heinemann, 1966), 37.10. I have adjusted the translation.

41. Tertullian's *Apologeticum* contains much condemnation of Roman imperial tyranny (4.1 [p. 92]). He argues, for instance, for efficacy of law (4.13 [p. 94]), freedom of conscience (24.6–7 [p. 134], 28.1 [p. 139], 39.5 [pp. 150–51], 49.4 [p. 169]), equality before the law (2.1–5 [pp. 87–88]), and the right of a free citizen to a fair and open trial (2.10–11 [p. 89], 3.3 [p. 91], 4.13 [p. 94], 37.4 [p. 148]). Some of his phrases suggest overthrow of the political system (20.2–3 [p. 122]), 42.8 [pp. 157–58], 45.7 [p. 160]). He even reads the male and female body in an even-handed fashion. See Perkins, "The Rhetoric of the Maternal Body in The *Passion of Perpetua*," in *Mapping Gender in Ancient Religious Discourses*, ed. Todd Penner and Caroline Vander Stichele (Leiden: Brill, 2007), p. 332. Many critics note that the professed egalitarianism of Christianity must be inimical to the political beliefs associated with the Roman Empire. See, for example, Giselle de Nie, "'Consciousness Fecund through God': From Male Fighter to Spiritual Bride-Mother in Late Antique Female Sanctity," in *Sanctity and Motherhood: Essays on Holy Mothers in the Middle Ages*, ed. Anneke B. Mulder-Bakker (New York: Garland, 1995), pp. 104, 108.
42. Pliny the Younger, *Epistularum Libri Decem*, ed. R. A. B. Mynors (Oxford: Clarendon Press, 1963), 10.96.9 (p. 339); translation: Henry Bettenson, ed. and trans., *Documents of the Christian Church* (London: Oxford University Press, 1943), p. 5.
43. This egalitarianism has been noted almost obsessively by critics down through the ages, but, almost certainly due to incorrigibly sexist attitudes and to a general discomfort in influential academic circles with ideals that are based on religious faith, it curiously and confoundedly still does not receive the attention that it deserves for its significance. See, for example, Evelyn Birge Vitz, "Gender and Martyrdom," *Medievalia et Humanistica*, new series 26 (1999): 92.
44. Tacitus, *Annales Livres XIII–XVI*, ed. Pierre Wuilleumier (Paris: Société d'Édition "Les Belles Lettres," 1978), 13.32; translation: Bettenson, *Documents*, p. 1.
45. Pliny the Younger, *Epistulae*, 10.96.8 (p. 339); translation: Bettenson, *Documents*, p. 5.
46. Eusebius, *History*, pp. 23, 418–20, 337, 341.
47. "Passion of Perpetua," p. 13, and n. 36. In the later Middle Ages, female saints typically drop to about 20 percent of the corpus. See Sanok, *Her Life Historical*, p. 39.
48. Eusebius, *History*, p. 192, n. 1.
49. Clement of Rome, *Epistle*, p. 4.
50. See Virginia Burrus, *Saving Shame: Martyrs, Saints, and Other Abject Subjects* (Philadelphia: University of Pennsylvania Press, 2008), p. 24. For female slaves, see Christine Trevett, *Christian Women and the Time of the Apostolic Fathers (AD c. 80–160): Corinth, Rome and Asia Minor* (Cardiff: University of Wales Press, 2006), pp. 201–03.
51. Susan Stanford Friedman, *Mappings: Feminism and the Cultural Geographies of Encounter* (Princeton, NJ: Princeton University Press, 1998), p. 25, and

see Rosi Braidotti, *Nomadic Subjects: Embodiment and Sexual Difference in Contemporary Feminist Theory* (New York: Columbia University Press, 1994), pp. 4, 268–77.
52. Burrus, *Saving Shame*, p. 25.
53. Burrus, *Saving Shame*, p. 27, and Elizabeth A. Castelli, *Visions and Voyeurism: Holy Women and the Politics of Sight in Early Christianity* (Berkeley: Center for Hermeneutical Studies, 1995), p. 19.
54. Bakhtin, *The Dialogic Imagination*, p. 105; Burrus, *Saving Shame*, p. 28. For class in these narratives, see Perkins, *The Suffering Self*, p. 113.
55. Shaw is particularly helpful in explaining the traditions and influence of the Greek athletic contest. See "Body," pp. 278, 289–90.
56. See Tertullian, *Apologeticum*, 50.1–9 (pp. 169–70); Clement of Rome, *Epistle*, p. 4; and Aldhelm's prose *De Virginitate*, composed c. 700 (Aldhelmi Opera Omnia, ed. R. Ehwald [Berlin: Monumenta Germaniae Historica, 1919], *De Virginitate*, p. 230).
57. Vitz, "Gender and Martyrdom," p. 80. See Clement of Rome, *Epistle*, p. 4; Tertullian, *Apologeticum*, 50.8 (p. 170).
58. See P. Vergili Maronis, *Opera*, ed. A. Sidgwick, 2 vols. (Cambridge, UK: Cambridge University Press, 1927) 1: *Aeneid* 1, lines 275–96. For the power that the martyrs gain through the spectacle of their tortures, see Peter Brown, *The Cult of the Saints: Its Rise and Function in Latin Christianity* (Chicago: University of Chicago Press, 1981), pp. 106–27.
59. See Robert Graves, *The Greek Myths*, 2 vols. (New York: George Braziller, 1955), 2:113–16, 121–22.
60. Shaw, "Passion of Perpetua," pp. 6, 18.
61. Bakhtin, *The Dialogic Imagination*, p. 108.
62. Vergil, *Aeneid* 1:378–79; see Mary R. Lefkowitz, "The Motivations for St. Perpetua's Martyrdom," *Journal of the American Academy of Religion* 44 (1976): 418.
63. Tacitus, *Annales* 13.33; translation: Bettenson, *Documents*, p. 1.
64. See Clare A. Lees, "At a Crossroads: Old English and Feminist Criticism," in *Reading Old English Texts*, ed. Katherine O'Brien O'Keeffe (Cambridge, UK: Cambridge University Press, 1997), p. 161.
65. 4 Maccabees 6:7; Peter Damian, *Opusculum* 40.9, *PL* 145:659–60.
66. Kirk, "'Who Suffreth More Than God?'" p. 92.
67. See Ignatius of Antioch, *Epistle to the Romans*, in Ignatius of Antioch, *Lettres*, ed. P. Th. Camelot, 4th ed. (Paris: Éditions du Cerf, 1969), 6.1–2. Subsequent references to Ignatius's *Epistles* will be to this edition. See also Acts 2:24, Galatians 4:19.
68. See Shaw, "Body," pp. 287–88, and n. 58; and Elizabeth A. Castelli, *Martyrdom and Memory: Early Christian Culture Making* (New York: Columbia University Press, 2004), pp. 71–77.
69. See Ignatius, *Epistle to the Trallians*, 4.1.
70. Achilles Tatius, *The Adventures of Leucippe and Clitophon*, with an English translation by S. Gaselee (London: William Heinemann, 1984), 6.21.345.

Subsequent references to this work will appear in the text. Cf. Musurillo, ed., pp. 79, 133, 159, and see Shaw, "Body," p. 271, and n. 3.
71. Perkins, "Space, Place, Voice," p. 117.
72. Perkins, "Space, Place, Voice," p. 118.
73. See Shaw, "Body," pp. 291–4; Susan Signe Morrison, *Women Pilgrims in Late Medieval England: Private Piety as Public Performance* (London: Routledge, 2000), p. 112; and Patricia Cox Miller, ed., *Women in Early Christianity: Translations from Greek Texts* (Washington, DC: Catholic University of America Press, 2005), pp. 253–86. For Seneca, see *De Ira* in *Seneca: Moral Essays*, ed. John W. Basore, 3 vols. (London: William Heinemann, 1952), 1:2.12.6; and Hanna, "Some Commonplaces," p. 77.
74. Michel Foucault, *The History of Sexuality Volume 1: An Introduction*, trans. Robert Hurley (New York: Vintage, 1990), pp. 97, 94, 98; Derrida, *Margins of Philosophy*, p. 17.
75. Perkins, *The Suffering Self*, pp. 116, 123.
76. See Jerome, *Epistola 1*, in *Select Letters of St. Jerome*, ed. F. A. Wright (London: William Heinemann, 1963), 1.7–9.
77. The slighting also appears in 4 Maccabees (see 15:4–5).
78. Pliny the Elder, *Naturalis historia Livre VII*, ed. Robert Schilling (Paris: Belles Lettres, 1977), 7.23.87 (p. 70); Tertullian, *Apologeticum*, 50.8 (p. 170). See Pausanias, *Graecia descripto*, ed. Maria Helena Rocha-Pereira, 3 vols. (Leipzig: Teubner, 1973–81), 1: 1.23.1–2.
79. Tertullian, *Apologeticum*, 50.8 (p. 170). The translation I use is that of Emily Joseph Daly, in Tertullian, *Apologetical Works*, FC 10 (Washington, DC: Catholic University of America Press, 1950), pp. 1-126. Subsequent references will appear in the text.
80. Pliny the Elder, *Naturalis historia*, 7.23.87 (p. 70).
81. See also Larissa Tracy, trans. and intro., *Women of the Gilte Legende: A Selection of Middle English Saints Lives* (Cambridge, UK: Brewer, 2003), p. 111; and Kevin Brownlee, "Martyrdom and the Female Voice: Saint Christine in the *Cité des dames*," in *Images of Sainthood in Medieval Europe*, pp. 124–32. The tongue-severing episode, suggestive of self-castration, is appropriated into the vita of Paul the Hermit. The roles of the major characters are exactly reversed: he is tempted by a prostitute (*LA*, 94).
82. Tertullian prefers the magnified version of her sexual history from Pliny. In Pausanias's account, she is not a prostitute but the mistress of one of the conspirators. See Pausanias, *Graecia descripto*, 1:1.23.1–2.
83. Roland Barthes, *A Lover's Discourse: Fragments*, trans. Richard Howard (New York: Hill and Wang, 1978), p. 154.
84. Tertullian, *Apologeticum*, 50.8 (p. 170); translation: Daly, in *Tertullian: Apologetical Works*, p. 124.
85. See Cicero, *De inventione*, 2.54.163: *Scripta quae manserunt omnia, fasc. 2: Rhetorici libri duo qui vocantur de inventione*, ed. E. Stroebel (Stuttgart: Teubner, 1965), p. 149; and Tertullian, *de Patientia*, 2, 3, 4.
86. Pausanias, *Graecia descripto*, 1:1.23.2.

87. Hélène Cixous, "The Laugh of the Medusa," *Signs* 1 (1967): 883; and *LA*, 420, 421.
88. This text has been dated to both pre-Christian and post-Christian times. The first century AD seems the most probable date. I use *The Testament of Job*, in *The Apocryphal Old Testament*, ed. H. F. D. Sparks (Oxford: Clarendon Press, 1984), pp. 617–48. Subsequent references will occur by chapter numbers parenthetically in the text.
89. For the original's term for these girdles, see *The Testament of Job According to the SV Text*, ed. Robert A. Kraft (Missoula: Society of Biblical Literature and Scholars' Press, 1974), p. 79, n. 46.8.
90. For Gregory the Great's *Regulae Pastoralis*, I use *PL* 77:9–128.
91. A major reason for these changes is that "masculine identity is itself rendered queerly malleable and unstable by its explicit linking with the suffering endurance of women." Burrus, *Saving Shame*, p. 32.
92. See Longus, *Daphnis and Chloe*, trans. George Thornley, revised J. M. Edmonds (London: William Heinemann, 1935), 1.28.50–52, 2.20.95–97. Subsequent references will appear in the text.
93. Frequently martyrs are placed in prison (Musurillo, ed., 70–73, 108–11, etc.), but this location is not a By Way. It merely suspends *and* continues the same kind of suffering process as the Suffering Portion.
94. Perpetua's narrative is an important transitional text with regard to By Ways. Her first dialogue with her father is quasi-judicial, even though it seems to occur in the family home, because (among other things) it includes a statement of Belief Identification and is reminiscent of a marriage dispute (Musurillo, ed., 108–09). Certainly the head of a Roman family can claim a kind of legal authority over his family members that is parallel to the judge-persecutor's authority in many passios.
95. Examples of varying translations are Musurillo, ed., 79; Eusebius, *History*, p. 202; Stevenson, *New Eusebius*, p. 39; Shaw "Passion of Perpetua," p. 18.
96. See Shaw, "Passion of Perpetua," pp. 7–9, and nn. 18, 20.
97. See Henry George Liddell and Robert Scott, eds., *A Greek-English Lexicon*, 9th ed., 2 vols. (Oxford: Clarendon Press, 1940), s. v. γυργαθὸν.
98. See Perkins, *The Suffering Self*, p. 200; Jacques Lacan, *Écrits: A Selection*, trans. Alan Sheridan (New York: Norton, 1977), p. 305. See also p. 306; and *The Four Fundamental Concept of Psychoanalysis: The Seminar of Jacques Lacan* Book XI, ed. Jacques-Alain Miller, trans. Alan Sheridan (New York: Norton, 1981), p. 72; and Castelli, *Visions and Voyeurism*, pp. 2–9.
99. Kirk, "'Who Suffreth More Than God?'" p. 89.
100. Lees, "At a Crossroads," p. 151.
101. See Braidotti, *Nomadic Subjects*, pp. 269–70.
102. Sheila Delany, "'Mothers to Think Back Through': Who Are They? The Ambiguous Example of Christine de Pizan," in *Medieval Texts and Contemporary Readers*, ed. Laurie A. Finke and Martin B. Shichtman

(Ithaca, NY: Cornell University Press, 1987), pp. 179–81, 196–97. The idea of a woman's tradition is continually refreshed by redefining that tradition. See *Gendering the Master Narrative: Women and Power in the Middle Ages*, ed. Mary C. Erler and Maryanne Kowaleski (Ithaca, NY: Cornell University Press, 2003).

103. See Scott Bukatman, *Terminal Identity: The Virtual Subject in Postmodern Science Fiction* (Durham, NC: Duke University Press, 1993), pp. 244–47, 260–61.

104. Elizabeth A. Castelli, "'I Will Make Mary Male': Pieties of the Body and Gender Transformation of Christian Women in Late Antiquity," in *Body Guards: The Cultural Politics of Gender Ambiguity*, ed. Julia Epstein and Kristina Straub (New York: Routledge, 1991), pp. 33 and 42. These glimpses work like the ideas of "the trace" and "the supplement" in Derrida's theories of language. See *Of Grammatology*, pp. 145, 178. Another way of understanding these glimpses is as occasional glimpses of the immanent Marxist revolution, endlessly delayed by culture. See Raymond Williams, *The Long Revolution* (London: Chatto and Windus, 1961), p. 50. See also Michel Foucault, *Language, Counter-Memory, Practice: Selected Essays and Interviews*, ed. Donald F. Bouchard, trans. Bouchard and Sherry Simon (Ithaca, NY: Cornell University Press, 1977), pp. 154–56.

105. Kristeva, *Desire in Language*, p. 116. See pp. 116–21.

106. Emmanuel Levinas, *Difficult Freedom: Essays on Judaism*, trans. Seán Hand (Baltimore: Johns Hopkins University Press, 1990), p. 293.

107. See McInerney, *Eloquent Virgins*, pp. 3–4, and n. 7; and Foucault, *Language, Counter-Memory, Practice*, pp. 154–56. Another important reason for repetition in the saints' lives has to do with attitudes toward the body. The bodies of martyrs have the same tortures visited upon them again and again because that is the way, as Barthes notes, that the bodies of victims of sadism nearly always appear in literary works and other artistic compositions: the victim's body is constantly renewed for new torture. See Barthes, *A Lover's Discourse*, p. 207; Musurillo, ed., 69.

108. See Augustine, *Sermones*, 280.1.1, *PL* 38:1281.

109. As Thomas J. Farrell has noticed. See "The Chronotopes of Monology in Chaucer's *Clerk's Tale*," in *Bakhtin and Medieval Voices*, ed. Thomas J. Farrell (Gainesville: University Press of Florida, 1995), pp. 150–1, and, more generally, E. P. Thompson, *The Making of the English Working Class* (New York: Pantheon, 1963), p. 4.

110. See Jo Ann McNamara, "Sexual Equality and the Cult of Virginity in Early Christian Thought," in *Women in Early Christianity*, ed. David M. Scholer (New York: Routledge, 1993), pp. 228–29.

111. See Robert Mills, "Can the Virgin Martyr Speak?" in *Medieval Virginities*, ed. Anke Bernau, Ruth Evans, and Sarah Salih (Toronto: University of Toronto Press, 2003), pp. 201; 187; and Castelli, *Visions and Voyeurism*, p. 10.

112. Bukatman, *Terminal Identity*, p. 265.

113. Homi K. Bhabha, *The Location of Culture* (London: Routledge, 1994), p. 90; Judith Butler, *Gender Trouble: Feminism and the Subversion of Identity* (New York: Routledge, 1990), p. 145. See also pp. 140–41, 148.
114. McInerney, *Eloquent Virgins*, p. 4. Explicit justification for the appropriation of hagiographical material from one life to another occurs in *The Earliest Life of Gregory the Great*, ed. Bertram Colgrave (Cambridge, UK: Cambridge University Press, 1985), pp. 130–32, and Gregory of Tours, *Vitam Patri*, Preface, in *Miracula et Opera Minora*, ed. B. Krusch. Monumenta Germaniae Historica, Scriptores rerum Merovingicorum 1 (Hanover: Hahnsche, 1885): 661–744.
115. See Hippolyte Delehaye, *Les légendes hagiographiques* (Brussels: Societé des Bollandistes, 1905), pp. ix, 71–106. Sherry L. Reames neatly summarizes Delehaye's complicated and influential but ultimately patronizing attitude toward the *Legenda Aurea*. See her *The Legenda aurea: A Reexamination of Its Paradoxical History* (Madison: University of Wisconsin Press, 1985), pp. 20–26; and Thomas J. Heffernan, *Sacred Biography: Saints and Their Biographers in the Middle Ages* (New York: Oxford University Press, 1988), pp. 55–67.
116. These attitudes began in the early modern period and have persisted. See Reames, *Legenda aurea*, pp. 27–63.
117. See Gregory the Great, *Dialogi* 3.28.
118. Bhabha, *Location of Culture*, p. 86. See also Michael Tausig, *Mimesis and Alterity*, (New York: Routledge, 1993), p. 19.
119. Judith Butler, *Gender Trouble*, p. 146. For a more positive version of mimicry through gender, see Luce Irigaray, *The Irigaray Reader*, ed. Margaret Whitford (Oxford: Basil Blackwell, 1991), p. 124; and Gail Ashton, "Patient Mimesis: Griselda and the *Clerk's Tale*," *Chaucer Review* 32 (1998): 233.
120. Jacobus, *LA*, 31. Jacobus's ultimate source for the passion of Lucy is the version now considered part of the *Acta Sanctorum*, most likely composed in the fifth century.
121. William Granger Ryan, trans., Jacobus de Voragine, *The Golden Legend: Readings on the Saints*, 2 vols. (Princeton, NJ: Princeton University Press, 1993), 1:29. Subsequent references will occur in the text.
122. Lives of Lucy in earlier texts contain the same idea of doubling (*duplicabitur*). See B. Mombritius, ed., *Sanctuarium seu Vitae Sanctorum*, 2nd ed., 2 vols. (Paris: Fontemoing, 1910) 2:108; and the Cotton-Corpus Legendary, CCCC 9, 220r.
123. McInerney, *Eloquent Virgins*, p. 4.
124. Bhabha, *Location of Culture*, p. 86.
125. Irigaray, *Irigaray Reader*, p. 124 (see also p. 134); N. Katherine Hayles, *How We Became Posthuman: Virtual Bodies in Cybernetics, Literature, and Informatics* (Chicago: University of Chicago Press, 1999), pp. 8–9.
126. See *Pearl*, ed. E. V. Gordon (Oxford: Clarendon Press, 1953), lines 169–240, 1101–07, 1115, 1147; *Sir Orfeo*, ed. A. J. Bliss, 2nd ed. (Oxford: Clarendon Press, 1966), lines 304, 321–22, 405–08.

127. Julian of Norwich, *The Writings of Julian of Norwich: A Vision Showed to a Devout Woman and A Revelation of Love*, ed. Nicholas Watson and Jacqueline Jenkins (University Park: Pennsylvania State University Press, 2006), p. 131; Margery Kempe, *The Book of Margery Kempe*, ed. Sanford Brown Meech and Hope Emily Allen (London: Oxford University Press, 1940, repr. 1997), pp. 8, 68–69.
128. Bhabha, *Location of Culture*, pp. 88–89. See also p. 91. I mean by the distressed canon that the traditional literary and intellectual canon is never "ready" for writing that is exclusively feminine, but it is also never "happy" with its impulse to exclude. See Lees, "At a Crossroads," p. 152.
129. See Laura Mulvey, "Visual Pleasure and Narrative Cinema," in *Contemporary Literary Criticism: Literary and Cultural Studies*, ed. Robert Con Davis and Ronald Schleifer, 3rd ed. (New York: Longman, 1994), p. 429.

1 The Female Patience Figure as Speaker

1. See Judith Perkins, *The Suffering Self: Pain and Narrative Representation in the Early Christian Era* (London: Routledge, 1995), p. 104. For the manuscripts and editions of this passio, see Carolyn Osiek, "Perpetua's Husband," *Journal of Early Christian Studies* 10 (2002): 287, n. 1. For the later manuscript versions of this passio and its reception in centuries after its first appearance, see Rex D. Butler, *The New Prophecy and "New Visions": Evidence of Montanism in "The Passion of Perpetua and Felicitas"* (Washington, DC: Catholic University of America Press, 2006), pp. 98–126.
2. See Brent D. Shaw, "The Passion of Perpetua," *Past and Present* 139 (1993): 45. The passio has been relatively neglected by specialists in literary analysis. A notable exception is Erin Ronsse, "Rhetoric of Martyrs: Listening to Saints Perpetua and Felicitas," *Journal of Early Christian Studies* 14 (2006): 283–327. See also Thomas J. Heffernan and James E. Shelton, "*Paradisus in carcere*: The Vocabulary of Imprisonment and the Theology of Martyrdom in the *Passio Sanctarum Perpetuae et Felicitatis*," *Journal of Early Christian Studies* 14 (2006): 217–23.
3. Perkins, *The Suffering Self*, pp. 105, 113, 112. See Barbara Baert, in "Mantle, Fur, Pallium: Veiling and Unveiling in the Martyrdom of Agnes of Rome," in *Weaving, Veiling, and Dressing: Textiles and Their Metaphors in the Late Middle Ages*, ed. Kathrun M. Rudy and Baert (Turnhout: Brepols, 2007), nn. 9 and 18.
4. See Heidi Vierow, "Feminine and Masculine Voices in the *Passion of Saints Perpetua and Felicitas*," *Latomus* 58 (1999): 618.
5. See Ronsse, "Rhetoric of Martyrs," pp. 292–93. See Brent D. Shaw, "Judicial Nightmares and Christian Memory," *Journal of Early Christian Studies* 11 (2003): 546; and Joyce E. Salisbury, *Perpetua's Passion: The Death and Memory of a Young Roman Woman* (New York: Routledge, 1997), p. 114.

6. Ross Shepard Kraemer, *Her Share of the Blessings: Women's Religions among Pagans, Jews, and Christians in the Greco-Roman World* (New York: Oxford University Press, 1992), pp. 159–61. For Montanism, see R. Butler, *New Prophecy*, pp. 9–43.
7. Elizabeth A. Castelli, "'I Will Make Mary Male': Pieties of the Body and Gender Transformation of Christian Women in Late Antiquity," in *Body Guards: The Cultural Politics of Gender Ambiguity*, ed. Julia Epstein and Kristina Straub (New York: Routledge, 1991), pp. 33 and 42, her emphasis.
8. See Shaw, "Passion of Perpetua," p. 29; Salisbury, *Perpetua's Passion*, pp. 105–06; and Giselle de Nie, "'Consciousness Fecund through God': From Male Fighter to Spiritual Bride-Mother in Late Antique Female Sanctity," in *Sanctity and Motherhood: Essays on Holy Mothers in the Middle Ages*, ed. Anneke B. Mulder-Bakker (New York: Garland, 1995), p. 119. The wound in Dinocrates's face may be allegorized in other ways. See F. J. Dölger, *"Antike Parallelen zum leidenden Dinocrates in der Passio Perpetuae," Antike und Christentum* 2 (1930): 28–31.
9. Julia Kristeva, *Desire in Language: A Semiotic Approach to Literature and Art*, ed. Leon S. Roudiez, trans. Thomas Gora, Alice Jardine, and Roudiez (New York: Columbia University Press, 1980), p. 135.
10. Kristeva, *Desire in Language*, p. 133. She calls the sounds of an infant that have no connection with signified objects examples of "chora," a term she gets from Plato. See pp. 133, 135.
11. Ronsse, "Rhetoric of Martyrs," p. 319; Kristeva, *Desire in Language*, p. 140.
12. Kristeva, *Desire in Language*, pp. 139, 134.
13. Kristeva, *Desire in Language*, p. 139. See Virginia Burrus, *Saving Shame: Martyrs, Saints, and Other Abject Subjects* (Philadelphia: University of Pennsylvania Press, 2008), p. 28.
14. This idea of domestic space also connects Perpetua with Jewish traditions. See Daniel Boyarin, *Dying for God: Martyrdom and the Making of Christianity and Judaism* (Stanford, CA: Stanford University Press, 1999), p. 81.
15. Kristeva, *Desire in Language*, pp. 133; 140. See also pp. 138, 142. The connection between the waterpot and transformational language recalls the Samaritan woman to whom Jesus describes "living water" and reveals Himself as the Messiah (John 4:6–30). She abandons her waterpot and urges the local townspeople to come and see Jesus (4:28–30). The parallel between water carried in a pot and her (potentially transformational) message is obvious.
16. Kristeva, *Desire in Language*, p. 142. He says *uideo* [I see], and then tries to blind his daughter.
17. Ronsse, "Rhetoric of Martyrs," p. 320. See Margaret R. Miles, *Carnal Knowing: Female Nakedness and Religious Meaning in the Christian West* (Boston: Beacon Press, 1989), p. 59. Within the Judeo-Christian tradition, a vase or waterpot calls to mind besides John 4:6–30 associations with Rebecca (Genesis 24:10–20). See Mary Douglas, *Purity and Danger: An*

Analysis of the Concepts of Pollution and Taboo (1966, repr. London: Ark, 1984), p. 158. For Jerome, a water pitcher is an image of a chaste woman's body. See *Epistola 22*, 64.

18. See Kristeva, *Desire in Language*, pp. 140–41.
19. See Eva C. Keals, "Attic Vase-Painting and the Home Textile Industry," in *Ancient Greek Art and Iconography*, ed. Warren G. Moone (Madison: University of Wisconsin Press, 1983), pp. 209, 210–14, and figs. 14.1–6. In ancient Greek art a woman carrying a water jar is subject to "male erotic fantasies," "voyeurism," and "rape." See pp. 212, 210, 214. For the vase in the passio, see Miles, *Carnal Knowing*, p. 59. For an early medieval artwork depicting a woman at a well, see Lynda L. Coon, *Sacred Fictions: Holy Women and Hagiography in Late Antiquity* (Philadelphia: University of Pennsylvania Press, 1997), p. 47, fig. 1.
20. However, this pattern is broken at the fourth vision. No use of *facio* appears just before this last dream, perhaps because Perpetua does not pray for a vision, or for anything else, at this juncture.
21. Kristeva, *Desire in Language*, p. 135. Perpetua uses a form of *facio* to indicate her famous transformation into a man: *et expoliata sum et facta sum masculus* (p. 118) [my clothes were stripped off, and suddenly I was a man] (p. 119).
22. Kristeva, *Desire in Language*, p. 137. In a later version of her passio, Perpetua uses wordplay with regard to her name, which makes her usurpation of the masculine power of naming even clearer. See Miles, *Carnal Knowing*, p. 60.
23. Ronsse, "Rhetoric of Martyrs," p. 311.
24. See Robert Rousselle, "The Dreams of Vibia Perpetua: Analysis of a Female Christian Martyr," *The Journal of Psychohistory* 14 (1987): 193–206, for a very convincing psychological reading that has received much acknowledgment, but little engagement.
25. See Alvyn Pettersen, "Perpetua—Prisoner of Conscience," *Vigiliae Christianae* 41 (1987): 144. "Caseo" certainly means "cheese," not "milk." The image makes heaven Eucharistic, but the substance that Perpetua consumes comes from a ewe, a female source, rather than from Christ's male body.
26. See also Jerome's *Commentarium in Ezekiel* 3.5 in *PL* 25.35d. The honey image appears in later saints' lives concerning women. See John Capgrave, *The Life of Saint Katherine*, ed. Karen Winstead (Kalamazoo, Middle English Text Series [TEAMS], 1999), Prologue, lines 83–107; IV, lines 43–71. More generally, see the discussion concerning a passage in Chaucer's *Prioress's Tale* that features a "greyn" representing powers of speech (lines 643–676, and p. 916, n. 662).
27. De Nie, "'Consciousness Fecund through God,'" pp. 102–03, 109–10. E. R. Dodds seems to have first made the cheese=semen connection. See *Pagan and Christian in an Age of Anxiety: Some Aspects of Religious Experience from Marcus Aurelius to Constantine* (Cambridge, UK: Cambridge University Press, 1965), p. 51.

28. Clement of Alexandria, *Le Pédagogue*, ed. Henri-Irénée Marrou, 3 vols. (Paris: Éditions du Cerf, 1960–83) 1:6.42.3, 43.3–4, 46.1. I found this reference in de Nie, "'Consciousness Fecund through God,'" pp. 113–14, and see Caroline Walker Bynum, *Jesus as Mother: Studies in the Spirituality of the High Middle Ages* (Berkeley: University of California Press, 1982), pp. 132–35; and Susan Signe Morrison, *Women Pilgrims in Late Medieval England: Private Piety as Public Performance* (London: Routledge, 2000), p. 10.
29. Ambrose, *De Virginibus*, ed. Egnatius Cazzaniga (Turin: G. B. Paravia, 1948), 1.5.22. Translation: Boniface Ramsey, trans. *Ambrose* (London: Routledge, 1997).
30. Evelyn Birge Vitz, "Gender and Martyrdom," *Medievalia et Humanistica*, new series 26 (1999): 90; *LA*, 163, 168, 171–72, 203–04, 398, 528, 794. For the reference to Tertullian, see his *Apologeticum*, 50.13 (p. 171); and Timothy David Barnes, *Tertullian: A Historical and Literary Study*, rev. ed. (Oxford: Clarendon Press, 1985), pp. 77–78.
31. *Hrotsvithae Opera*, ed. Paulus de Winterfeld (Munich: Monumenta Germaniae Historica, 1978), p. 188, lines 5–7.
32. *The Plays of Hrotswitha of Gandersheim*, trans. Larissa Bonfante (New York: New York University Press, 1979), p. 159. I found these references in Vitz, "Gender and Martyrdom," p. 81.
33. Vitz, "Gender and Martyrdom," p. 90. See n. 20, and de Nie, "'Consciousness Fecund through God,'" p. 114, and nn. 59, 60, and 61. The image is common. See *LA*, 168, 203–04, 794, and Thomas J. Heffernan, *Sacred Biography: Saints and Their Biographers in the Middle Ages* (New York: Oxford University Press, 1988), p. 288.
34. De Nie, "'Consciousness Fecund through God,'" p. 119, and see n. 82. For a summary of the various interpretations of Perpetua's first dream, see Patricia M. Davis, "The Weaning of Perpetua: Female Embodiment and Spiritual Growth Metaphor in the Dream of an Early Christian Martyr," *Dreaming* 15 (2005): 263–64.
35. See Walter J. Ong, *Orality and Literacy: The Technologizing of the Word* (London: Routledge, 1981), pp. 38–39, 43–45.
36. Kristeva, *Desire in Language*, p. 139.
37. R. Butler, *New Prophecy*, pp. 70, 91–92. For the terms for "prayer" and "sigh" in Greek and Latin, see p. 70. He also refers to Romans 8:26.
38. Tertullian, *Apologeticum*, 50.1–9 (pp. 169–70); *de Patientia*, 4.4; Salisbury, *Perpetua's Passion*, pp. 109–10.
39. See Perkins, "The Rhetoric of the Maternal Body," p. 316.
40. Ronsse, "Rhetoric of Martyrs," pp. 307; 321–22.
41. The child can of course represent other things besides language and/or female inheritance.
42. Cf. Maud Burnett McInerney, *Eloquent Virgins: From Thecla to Joan of Arc* (New York: Palgrave Macmillan, 2003), p. 21; and Perkins, *Roman Imperial Identities in the Early Christian Era* (London: Routledge, 2009), pp. 163–69.
43. Ronsse, "Rhetoric of Martyrs," pp. 323–24. See also p. 325.

44. See Ronsse, "Rhetoric of Martyrs," p. 325. One may take this idea of inheritance further, into, for instance, the careers of women who found and organize exclusively female monastic societies. See de Nie, "'Consciousness Fecund through God,'" p. 128, who observes that Saint Eugenia inspires other women to found convents of nuns. See also p. 136. For Eugenia, see *Vita Sanctae Eugeniae Virginis ad Martyris*, in *De Vitis Patrum* 1, *PL* 73:606–24.
45. See Miles, *Carnal Knowing*, p. 61. M. Louise Robert, "Une vision de Perpétue martyre en 203," *Comptes rendus de l'académie des inscriptions et belles-lettres* (1982): 256–58, puts the strongest case that Perpetua must change into a man in order to participate in the wrestling match. For analogues to Perpetua's battle with the devil, see Lloyd A. Thompson, *Romans and Blacks* (London: Routledge, 1989), pp. 110–13. The Egyptian may be an image suggested by Tertullian. See R. Butler, *New Prophecy*, pp. 74–76.
46. See Pettersen, "Perpetua—Prisoner of Conscience," p. 149, and n. 79; and de Nie, "'Consciousness Fecund through God,'" pp. 122, 149–50. If it is necessary for Perpetua to become a man in order to triumph and to gain heaven, why in her first dream does she tread on the dragon's head, an openly Christlike (and hence male) act, and then get to a kind of heaven without needing any gender transformation? See Burrus, *Saving Shame*, p. 29.
47. See Wayne A. Meeks, "The Image of the Androgyne: Some Uses of a Symbol in Earliest Christianity," *History of Religions* 13 (1974): 165–208. McInerney notes that *masculus* could be an adjective rather than a noun, so Perpetua might become "masculine" rather than "a man" at this juncture. The treatment of her by the attendants, in my view, suggests instead an actual change of sex. See *Eloquent Virgins*, p. 26.
48. See Tertullian, *Spectaculis*, 3.8.
49. Perkins, *The Suffering Self*, p. 112; de Nie, "'Consciousness Fecund through God,'" p. 120. In the passio, see *hanc ... hunc ... Filia* (118) [her ... her ... Daughter] (119).
50. Perkins, "The Rhetoric of the Maternal Body," p. 326. See Shaw, "Judicial Nightmares," p. 546, for an analogous dream by a man who fights the emperor in the arena.
51. See Castelli, "'I Will Make Mary Male,'" p. 37. Critics are perhaps wary of calling a text "feminist" when it cannot be described as such. See p. 46. Feminism, in its twentieth-century and twenty-first-century manifestations, is a body of attitudes that late antique people could not possibly have held or even considered. At best a kind of "locational feminism" may be detected in previous eras. See Susan Stanford Friedman, *Mappings: Feminism and the Cultural Geographies of Encounter* (Princeton, NJ: Princeton University Press, 1998), pp. 3–13, 102–03.
52. Perkins, *The Suffering Self*, p. 106.
53. Perkins, *The Suffering Self*, p. 107; R. Butler, *New Prophecy*, p. 65.
54. See Robert, "Une vision de Perpetué," pp. 255–56.

55. Perpetua fulfills the text in Genesis 3:15 by bruising the head of the serpent. For Rousselle, the weapons are phallic symbols, and this dream, like the others, represents a wish for sexual activity, suggested by words like *ascendo*. See "Dreams of Vibia Perpetua," p. 195. This interpretation only shores up the masculine soldier-ideal embodied in the weapons, which Perpetua overcomes.
56. Perkins, *The Suffering Self*, pp. 109, 107. See the passio, 112–13, 116–17.
57. Castelli, "'I Will Make Mary Male,'" p. 39; Burrus, *Saving Shame*, p. 29.
58. Mary R. Lefkowitz, "The Motivations for St. Perpetua's Martyrdom," *Journal of the American Academy of Religion* 44 (1976): 421. See also Miles, *Carnal Knowing*, p. 59, who notes that her dreams tend to be of men—lots of men. She never dreams of a woman, save herself. Examples of benign, supportive men would be the old shepherd, Dinocrates, the trainer, and Perpetua's seconds at the wrestling match.
59. His position on the ladder ahead of Perpetua in the first vision works as a prophecy of his death before hers in the martyrdoms. Saturus first appears in this vision, where he gets the description of leader and teacher. He is not arrested with the same group of catechumens as Perpetua's (110–11). He reappears rather suddenly when the narrator intrudes Saturus's vision right after her diary concludes (118–23). Saturus then has a leading role in the martyrdoms, rightly predicting the manner of his death (126–27). He is killed first, and this position seems to be interpreted as a point of honor among the catechumens (128–31). None of Perpetua's subsequent visions need prompting from a man in order to occur.
60. Saturus's vision is unexpected and seems slightly out of place when otherwise the narrative reads quite smoothly. The ending of Perpetua's section leads the audience to expect a description of martyrdoms, not a vision by another prisoner.
61. In heaven, Saturus announces to her *Habes quod uis* (120) ["Your wish is granted"] (121), as if he had a higher position than her in the heavenly hierarchy and maintained some authority over her. Perpetua's narrative, on the other hand, does not suggest that Saturus is superior to her.
62. A deacon, he first appears as a briber of Perpetua's prison guards (108), then as a messenger from her to her father (114), and finally in Perpetua's fourth vision (116).
63. Shaw, "Passion of Perpetua," p. 7.
64. Shaw, "Passion of Perpetua," pp. 7–8, 6.
65. Burrus, *Saving Shame*, p. 31.
66. See John Anson, "The Female Transvestite in Early Monasticism: The Origin and Development of a Motif," *Viator* 5 (1974): 1–32; and Mathew Kuefler, *The Manly Eunuch: Masculinity, Gender Ambiguity, and Christian Ideology in Late Antiquity* (Chicago: University of Chicago Press, 2001), pp. 241–42.
67. See Paul E. Szarmach, "Ælfric's Women Saints: Eugenia," in *New Readings on Women in Old English Literature*, pp. 146–57, and his "St. Euphrosyne: Holy Transvestite," in *Holy Men and Holy Women: Old English Prose Saints' Lives*

and Their Contexts, ed. Szarmach (Albany: State University of New York Press, 1996), pp. 356–65.
68. But see Kuefler, *The Manly Eunuch*, p. 231. For female transvestism, see *LA*, 353, 397, 603, 674–77; for male, 654. Boyarin fully discusses the story's origin in a narrative of a Jewish virgin who saves her chastity through tricking her adversaries. See Boyarin, *Dying for God*, pp. 81–82.
69. Kuefler, *The Manly Eunuch*, pp. 147. See also pp. 243–44, and Virginia Burrus, *"Begotten, Not Made": Conceiving Manhood in Late Antiquity* (Stanford, CA: Stanford University Press, 2000), pp. 138–40.
70. McInerney, *Eloquent Virgins*, p. 67. The translation from Ambrose is that of Boniface Ramsey, in *Ambrose* (London: Routledge, 1997), pp. 71–116 (future references will occur in the text). The narrative is vastly concerned with place, constantly mentioning specific buildings and allegorical connections between buildings and people: *Ubicumque virgo Dei est, templum Dei est* [Wherever a virgin of God is, there is a temple of God] (4.26; see also 4.27, 4.30, 4.32).
71. See Kuefler, *The Manly Eunuch*, p. 243, and n. 130. See also Deuteronomy 22:5.
72. All of the characters in the *De Virginibus* speak in Ambrose's own peculiar style, which remains "shrill" throughout his writing career. Burrus, "*Begotten, Not Made*", p. 138.
73. For masquerades and sexual differences see Judith Butler, *Gender Trouble: Feminism and the Subversion of Identity* (New York: Routledge, 1990), pp. 47–48, 50, 137–39.
74. Ambrose uses the language of athletic competition throughout the text in a manner similar to Tertullian. See, for example, Ambrose, *De Virginibus*, 4.33.
75. Indeed the possession of a woman's underclothes is often seen among men as a trophy representative of sexual conquest, even if the possessor did not engage in sex.
76. Burrus, "Reading Agnes: The Rhetoric of Gender in Ambrose and Prudentius," *Journal of Early Christian Studies* 3 (1995): 33. See also pp. 25, 42–43.
77. See Burrus, *Begotten, Not Made*, p. 148.
78. Cf. Kuefler, *The Manly Eunuch*, p. 243.
79. If the miracle, in the less modest one's eyes, of the soldier's transformation includes not only a metamorphosis into a woman but also into a virgin, the newcomer also reflects the soldier's presumed desire for a new life as a devout Christian.
80. See Ramsey, *Ambrose*, p. 100, n. 21. This highly learned reference obviously is meant to appeal to a literary audience and shows most clearly how Ambrose's own voice is behind the discourse of all of his characters.
81. Burrus, *"Begotten, Not Made,"* p. 150.
82. See Kuefler, *The Manly Eunuch*, pp. 231, 243–44.
83. The difference between the two characters' disguises are many. For instance, surely the virgin would be as ridiculous and unconvincing in

her new garb as the soldier is were anyone to inspect her closely, but apparently no-one does. A typical Roman soldier, familiar to local citizens yet anonymous and indistinguishable from other soldiers through the wearing of a kind of uniform, is not a typical object of the male gaze. The cross-dressing soldier is recognized immediately as a man because (among other reasons) he replaces a woman when a woman in a brothel *is* typically an object of the male gaze. In more practical terms, there is more substance to the dress of a Roman legionnaire than the dress of prostitute in a bedroom, so the soldier's armor can do a better job of covering up the person wearing it. Indeed, his armor has been designed for the exact purpose of shielding and covering.

84. Boyarin, *Dying for God*, p. 86.
85. I thus disagree with McInerney when she calls Ambrose's typical female martyr "pure symbolic object, perfectly passive and perfectly silent." See *Eloquent Virgins*, p. 11.
86. Virginia Burrus, "'Equipped for Victory': Ambrose and the Gendering of Orthodoxy," *Journal of Early Christian Studies* 4 (1996): 472.
87. McInerney, *Eloquent Virgins*, p. 50. She is thinking of Jerome's exhortations that women be learned, but largely silent. See pp. 64–65. I part company with McInerney completely when she finds the Virgin of Antioch to be "silenced by her own virginity, paralyzed by shame and fear of public opinion" (p. 72).
88. Bruno Krusch, ed., *Ionae Vitae Sanctorum Columbani, Vedastis, Iohannis* (Hanover: Impensis Bibliopolii Hahniani, 1905), 1–294; Jo Ann McNamara, John E. Halborg, and E. Gordon Whatley, eds. and trans., *Sainted Women of the Dark Ages* (Durham, NC: Duke University Press, 1992), pp. 155–75. See also Coon, *Sacred Fictions*, pp. 24–26, 120–41; and Jane Tibbetts Schulenberg, *Forgetful of Their Sex: Female Sanctity and Society ca. 500–1100* (Chicago: University of Chicago Press, 1998).
89. The translation is that of McNamara and Halborg in *Sainted Women of the Dark Ages*, pp. 155–75.

2 The Female Patience Figure as Frozen Speaker

1. Later, male figures become more common, for example, the male personification of Patience in William Langland's *Piers Plowman: An Edition of the C-Text*, ed. Derek Pearsall (Berkeley: University of California Press, 1978). See Passus 15, lines 33–34.
2. The complexity is surprising because critics have often treated Tertullian as strongly antifeminist. See Maud Burnett McInerney, *Eloquent Virgins: From Thecla to Joan of Arc* (New York: Palgrave Macmillan, 2003), p. 17.
3. Tertullian, *de Patientia*, 15.4. The translation I use is that of Emily Joseph Daly, in Tertullian, *Disciplinary, Moral and Ascetical Works*, FC 40 (Washington, DC: Catholic University of America Press, 1959), pp. 189–222. Subsequent references will appear in the text.

4. Shaw says that Tertullian "imagines *patientia* as a woman in dress and deportment—demure, shy, withdrawn, passive—the *alumna* or foster child of god. Tertullian accept[s] that this was, indeed, not just a female, but also a servile virtue." "Body," p. 297.
5. Men did not typically wear garments described as close-fitting in Tertullian's day. Ambrose links patience itself with the idea of clothing. In his *de Iacob*, he says *induatur patientia* (4.14), "let us put on patience," ed. C. Schenkl, CSEL 32, part 2 (Vienna: F. Tempsky, 1897), pp. 1–70; Michael P. McHugh, trans. *Ambrose: Seven Exegetical Works*, FC 65 (Washington: Catholic University of America Press, 1972), p. 155. Ambrose also says *sume operimentum fidei atque patientiae* (4.10), [take up the covering of faith and of patience] in his *de Interpellatione Iob et David*, (ed. C. Schenkl, CSEL 32, part 2), pp. 209–96; trans., p. 375.
6. See Michel Foucault, *The History of Sexuality, Volume 2: The Use of Pleasure*, trans. Robert Hurley (New York: Vintage, 1990), pp. 46–47.
7. The presumption is far too reductive.
8. Tertullian can be quite egalitarian in general, and certainly praises women martyrs as much as men, with little in the way of distinction between their personal qualities. See Daniel L. Hoffman, *The Status of Women and Gnosticism in Irenaeus and Tertullian* (Lewiston: Edwin Mellen Press, 1995), pp. 169–70. For critical works concerning Tertullian's rhetorical skill, see Erin Ronsse, "Rhetoric of Martyrs: Listening to Saints Perpetua and Felicitas," *Journal of Early Christian Studies* 14 (2006): n. 15.
9. Tertullian, *De Cultu Feminam*, ed. A. Kroymann, *Opera* 1:341–70. See McInerney, *Eloquent Virgins*, pp. 17–20; and Brad Windon, "The Seduction of Weak Men: Tertullian's Rhetorical Construction of Gender and Ancient Christian 'Heresy,'" in *Mapping Gender in Ancient Religious Discourses*, ed. Todd Penner and Caroline Vander Stichele (Leiden: Brill, 2007), pp. 459, 469.
10. See Perkins, "The Rhetoric of the Maternal Body," pp. 320–23.
11. See Gregory's letters in Bede, *Bede's Ecclesiastical History of the English People*, ed. Bertram Colgrave and R. A. B. Mynors (Oxford: Clarendon Press, 1969), 1.27 and 30.
12. A. N. Doane, ed., *Genesis A: A New Edition* (Madison: University of Wisconsin Press, 1978), pp. 36–37. I use the edition in *The Junius Manuscript*, ed. George Philip Krapp (New York, Columbia University Press, 1931), pp. 3–87. For a review of criticism concerning this poem, see Paul G. Remley, *Old English Biblical Verse: Studies in Genesis, Exodus, and Daniel* (Cambridge, UK: Cambridge University Press, 1996), pp. 18–19, 97.
13. Remley, *Old English Biblical Verse*, pp. 114, 143–49.
14. See Malcolm R. Godden, "The Trouble with Sodom: Literary Responses to Biblical Sexuality," *Bulletin of the John Rylands Library* 77 (1995): 118, 119.
15. See M. Nussbaum, *The Therapy of Desire: Theory and Practice in Hellenistic Ethics* (Princeton, NJ: Princeton University Press, 1994), pp. 359–401.

16. See *Andreas and The Fates of the Apostles*, ed. Kenneth R. Brooks (Oxford: Clarendon Press, 1961), *Andreas*, lines 713, 717.
17. Julia Kristeva, "Women's Time," in *The Kristeva Reader*, ed. Toril Moi (New York: Columbia University Press, 1986), pp. 187–213.
18. Geoffrey W. Bromley, ed., *The International Standard Bible Encyclopedia*, 4 vols. (Grand Rapids: Eerdmans, 1986), 3:172; J. D. Douglas and Merrill C. Tenney, eds., *The New International Dictionary of the Bible: Pictorial Edition* (Basingstoke: Marshall Pickering, 1987), p. 602. See Martin Harries, *Forgetting Lot's Wife: On Destructive Spectatorship* (New York: Fordham University Press, 2007), p. 28, fig. 3; p. 7, n. 5.
19. See Harries, *Forgetting Lot's Wife*, p. 104.
20. Some early texts interpret Lot's wife as a pillar, on the basis of their understanding of the Hebrew word used to describe her in her transformed state. See Josephus, *Jewish Antiquities Books I-IV*, in *Josephus*, ed. and trans. H. St. J. Thackeray, 9 vols. (London: William Heinemann, 1961), 4:101.
21. See *The Cædmon Manuscript of Anglo-Saxon Biblical Poetry. Junius xi in the Bodleian Library*, intro., Israel Gollancz (Oxford: Oxford University Press, 1927), pp. 119–21. There is a space of about a page and a half for illustrations immediately after the transformation of Loth's wife appears in the poem.
22. C. R. Dodwell and Peter Clemoes, eds., *The Old English Illustrated Hexateuch: British Museum Cotton Claudius B. IV EEMF 18* (Copenhagen: Rosenkilde and Bagger, 1974), p. 56; and Benjamin C. Withers, *The Illustrated Old English Hexateuch, Cotton Claudius B. iv: The Frontier of Seeing and Reading in Anglo-Saxon England* (Toronto: British Museum and University of Toronto Press, 2007), pp. 18, 21.
23. See C. R. Dodwell, *Anglo-Saxon Gestures and the Roman Stage* (Cambridge, UK: Cambridge University Press, 2000), p. 134, and plates XLIX a and b.
24. *The Old English Heptateuch and Ælfric's Libellus de veteri Testamento et novo*, ed. Richard Marsden (Oxford: Oxford University Press, 2008), p. 43 (Genesis 19:26). Hereafter, referred to as *Heptateuch* with page references in the text.
25. Peter Kidd at the British Library provided information concerning the illustration (personal communication). In other illustrations, Loth's wife's robe is light-colored. Cf. Cotton Claudius B. iv, 32r.
26. Angel-messengers tend to appear on the left in the illustrations to *Genesis A* in the Junius 11 manuscript as well. See the facsimile, pp. 65, 74, 82, 84, and 87.
27. See also *Ælfric's Anglo-Saxon Version of Alcuini Interrogationes Sigewulfi Presbyteri in Genesin*, ed. George Edwin MacLean (Hallé: E. Karras, 1883) (hereafter *Interrogationes Sigewulfi*), pp. 104-07. The traditions of how to depict the ruined cities and Lot's wife in artworks vary.
28. See Allen J. Frantzen, "The Disclosure of Sodomy in *Cleanness*," *PMLA* 111 (1996): 459–60, where he describes the landscape of the destroyed

cities as anal. See also his *Before the Closet: Same-Sex Love from "Beowulf" to "Angels in America"* (Chicago: University of Chicago Press, 1998), pp. 184–226.

29. *Cleanness*, in *The Poems of the Pearl Manuscript: Pearl, Cleanness, Patience, Sir Gawain and the Green Knight*, ed. Malcolm Andrew and Ronald Waldron (Berkeley, University of California Press, 1978), lines 981–84.

30. Martin Harries, "Forgetting Lot's Wife: Artaud, Spectatorship, and Catastrophe," *Yale Journal of Criticism* 11 (1998): 227. Bede also stresses the sounds of destruction that reach her. See Charles W. Jones, ed., *Bedae Venerabilis Opera, In Principium Genesis*. CCSL 118a (Turnhout: Brepols, 1967), 19.26, p. 227.

31. Harries, *Forgetting Lot's Wife*, p. 28. See also pp. 106–07, and Jacques Lacan, *Écrits: A Selection*, trans. Alan Sheridan (New York: Norton, 1977), p. 43.

32. See Jean Baudrillard, "Simulacra and Simulations," in *Modern Criticism and Theory: A Reader*, ed. David Lodge with Nigel Wood (Harlow: Longman, 2000), p. 405. An anonymous third-century (?) Latin poem describes her as *ipsa et imago sibi* [herself an image of herself]. *Incertu de Sodoma*, ed. Rudolf Peiper, *Cypriani Galli Poetae Heptatevchos*. CSEL 23, Part 3 (Vienna: F. Tempsky, 1881), pp. 212–20, line 120. The poem has been attributed to Tertullian and Cyprian. Its authorship remains unknown.

33. S. J. Crawford supplied parentheses that clearly demark the phrase as an addition to the Vulgate text. They are not in the manuscript. See Crawford, ed., *The Old English Version of the Heptateuch, Ælfric's Treatise on the Old and New Testament and His Preface to Genesis* (London: Oxford University Press, 1922), p. 134; Frederick M. Biggs, "Biblical Glosses in Ælfric's Translation of Genesis," *Notes and Queries* 38 (1991): 291, *Heptateuch*, p. 43; and Rebecca Anne Barnhouse, "Shaping the Hexateuch Text for an Anglo-Saxon Audience," in *The Old English Hexateuch: Aspects and Approaches*, ed. Rebecca Anne Barnhouse and Benjamin C. Withers (Kalamazoo: Medieval Institute Publications, 2000), pp. 97–98.

34. Biggs notices the parallel uses of *getacnunge* for the requisite Genesis passages in Ælfric's works. See Biggs, "Biblical Glosses," p. 291.

35. For "sense for sense" translation as opposed to "word for word" (the idea came originally from Cicero, and was further popularized by Jerome and King Alfred), see Robert Stanton, *The Culture of Translation in Anglo-Saxon England* (Cambridge, UK: Brewer, 2002), pp. 75, 82, 110–11.

36. She contrasts with the personified female figure of Wisdom that is a major feature of the text and supposedly "rescues" Lot (Wisdom 10:6).

37. Clement of Rome, *The First Epistle of Clement to the Corinthians*, in *The Epistles of St. Clement of Rome and St. Ignatius of Antioch*, trans. James A. Kleist. Ancient Christian Writers 1 (Westminster, MD: The Newman Press, 1961), p. 15.

38. Bede, *In Lucae Evangelium expositio*, ed. D. Hurst, CCSL 120 (Turnhout: Brepols, 1960), 17.32, p. 319. Bede is similarly moralistic in his *In Principium Genesis*. See 19.26, pp. 227–28.

39. The translation is from Dolores Warwick Frese, "Sexing Political Tropes of Conquest: 'The Wife's Lament' and Laȝamon's *Brut*," in *Sex and Sexuality in Anglo-Saxon England: Essays in Memory of Daniel Gillmore Calder*, ed. Carol Braun Pasternack and Lisa M. C. Weston (Tempe: Arizona Center for Medieval and Renaissance Studies, 2004), p. 211, n. 22.
40. For instance, according to the poem *Sodoma*, trees in the area bear fruits that turn to ashes in one's mouth. *Incerti de Sodoma*, lines 137–38, and see *The Defective Version of Mandeville's Travels*, ed. M. C. Seymour (Oxford: Oxford University Press, 2002), p. 42. The desert also has associations with the lives of hermits and ascetics.
41. The complete passage is *Denique uxor Loth, ubi respexit, remansit et in salem conuersa hominibus fidelibus quoddam praestitit condimentum, quo sapiant aliquid, unde illud caueatur exemplum*. Augustine, *Civitas Dei*, ed. Bernard Dombart and Alphonse Kalb, 4th ed. CCSL 48 (Turnhout: Brepols, 1955), 16.30.535, "Furthermore, Lot's wife was rooted to the spot where she looked back; and by being turned into salt she supplied a kind of seasoning for the faithful—a seasoning of wisdom to make them beware of following her example." Henry Bettenson, trans., *Concerning the City of God Against the Pagans* (Harmondsworth: Penguin, 1972), p. 692.
42. *Incerti de Sodoma*, line 125. See Irénée de Lyon [Irenaeus], *Contre les Hérésies Livre IV: Édition Critique [Adversus Haereses]*, ed. Adelin Rousseau, Bertrand Memmerdinger, Louis Doutreleau, and Charles Mercier, 2 vols. (Paris: Éditions du Cerf, 1965), 2:794, 4.31.3.
43. Salt-stone is not one of the harder or more durable varieties of stone, but the Old English accounts of Loth's wife stress the "stone" of her new substance, whereas the vulgate stresses *salis*, "salt." For the "stoniness" of certain female saints, see Andrea Rossi-Reder, "Embodying Christ, Embodying Nation: Ælfric's Accounts of Saints Agatha and Lucy," in Pasternack and Weston, eds., *Sex and Sexuality in Anglo-Saxon England*, pp. 187, 190.
44. Clement of Rome, *Corinthians 1*, pp. 15-16.
45. Bede associates her motives for looking back with a rejection of Christ's promise to redeem humanity (*In Lucae Evangelium expositio*, p. 319). This reading only makes sense if one accepts the Old Testament as figuring the New.
46. See *Klaeber's Beowulf and The Fight at Finnsburg*, ed. R. D. Fulk, Robert E. Bjork, and John D. Niles, 4th ed. (Toronto: University of Toronto Press, 2008), *Beowulf*, lines 1384–87.
47. *Incerti de Sodoma*, lines 121–26. It is difficult to ascertain how influential this poem would be. See also Augustine, *Civitas Dei*, 16.30.535.
48. Irenaeus, *Adversus Haereses*, 4.31.3.
49. Henry Bettenson, ed. and trans., *The Early Christian Fathers: A Selection from the Writings of the Fathers from St. Clement of Rome to St. Athanasias* (London: Oxford University Press, 1963), p. 122.
50. Niobe's story is an analogue to Lot's wife's in that the former is transformed into a physical object, the rock of Sipylos, which one may still visit. According to tradition, the rock still weeps. See Robert Graves,

The Greek Myths, 2 vols. (New York: George Braziller, 1955), 1:259. *The Adventures of Leucippe and Clitophon* also connects the immovability of its heroine with Niobe (Achilles Tatius 3.15.167). In Aesop's *Fables*, truth is "a woman standing all alone" out in the desert, having left "the town," which is full of liars. See B. E. Perry, ed., *Aesopica*, vol. 1 (Urbana: University of Illinois Press, 1952), Number 355. For the translation, see *Fables of Aesop*, trans. S. A. Handford (Harmondsworth: Penguin, 1964), Number 160, p. 164.

51. See Harries, *Forgetting Lot's Wife*, p. 20. Augustine notes that she is rooted to her spot (*Civitas Dei*, 16.30.535; Bettenson, trans., *City of God*, p. 692).
52. Julia Kristeva, *Tales of Love*, trans. Leon S. Roudiez (New York: Columbia University Press, 1987), pp. 376, 375.
53. Lacan, *Écrits*, pp. 305, 43; Harries, "Forgetting Lot's Wife," p. 233.
54. For connections between landscape, body, and the surface of a manuscript page, see Withers, *The Illustrated Old English Hexateuch*, p. 264; and Patricia Cox Miller, "The Blazing Body: Ascetic Desire in Jerome's *Letter to Eustochium*," *Journal of Early Christian Studies* 1 (1993): 27–30.
55. See Withers, *The Illustrated Old English Hexateuch*, p. 293, for the tendency of Old Testament manuscripts to promote the written word while retaining oral aspects. He also connects manuscripts, monumental objects, and law. See pp. 157–58.
56. In the Old English *Heptateuch*, the word *getacnunge* is followed immediately by *Ða beheold Abraham on ærne mergen þyderweard* [then Abraham looked over there in the early morning], so that the translator's addition to the biblical account implies that Abraham looks "over there" to the *getacnunge*: Loth's wife in her changed form. However, unexpectedly, no further mention is made of her image by him or by the translator (p. 43).
57. For instance, a church is built on the site of Cecilia's martyrdom. The texts concerning her therefore suggest that readers should visit this site (*LA*, 777). See also Josephus, *Antiquities*, 4:101, Rabanus Maurus, *De universo*, 2.2, *PL* 111:36, and *Mandeville's Travels*, p. 42, where "dwelliþ Lothis wyf a stoon of salt." The landscape is hellish (pp. 41–42).
58. Even Jesus's injunction to remember Lot's wife could make the rememberer complicit in these desires (Luke 18:2). See Pasternack and Weston, eds., *Sex and Sexuality in Anglo-Saxon England*, p. xlviii. As Harries notes, the desire of Lot's wife could be masochistic or even self-destructive. See *Forgetting Lot's Wife*, pp. 15, 98.
59. I am ignoring other possibilities: one might parachute in; one might go straight to the sites of Sodom and Gomorrah. I assume that a typical traveler would approach Lot's wife with a view to receiving some kind of information from her. For medieval understanding of the site, see, for instance, Ælfric's *Interrogationes Sigewulfi: for barn seo eorþe. ⁊ bið æfre unwæstmbære. ⁊ mid fulum wætere ofer gan* [the ground was all scorched and will be barren forever and covered with poisoned water] (p. 104),

Josephus, *The Jewish War*, trans. G. A. Williamson (Harmondsworth: Penguin Books, 1959), 4.483–85, 385–86, *Mandeville's Travels*, pp. 41–42, and *Cleanness*, lines 1008–48.

60. *Incerti de Sodoma*, lines 125–26. The menstruation confirms that she is alive and remains premenopausal. Hence, Eve's punishment for disobedience is extended until the end of time for Lot's wife, who thus connects with Genesis's theme of fertility in language. This portrayal of Lot's wife as still menstruating in her transformed state appears much more rarely during the Middle Ages as compared to other traditions concerning her. Her blood recalls the blood of the martyrs, often associated with relics and cults. See Peggy McCracken, *The Curse of Eve, the Wound of the Hero: Blood, Gender, and Medieval Literature* (Philadelphia: University of Pennsylvania Press, 2003), pp. 2–8, 22–37.
61. Menstrual blood connects with the early medieval idea of learning through breast milk. See Susan Signe Morrison, *Women Pilgrims in Late Medieval England: Private Piety as Public Performance* (London: Routledge, 2000), p. 32; Joyce E. Salisbury, *Perpetua's Passion: The Death and Memory of a Young Roman Woman* (New York: Routledge, 1997), p. 142; and Julia Kristeva, *Powers of Horror: An Essay on Abjection*, trans. Leon S. Roudiez (New York: Columbia University Press, 1982), p. 71.
62. Many ancient monuments present the human figure as larger or smaller than life. See Max Wegener, *Greek Masterworks of Art*, trans. Charlotte La Rue (New York: George Braziller, 1961), plates 2, 3, 6, 7, 12, 58, 63, 64, 108–11. Most medieval depictions of Lot's wife in artworks suggest that she is life-sized.
63. *Genesis A* frequently refers to written scriptural authority (lines 227, 969, 1121, 1239, 1630, 1723, 2565, 2612–13) though it, as other Old English poems do, refers to oral authority as well. The illustrations of the Loth-narrative in MS Claudius B. iv depict God and one of His angel-messengers carrying what seem to be tablets. See folio 31r.
64. See *The Old English "Apollonius of Tyre,"* ed. Peter Goolden (London: Oxford University Press, 1958), chap. 10, p.16.
65. See Peter Brown, *Society and the Holy in Late Antiquity* (Berkeley: University of California Press, 1982), pp. 103–65; Graves, *Greek Myths*, 1:11. For what cities represent to Anglo-Saxons, see Nicholas Howe, "Rome: Capital of Anglo-Saxon England," *Journal of Medieval and Early Modern Studies* 34 (2004): 147–72.
66. By associating Lot's wife with people *in tribulatione*, "in tribulation," in his *In Lucae Evangelium expositio* (p. 319), Bede suggests that she had conflicted desires.
67. The distinction suggests the illustration in MS Claudius B. iv, with its depiction of many dead people lying about. Many depictions of the destruction of the cities of the plain show only burning cities, with no obvious casualties. If she empathizes with suffering, she follows Christ's later teachings.

68. See Bernard F. Huppé, *Doctrine and Poetry: Augustine's Influence on Old English Poetry* (Albany: State University of New York Press, 1959), pp. 203–04; Bede, *In Lucae Evangelium expositio*, p. 319; Godden, "The Trouble with Sodom," p. 99. On the other hand, were one to treat the tribes that descend from Lot's daughters as the products of evil deeds, under the taint of incest, one would have to acknowledge that Lot's wife, by being turned into a salt-stone, "never becomes part of the incestuous community after the destruction of the cities" and thus might also be considered a figure of "salvation" (Harries, *Forgetting Lot's Wife*, p. 32).
69. See Augustine, *Civitas Dei*, 16.30.535.
70. MacLean conveniently supplies Alcuin's Latin version of the source passages for *Interrogationes Sigewulfi* as a parallel text in his edition of the Old English translation. For a complete edition, see *PL* 100:542, in particular *Interrogationes Sigewulfi*, 188.
71. In a more general discussion of the Genesis material. The bargaining scene is omitted from the poem.
72. Godden, "The Trouble with Sodom," p. 111. See Frantzen, *Before the Closet*, p. 186. Of course, God punishes these Sodomites further when the cities are leveled. One must acknowledge that Christian commentators on Genesis display a general tendency, which Ælfric seems to be following, "to invest the Genesis narrative with sharp and weighty moral distinctions," as Godden notes. "The Trouble with Sodom," p. 99.
73. Bede, at the end of his *De Schematibus et Tropis*, reverses the pattern of reference with regard to these passages, which suggests that biblical scholars tended to treat these passages as making up a whole. After quoting Jesus's statement about who will be taken on judgment day and who will not, he adds *Et memores estote uxoris Loth*, "And remember Lot's wife" (Bede, *Libri II De Arte Metrica et de Schematibus et Tropis—The Art of Poetry and Rhetoric*, ed. and trans. Calvin B. Kendal, Bibliotheca Germanicus, new series 2 [Saarbrücken: Verlag, 1991], pp. 202, 209). Frese sees the addition as a "pointed" comment against the unguarded use of non-Christian learning ("Sexing Political Tropes of Conquest," pp. 210–11, 216–17), when I believe that Bede uses it merely as an example of an "illustrative story" that warns (Bede, *De Schematibus et Tropis*, p. 209). By simply appearing very near in Luke's gospel to the previously quoted scriptural passage, the example suggested itself to Bede.
74. Concerns about the arbitrariness of God's punishment of the people in the cities of the plain were certainly current in the early Middle Ages. Obvious questions would be why do the women have to die if anal intercourse between men seems to be what God abhors? Why do the children have to die? See Godden, "The Trouble with Sodom," pp. 100–01. As Frantzen notes, certain medieval writers tried to answer these questions. Sometimes women were blamed for engendering the illicit sexual practices of the men in Sodom. See Frantzen, "Disclosure of Sodomy," p. 456.
75. See *Interrogationes Sigewulfi*, pp. 104–05.

76. Harries, "Forgetting Lot's Wife," pp. 222, 228.
77. In *Genesis A*, the figure of Loth's wife is also an image of the poet's individual art. By mentioning explicitly that the story of her transformation is *mære*, "famous," the poet emphasizes that such a story can only remain famous because poets and other artists choose to make it so in an oral-traditional society.
78. Graves, *Greek Myths*, 2:316. Not to mention the stone figure in *Andreas* that speaks explicitly (line 713). For emblems of Patience, see Gerald J. Schiffhorst, ed., *The Triumph of Patience: Medieval and Renaissance Studies* (Orlando: University Presses of Florida, 1978), frontispiece, and pp. 16–19, and 116.
79. In a significant parallel, Catherine E. Karkov notices that the illustrations in MS Junius 11 are particularly concerned with depicting inheritance, usually through the male line ("The Anglo-Saxon Genesis: Text, Illustration, and Audience," in *The Old English Hexateuch*, p. 214). Junius 11 also contains an unexpectedly large number of depictions of women, typically as wives and mothers (p. 225)
80. See "The Trouble with Sodom," pp. 101, 103–04. Godden concludes that Lot's incest seems to have been more a matter of curiosity than horror among the Anglo-Saxons. See pp. 112–13, and *Riddle 46* of *The Exeter Book*, ed. George Philip Krapp and Elliott Van Kirk Dobbie (New York: Columbia University Press, 1936), p. 205. In Godden's view, the illustrations of the seduction and subsequent births in Cotton MS. Claudius B. iv suggest "cosy domesticity rather than shock or sensuality" ("The Trouble with Sodom," p. 104, and figs. 3, 4). Frantzen observes that Lot's incest generally receives little attention from early medieval commentators, as compared to the harsh condemnations that the assumed acts of the Sodomites inspire. Presumably, though this incest is illicit, it is more acceptable than the Sodomites' practices because it is heterosexual (*Before the Closet*, pp. 222–23; Jerome, *Epistola 22*, p. 72).
81. Joseph Bosworth, ed., *An Anglo-Saxon Dictionary* (Oxford: Oxford University Press, 1882), with a *Supplement* by T. Northcote Toller (Oxford: Clarendon Press, 1921), *Enlarged Addenda and Corrigenda to the Supplement* by Alastair Campbell (Oxford: Clarendon Press), 1972, s. v. "Sið".
82. Godden, "The Trouble with Sodom," p. 111.
83. Godden, "The Trouble with Sodom," p. 103; cf. Marsden, ed. *Heptateuch*, p. 43.
84. Jonathan Wilcox explains the sources for this scene, identifying thoroughly the differences in the various depictions. See "The First Laugh: Laughter in Genesis and the Old English Tradition," in *The Old English Hexateuch*, pp. 259–60.
85. This abrupt shift occurs in part because the poet omits the content of about nine verses at this juncture. Cf. Genesis 18:13–21.
86. The sex with them that the Sodomites demand then is a further offense against God's plans because it presumably has the potential to change

their fertility-message physically. Once again semen can be associated with God's word, promise, and powers of creation.
87. For *Elene*, I use *The Vercelli Book*, ed. George Philip Krapp (New York: Columbia University Press, 1932), pp. 66–102.
88. Brown has associated the political concept of civic authority with early saints in late antiquity. The role of female saints and other authoritative women in such positions has been relatively neglected. See Brown, *Society and the Holy*, pp. 103–65.
89. See Bosworth and Toller, eds., *An Anglo-Saxon Dictionary*, s. v. "Wic"; Richard L. Venezky and Antonette DiPaolo Healey, eds., *A Microfiche Concordance to Old English* (Toronto: Dictionary of Old English Project, University of Toronto, 1980), s. v. "Wic." Both the abode of the Grendel family and the dragon's barrow are described as examples of *wic*, so the term is not unambiguously positive. See *Beowulf*, lines 1612a, 3083a. I gratefully acknowledge Richard Firth Green who drew my attention to the use of this term in the *Genesis A* passage.
90. *Travels of John Mandeville*, p. 42.
91. Anita R. Riedinger, "The Englishing of Arcestrate: Woman in Apollonius of Tyre," in *New Readings on Women in Old English Literature*, ed. Helen Damico, Alexandra Hennesey Olsen, and Marijane Osborn (Bloomington: Indiana University Press, 1990), p. 301.

3 The Female Patience Figure as Counterfeit

1. See Sherry L. Reames, *The Legenda aurea: A Reexamination of its Paradoxical History* (Madison: University of Wisconsin Press, 1985), pp. 198–99.
2. William Granger Ryan, trans., Jacobus de Voragine, *The Golden Legend: Readings on the Saints*, 2 vols. (Princeton, NJ: Princeton University Press, 1993), p. xv; Martha Easton, "Pain, Torture and Death in the Huntington Library *Legenda aurea*," in *Gender and Holiness: Men, Women and Saints in Late Medieval Europe*, ed. Samantha J. E. Riches and Sarah Salih (London: Routledge, 2002), p. 49.
3. See Maud Burnett McInerney, *Eloquent Virgins: From Thecla to Joan of Arc* (New York: Palgrave Macmillan, 2003), pp. 67–73.
4. *Life of Syncletica*, PG 28:1487–558. See Virginia Burrus, *Saving Shame: Martyrs, Saints, and Other Abject Subjects* (Philadelphia: University of Pennsylvania Press, 2008), pp. 100–07.
5. I am thinking of Jacobus's habit of including the etymologies of saints' names.
6. The collection is patterned after the many earlier medieval martyrologies, which played a large part in organizing people's time. See Easton, "Pain, Torture and Death," p. 49. The *Legenda Aurea* survives in about 1,000 manuscripts and in hundreds of adaptations and printed editions, "both in the original Latin and in every Western European language." Ryan, *Golden Legend* 1:xiii.
7. Easton, "Pain, Torture and Death," pp. 50–51.

8. For differences between the treatment of male and female martyrs' bodies, see Kirsten Wolf, "The Severed Breast: A Topos in the Legends of Female Virgin Martyr Saints," *Arkiv för Nordisk Filologi* 112 (1997): 100–104.
9. Easton, "Pain, Torture and Death," p. 51.
10. See Easton, "Pain, Torture and Death," p. 57. For the treatment of rape in the *Legenda Aurea*, see Mills, "Can the Virgin Martyr Speak?" pp. 190–91. For discussion of Ambrose's and Prudentius's depictions of female martyrs, see McInerney, *Eloquent Virgins*, pp. 70–75. As the readership for lives of women saints is increasingly associated with women, the idea of these lives as pornography becomes more problematic. See Catherine Sanok, *Her Life Historical: Exemplarity and Female Saints' Lives in Late Medieval England* (Philadelphia: University of Pennsylvania Press, 2007), p. 27.
11. See Larissa Tracy, trans. and intro., *Women of the Gilte Legende: A Selection of Middle English Saints Lives* (Cambridge, UK: Brewer, 2003), p. 6, and n. 14; p. 109. Later hagiography in turn tends to treat female saints in a "gentler" fashion even than the *Legenda Aurea*. See Reames, *Legenda aurea*, pp. 206–07.
12. Easton, "Pain, Torture and Death," p. 57 (See also p. 61); McInerney, *Eloquent Virgins*, p. 81.
13. Easton detects a tendency for genders to be blurred in later hagiography, perhaps, an effect of the gendering of patience literature. See "Pain, Torture and Death," pp. 52–53.
14. McInerney, *Eloquent Virgins*, pp. 73, 75.
15. Carol F. Heffernan, "Praying before the Image of Mary: Chaucer's *Prioress's Tale*, VII 502–12," *Chaucer Review* 39 (2004): 109. See pp. 109–10, n. 24, and Lee Patterson, *Temporal Circumstances: Form and History in the Canterbury Tales* (New York: Palgrave Macmillan, 2006), pp. 135, 137–38. For the treatment of images of Mary, see also Susan Signe Morrison, *Women Pilgrims in Late Medieval England: Private Piety as Public Performance* (London: Routledge, 2000), p. 12.
16. Patterson, *Temporal Circumstances*, p. 129. See William Orth, "The Problem of the Performative in Chaucer's Prioress Sequence," *Chaucer Review* 42 (2007): 202, 204.
17. See C. Heffernan, "Praying Before the Image of Mary," pp. 104, 112. The abbot's treatment of the clergeon's body suggests an image of the pietà and thus the reproduction of such images. See p. 114.
18. The *Tale*'s rather abrupt mention of Saint Hugh of Lincoln is another example of how the narrator apparently thinks of the saints as largely interchangeable (684–87). See Patterson, *Temporal Circumstances*, p. 153.
19. See Orth, "Problem of the Performative," pp. 205–06, nn. 25–28.
20. See Patterson, *Temporal Circumstances*, p. 151. Chaucer hints at parody of rote learning when the next tale after the *Prioress's Tale* is an obvious burlesque. The narrator "lerned" it "longe agoon." *Prologue to Sir Thopas* (Fragment VII, line 709).

4 The Female Patience Figure as Frozen Empress

1. See Alison Weir, *Eleanor of Aquitaine: A Life* (New York: Ballantyne Books, 1999), pp. 175–76. See also Eric Hicks, *Le Débat sur "Le Roman de la Rose,"* Bibliothèque du XVe siècle, no. 43 (Paris: Honoré Champion, 1977), pp. li–liv, 187–94.
2. Chrétien de Troyes, *Les Romans de Chrétien de Troyes: II Cligés*, ed. Alexandre Micha (Paris: Honoré Champion, 1957). Further references will be by line in the text.
3. Critics have considered this feigned death episode to be much more in a comic vein than the romance's style and subject-matter maintain elsewhere. See Laine E. Doggett, "On Artifice and Realism: Thessala in Chrétien de Troyes's *Cligés*," *Exemplaria* 16 (2004): 66, n. 87. The episode seems to have been popular with medieval audiences because it appears as a discrete excerpt. See Joan Tasker Grimbert, "*Cligés* and the Chansons: A Slave to Love," in *A Companion to Chrétien de Troyes*, ed. Norris J. Lacy and Grimbert (Cambridge, UK: Brewer, 2005), p. 134, and nn. 48 and 49.
4. For the parallels between the legendary phoenix and Christ, see *The Phoenix*, ed. N. F. Blake (Manchester: Manchester University Press, 1964), pp. 8–13.
5. See Doggett, "On Artifice and Realism," pp. 67–71.
6. See Kathleen Coyne Kelly, *Performing Virginity and Testing Chastity in the Middle Ages* (London: Routledge, 2000), pp. 64–65.
7. Translation: Chrétien de Troyes. *Arthurian Romances*, trans. William W. Kibler (London: Penguin Books, 1991), pp. 123–205, at p. 195. Subsequent references by page number in the text.
8. The four lines in brackets are not in all manuscripts. See Micha, ed., *Cligés*, p. 215.
9. She creates an new version of herself as dead, like a funeral effigy: a conventional artistic representation.
10. For *Cligés* as satire of the story of Tristan and Ysold, see 3125–36, 5239–43; Jean Frappier, *Chrétien de Troyes: l'homme et l'œuvre*, 2nd ed. (Paris: Hatier, 1957), pp. 112–13; and Doggett, "On Artifice and Realism," p. 44, n. 8.
11. Brigitte Cazelles, *The Lady as Saint: A Collection of French Hagiographic Romances of the Thirteenth Century* (Philadelphia: University of Pennsylvania Press, 1991), pp. 59, 81.
12. Just such a discovery scene occurs later in the narrative (6362–63).
13. Roland Barthes, *A Lover's Discourse: Fragments*, trans. Richard Howard (New York: Hill and Wang, 1978), p. 207.
14. Grimbert, "*Cligés* and the Chansons," p. 131. Grimbert concludes that Fénice is "a slave to love" (p. 136).

5 The Female Patience Figure at an Extreme

1. See, for example, A. C. Spearing, "Narrative Voice: The Case of Chaucer's *Man of Law's Tale*," *New Literary History* 32 (2001): 738.

2. See Lisa J. Kiser, *Telling Classical Tales: Chaucer and the Legend of Good Women* (Ithaca, NY: Cornell University Press, 1983), pp. 101–11; Anne Middleton, "The *Physician's Tale* and Love's Martyrs: 'Ensamples mo than ten' as a Method in the *Canterbury Tales*," *Chaucer Review* 8 (1973): 9–32; Sheila Delany, *The Naked Text: Chaucer's Legend of Good Women* (Berkeley: University of California Press, 1994), pp. 64, 68–69; and Catherine Sanok, "Reading Hagiographically: *The Legend of Good Women* and its Feminine Audience," *Exemplaria* 13 (2001): 339–54.
3. See Sanok, "Reading Hagiographically," pp. 333–39.
4. For the work as explicitly addressed to a mostly female audience, see *The Legend of Good Women*, 1254–59, 1263–64, 1879–85; Nicola F. MacDonald, "Chaucer's *Legend of Good Women*, Ladies at Court and the Female Reader," *Chaucer Review* 35 (2000): 22, 34–39; and Kara A. Doyle, "Thisbe out of Context: Chaucer's Female Readers and the Findern Manuscript," *Chaucer Review* 40 (2006): 231–32, 238–52, 256–57.
5. See Sanok, "Reading Hagiographically," pp. 340, 350.
6. See Sarah Stanbury, "Regimes of the Visual in Premodern England: Gaze, Body, and Chaucer's *Clerk's Tale*," *New Literary History* 28 (1997): 262.
7. The more usual reading of this passage is that Grisilde makes this request of Walter because she is charitable, a reading that is consistent with her character as described in the poem. See note 4 in the introduction for critics who find Grisilde heroic.
8. See Amy W. Goodwin, "The Griselda Game," *Chaucer Review* 39 (2004): 54–56.
9. For a discussion of the precise ways in which Grisilde is "translated," see Carolyn Dinshaw, *Chaucer's Sexual Poetics* (Madison: University of Wisconsin Press, 1989), p. 144; and Sarah Stanbury, *The Visual Object of Desire in Late Medieval England* (Philadelphia: University of Pennsylvania Press, 2008), p. 131. Walter's subsequent acts of "counterfeiting" confirm that the entire sign system of clothing is hollow.
10. Grisilde's thoughts here are an addition by Petrarch. For his *Epistolae seniles* 17.3, I use J. Burke Severs, *Literary Relationships of Chaucer's "Clerkes Tale"* (New Haven: Yale University Press, 1942), pp. 254–92, referred to from now on as "Petrarch." See p. 260. I also use Severs's text (pp. 255–89) for the anonymous French version of Grisilde's story from Paris, Bibliothèque Nationale, MS fr. 12459. 260.
11. See Andrew Sprung, "'If it youre wille be': Coercion and Compliance in Chaucer's *Clerk's Tale*," *Exemplaria* 7 (1995): 349, 364–65. Grisilde's body is so important to the narrative that I disagree with Stanbury's argument that Grisilde, particularly when Walter first publicly designates her as his bride, seems "to escape categorical definition by gender through assimilation with devotional schema." "Regimes of the Visual," p. 283. Such devotional schema do not eclipse the marquis's desire, which is for (among other things) a woman's body.
12. Anne Cranny-Francis, "From Extension to Engagement: Mapping the Imaginary of Wearable Technology," *Visual Communication* 7 (2008): 366;

Barbara Czarniawska and Eva Gustavsson, "The (D)evolution of the Cyberwoman?" *Organization* 15 (2008): 666. See also Donna Haraway, *Simians, Cyborgs and Women: The Reinvention of Nature* (London: Free Association Books, 1991), p. 152.

13. Haraway, *Simians, Cyborgs and Women*, p. 152. For intelligent machines, see N. Katherine Hayles, *How We Became Posthuman: Virtual Bodies in Cybernetics, Literature, and Informatics* (Chicago: University of Chicago Press, 1999), pp. 7, 161. McKinley captures something of Grisilde's artificiality with the phrase "a hagiographic 'Barbie.'" Kathryn McKinley, "The *Clerk's Tale*: Hagiography and the Problematics of Lay Sanctity," *Chaucer Review* 33 (1998): 96.

14. Delany argues that there "is an element of irony associated with" most of Chaucer's hagiographical references. See *The Naked Text*, p. 61. For various kinds of parody in *The Clerk's Tale*, see M. Keith Booker, "'Nothing that is so is so': Dialogic Discourse and the Voice of the Woman in the *Clerk's Tale* and *Twelfth Night*," *Exemplaria* 3 (1991): 527; Engle, "Chaucer, Bakhtin, and Griselda," pp. 429–59; Linda Georgianna, "*The Clerk's Tale* and the Grammar of Assent," *Speculum* 70 (1995): 805, 818.

15. But see *The Franklin's Tale*, 771–90. The point of this passage is undercut by the impatience of the characters in the tale. See Alcuin Blamires, *Chaucer, Ethics, and Gender* (Oxford: Oxford University Press, 2006), p. 163.

16. The translation is by Earl Jeffrey Richards. Christine de Pizan, *The Book of the City of Ladies*, trans. Earl Jeffrey Richards (New York: Persea, 1982), p. 255.

17. Though Christine's attitudes are perhaps no more unexpected than the humility and repentance that appear in Chaucer's retraction at the end of *The Canterbury Tales* (X [1], 1081–92).

18. See Roberta L. Krueger, "Uncovering Griselda—Christine de Pizan, 'une seule chemise,' and the Clerical Tradition: Boccaccio, Petrarch, Philippe de Mézières and the Ménagier de Paris," in *Medieval Fabrications: Dress, Textiles, Clothwork, and Other Cultural Imaginings*, ed. E. Jane Burns (New York: Palgrave Macmillan, 2004), pp. 86–88.

19. Maureen Quilligan, *The Allegory of Female Authority: Christine de Pizan's "Cité des Dames"* (Ithaca, NY: Cornell University Press, 1991), p. 167.

20. See Sheila Delany, "'Mothers to Think Back Through': Who Are They? The Ambiguous Example of Christine de Pizan," in *Medieval Texts and Contemporary Readers*, ed. Laurie A. Finke and Martin B. Shichtman (Ithaca, NY: Cornell University Press, 1987), pp. 177–97.

21. See Elizabeth Allen, "Chaucer Answers Gower: Constance and the Trouble with Reading," *ELH* 64 (1997): 642–43, 645; and Henry Barnett Hinckley, "The Debate on Marriage in *The Canterbury Tales*," in *Chaucer: Modern Essays in Criticism*, ed. Edward Wagenknecht (New York: Oxford University Press, 1959), p. 220.

22. Virginia Woolf, "Professions for Women," in *The Death of the Moth and Other Essays* (Harmondsworth: Penguin Books, 1961), p. 202.

23. By being human and divine, Christ is a hybrid. Both His wounds and His powers fit with aspects of the cyborg. See Cranny-Francis, "From Extension to Engagement," pp. 368–69. For Grisilde as a type of Christ in *The Clerk's Tale*, see Stanbury, *Visual Object of Desire*, p. 130. "Robotic wives are fully directed towards productivity" and "are forever busy with their duties." Czarniawska and Gustavsson, "The (D)evolution of the Cyberwoman?", p. 672. See also p. 678 and Haraway, *Simians*, p. 151. Such wives as depicted in science fiction are often duplicatable like simulacra and often unable "to feel empathy." They often cause and represent schizophrenia similar to Walter's. Hayles, *How We Became Posthuman*, pp. 161–62, 165–67. Yet, robotic performances can involve parody of human and of robotic behaviors, including behaviors associated with gender. See Yuji Sone, "Realism of the Unreal: The Japanese Robot and the Performance of Representation," *Visual Communication* 7 (2008): 347–49, 355.
24. See Hayles, *How We Became Posthuman*, pp. 2–3, for the best articulation of the assumptions behind posthumanism.
25. Woolf, "Professions," pp. 202, 206; Chaucer, *Clerk's Tale*, line 1177. See Stanbury, *Visual Object of Desire*, p. 149. Cf. Charlotte C. Morse, "The Exemplary Griselda," *Studies in the Age of Chaucer* 7 (1985): 55.
26. "Feminist readings tend to literalism" (Mitchell, "Chaucer's *Clerk's Tale*," n. 16), so I am in good company.
27. Anne Middleton, "The Clerk and His Tale: Some Literary Contexts," *Studies in the Age of Chaucer* 2 (1980): 149. See n. 37, and Andrea Denny-Brown, "Povre Griselda and the All-Consuming Archewyves," *Studies in the Age of Chaucer* 28 (2006): 99, n. 50, and pp. 104–08. A "song" in mixed company implies dancing, when such pairing off into couples would have a particular effect after the relating of any tale concerning marriage.
28. Scott Bukatman, *Terminal Identity: The Virtual Subject in Postmodern Science Fiction* (Durham, NC: Duke University Press, 1993), p. 9.
29. More than the "flicker … of irony" that Jill Mann suggests. See *Feminizing Chaucer*, 2nd ed. (Cambridge, UK: Brewer, 2002), p. 118.
30. See Sprung, "'If it youre wille be,'" p. 364. See Allen, "Chaucer Answers Gower," p. 629, for Chaucer's similar treatment of Custance in *The Man of Law's Tale*.
31. William McClellan, "Bakhtin's Theory of Dialogic Discourse, Medieval Rhetoric Theory, and the Multi-Voiced Structure of the *Clerk's Tale*," *Exemplaria* 1 (1989): 478.
32. Harold Bloom, *The Anxiety of Influence: A Theory of Poetry* (Oxford: Oxford University Press, 1980), p. 95; Bakhtin, "From Notes Made in 1970–1," in *Speech Genres and Other Late Essays*, ed. C. Emerson Michael Holquist, trans. Vern McGee (Austin: University of Texas Press, 1986), pp. 132–33.
33. The *Livre* is directed explicitly against antifeminist literature to which Christine feels she must respond (2.43.2, 2.47.1, 2.49.5). See also Joseph Baird and John Kane, trans., *La Querrele de la Rose: Letters and Documents*

(Chapel Hill: University of North Carolina Press, 1978), p. 112; and Judith Laird, "Good Women and *Bonnes Dames*: Virtuous Females in Chaucer and Christine de Pizan," *Chaucer Review* 30 (1995): 62, 68. For examples of studies of Christine's feminism, see the notes on p. 69 of Laird's article.

34. See Mann's investigation of the meanings of "ynogh" in *The Clerk's Tale*, in *Feminizing Chaucer*, pp. 120, 123–24.
35. The moral aspects of this look by Valterius occur in all versions of the story under investigation.
36. At the abduction of Walter's son, Chaucer, like Christine, removes any reference to sight (673–86). Perhaps Chaucer wants to stress that Grisilde only has eyes for Walter. Certainly this omission shows that Chaucer carefully thinks about each character's use of a gaze and does not merely expand upon images of sight when he happens upon them, or whimsically insert them when they seem to suit his momentary designs.
37. Thomas J. Farrell, "The Chronotopes of Monology in Chaucer's *Clerk's Tale*," in *Bakhtin and Medieval Voices*, ed. Thomas J. Farrell (Gainesville: University Press of Florida, 1995), p. 146.
38. See, for instance, *The Wedding of Sir Gawain and Dame Ragnell*, in *Middle English Verse Romances*, ed. Donald B. Sands (New York: Holt, Rinehart and Winston, 1966), pp. 323–47, lines 19–63.
39. See Genesis 24:13–67, 29:7–11, and Sprung, "'If it youre wille be,'" p. 349, and n. 13.
40. See M. Mills, ed., *Lybeaus Desconus* (London: Oxford University Press, 1969), pp. 42–60, and p. 242, nn. 2029–31; p. 243, note L (Lambeth) 2192, for recognition scenes and weddings. See also the romance of *La Cote Mal Taillé* in *Le Roman de Tristan en Prose*, vol. 1, ed. Philippe Ménard (Geneva: Librairie Droz S. A., 1987), pp. 88–127. Marriage is often inimical to a knightly career. See Chaucer's *Franklin's Tale*.
41. In Chaucer's version, Walter notices his love-object when he is "on huntyng ... paraventure" (234), a journey that parallels and contrasts with Grisilde's daily journey from tending her sheep (his aim is self-indulgence; hers is service). In this version Grisilde does not replace Walter on horseback, but all versions present her replacing him in the castle, the space of civic responsibility. The satire of political precepts becomes more extreme when Walter's lies cause the spreading of ill-fame about himself (722–25). The public is shown to be fickle in its loyalties, and subject to misinformation and error (995–1005). The role of public opinion in the political sphere is at best paradoxical.
42. See *Lybeaus Desconus*, Lambeth, lines 2178–201.
43. Stanbury has produced much work on this subject. See *Visual Object of Desire*, pp. 101–02.
44. See David Wallace, *Chaucerian Polity: Absolutist Lineages and Associational Forms in England and Italy* (Stanford, CA: Stanford University Press, 1997), p. 284. Both Chaucer and Christine seem to work from Petrarch's

version together with a French translation of the *Epistola*, though Chaucer's French translation is almost certainly a different one from the one Christine uses. See Severs, *Literary Relationships*, p. 27; Richards, trans., *The Book of the City of Ladies*, pp. 265–66. Walter's unique sense of sight also seems to work in reverse in that he plays a game of secrets with his people. He desires to conceal whatever is his desire, to the point that his concealment amounts to political, social, and individual abnegation of his responsibilities as ruler, husband, and father. See Patricia Cramer, "Lordship, Bondage, and the Erotic: The Psychological Bases of Chaucer's 'Clerk's Tale,'" *Journal of English and Germanic Philology* 89 (1990): 497. Walter's secret life suggests connections between him and such hypocrites as Faux Semblant in Guillaume de Lorris and Jean de Meun, *Le Roman de la Rose*, ed. Ernest Langlois, 5 vols. (Paris: Société des anciens textes français, 1914–24), Book 11: 23–26, 67, 219–22.

45. See McKinley, "The *Clerk's Tale*: Hagiography," p. 92, and Mann, *Feminizing Chaucer*, p. 119, who says: "patience conquers ... through pity." See also pp. 124–25. The Clerk notes that the testing of Grisilde is both needless and the product of obsession (*The Clerk's Tale*, lines 455–62, 696–707).

46. Stanbury, however, notes that the split between a male-traditional gaze and its objects is not as simple in the Middle Ages as has often been assumed. See "Regimes of the Visual," p. 268.

47. Dinshaw, *Chaucer's Sexual Poetics*, p. 150; Seth Lerer, *Chaucer and His Readers: Imagining the Author in Late-Medieval England* (Princeton, N J: Princeton University Press, 1993), pp. 30; 28–29. In contrast to Lerer, I think that the appropriation of Petrarch's gaze by the Clerk makes the Italian poet into a "maker" who goes beyond the status Lerer gives him: "only ... another maker for a locally and temporarily defined community." See *Chaucer and His Readers*, p. 30.

48. Dinshaw, *Chaucer's Sexual Poetics*, pp. 152–53; 137. For further discussion, see Emma Campbell, "Sexual Poetics and the Politics of Translation in the Tale of Griselda," *Comparative Literature* 55 (2003): 204–05.

49. Kathryn L. Lynch, "Despoiling Griselda: Chaucer's Walter and the Problem of Knowledge in *The Clerk's Tale*," *Studies in the Age of Chaucer* 10 (1988): 69. Part of the (erotic) appeal of the cyborg is that it may be replicated. It can become a simulacrum. See Haynes, *How We Became Posthuman*, pp. 165–67.

50. The passage is probably not Petrarch's and may well not have been in the sources that Chaucer uses. The French text also omits this action. See Severs, *Literary Relationships*, p. 284, n. 25, and pp. 274–75. Later still, at the casting out scene, Walter leaves her presence before she strips.

51. For a profeminine view of Grisilde at the casting out, see, for instance, Alcuin Blamires, *The Case for Women in Medieval Culture* (Oxford: Clarendon Press, 1997), pp. 164–71.

52. See A. C. Spearing, *Criticism and Medieval Poetry*, 2nd ed. (London: Arnold, 1972), pp. 95–96.

53. See Michel Foucault, *Discipline and Punish: The Birth of the Prison*, trans. Alan Sheridan (New York: Vintage, 1979), p. 202. For the critics who see Grisilde as genuinely a paragon of patience, see Kathy Lavezzo, "Chaucer and Everyday Death: *The Clerk's Tale*, Burial, and the Subject of Poverty," *Studies in the Age of Chaucer* 23 (2001): 257, n. 7. To actually see someone's moral qualities is impossible, even if Walter finally seems to gain his desire when he "sees" in Grisilde an abstract virtue along with the countenance that he usually surveys: "And whan this Walter saugh hire pacience, / Hir glade chiere, and no malice at al" (lines 1044–45). Perhaps one may "see" a virtue only as a written text (Chaucer, *Nun's Priest's Tale* [VII], lines 3438–43), or as a work of art.
54. Robin Kirkpatrick, "The Griselda Story in Boccaccio, Petrarch, and Chaucer," in *Chaucer and the Italian Trecento*, ed. Piero Boitano (Cambridge, UK: Cambridge University Press, 1983), p. 244.
55. M. M. Bakhtin, *The Dialogic Imagination: Four Essays*, ed. Michael Holquist, trans. Caryl Emerson and Holquist (Austin: University of Texas Press, 1981), p. 108 (he is talking about the protagonists of early Greek romances); Stanbury, "Regimes of the Visual," p. 281. See also the infinitely fractured images of women in Bukatman, *Terminal Identity*, pp. 244–47.
56. Chaucer's examples of hagiography and secular hagiography tend to be more sophisticated than previous examples. See Spearing, "Narrative Voice," p. 741.
57. The most stalwart defender of Griselda's exemplary role is Morse, "The Exemplary Griselda," pp. 51–86. More generally, see Catherine Sanok, *Her Life Historical: Exemplarity and Female Saints' Lives in Late Medieval England* (Philadelphia: University of Pennsylvania Press, 2007), pp. xi–xii, xiv, 2–5, 8.
58. Morse, "Exemplary Griselda," p. 76.
59. See Stanbury, *Visual Object of Desire*, p. 149, Goodwin, "The Griselda Game," p. 46, and Lynch "Despoiling Griselda," pp. 42–43.
60. Francis Lee Utley, "The Five Genres of Chaucer's *Clerk's Tale*," *Chaucer Review* 6 (1971): 210. The exemplarity argument is a refusal to acknowledge this dead end—often, in fact, a refusal to admit into discussion the specific context of the *Tale*, particularly the Envoy. See, for example, Gerald Morgan, "The Logic of the *Clerk's Tale*," *Modern Language Review* 104 (2009): 25.
61. See Goodwin, "Griselda Game," pp. 45–46, 49, 54, 57–58.
62. One might argue that this speech completely contradicts the false inheritance on view in much of the French Griselda material that is openly misogynist. See Morse, "Exemplary Griselda," pp. 74–76; Stanbury, *Visual Object of Desire*, p. 143.
63. I am not so "literalist" so as to miss the fact that Chaucer (or the Clerk) undercuts this feminine inheritance of language by prefacing it with the advice: "Folweth Ekko, that holdeth no silence, / But evere answereth at

the countretaille" (lines 1198–99), a phrase that suggests empty repetition and contradiction merely for its own sake. Perhaps any such language inheritance is empty repetition and any search for an exemplar is useless.

64. For discussion of the significance of Griselda's immovable expression, see Thomas H. Bestul, "True and False *Cheere* in Chaucer's *Clerk's Tale*," *Journal of English and Germanic Philology* 82 (1983): 500–14; and Sprung, "'If it youre wille be,'" pp. 350–52. For Griselda as a work of art, see Muriel Whitaker, "The Artist's Ideal Griselda," in *Sovereign Lady: Essays on Women in Middle English Literature* (New York: Garland, 1995), pp. 87–91. More generally, see Roland Barthes, *S/Z: An Essay*, trans. Richard Miller (New York: Hill and Wang, 1975), pp. 40–43.
65. See Lavezzo, "Chaucer and Everyday Death," p. 269, for the pietà image.
66. Kirkpatrick, "The Griselda Story," p. 243.
67. It is possible to interpret Walter as "tamed" by Grisilde, so that her example has worked on him, but there is little evidence in the *Tale* to suggest that he has changed, as one may see through examining his relations with his people (his eventual "conversion" involves only his dubious and absurdly belated understanding of his wife, so far as readers can tell). By the end of the narrative, Walter has both fooled and completely subjected a previously interventionist populace. He would even seem to choose Grisilde as his wife in order to spite them, once they have insisted that he marry (181–85). He then removes his children from their mother and from public view for several years (so that his own influence over them will dominate: once again the sign of a tyrant), without apparently caring that the people think that he has murdered his children when the prospect of an heir was their principal reason that he marry. Finally, one might note that Walter does not explicitly release Grisilde from her vow at the end of the *Tale*.
68. See Robin Waugh, "A Woman in the Mind's Eye (and not): Narrator's and Gazes in Chaucer's *Clerk's Tale* and in Two Analogues," *Philological Quarterly* 79 (2000): 9–10. Mann says "in this tale, patience is shorn of its quality of movement . . . is frozen into the marble stillness of endurance." *Feminizing Chaucer*, p. 117.
69. See Severs, *Literary Relationships*, pp. 278–79. See Chaucer's *Nun's Priest's Tale*, line 3217, for "heigh" as a vantage point where one may see widely, almost with divine omniscience.
70. See Lynn Staley, "Chaucer and the Postures of Sanctity," in *The Powers of the Holy: Religion, Politics, and Genders in Late Medieval English Culture*, ed. David Aers and Lynn Staley (University Park: Pennsylvania State University Press, 1996), p. 241.
71. See Elizabeth A. Castelli, "'I Will Make Mary Male': Pieties of the Body and Gender Transformation of Christian Women in Late Antiquity," in *Body Guards: The Cultural Politics of Gender Ambiguity*, ed. Julia Epstein and Kristina Straub (New York: Routledge, 1991), pp. 3, 42, 46–47.

6 The Female Patience Figure as Shrine

1. See the bibliography in John H. Arnold and Katherine J. Lewis, eds., *A Companion to The Book of Margery Kempe* (Cambridge, UK: Brewer, 2004), pp. 223–40.
2. See, for example, Stanley Hussey, "The Rehabilitation of Margery Kempe," *Leeds Studies in English*, new series 32 (2001): 171–94.
3. See Catherine Sanok, *Her Life Historical: Exemplarity and Female Saints' Lives in Late Medieval England* (Philadelphia: University of Pennsylvania Press, 2007), pp. xvi, 116–42.
4. See Timea K. Szell, "From Woe to Weal and Weal to Woe: Notes on the Structure of *The Book of Margery Kempe*," in *Margery Kempe: A Book of Essays*, ed. Sandra J. McEntire (New York: Garland, 1992), pp. 73–91.
5. In some ways I agree with Sanok that such extreme material is meant to satirize the society that Margery tries to both live in and transcend. See *Her Life Historical*, pp. 140–41.
6. Sanok, *Her Life Historical*, pp. 124; 18, 136–37.
7. Julia Kristeva, *Desire in Language: A Semiotic Approach to Literature and Art*, ed. Leon S. Roudiez, trans. Thomas Gora, Alice Jardine, and Roudiez (New York: Columbia University Press, 1980), p. 240; Cynthia Hahn, "Seeing and Believing: The Construction of Sanctity in Early-Medieval Saints' Shrines," *Speculum* 72 (1997): 1079–87; and Virginia Chieffo Raguin and Stanbury, eds., *Women's Space: Patronage, Place, and Gender in the Medieval Church* (Binghamton: State University of New York Press, 2005). One could argue that a kind of feminine language exists in and from the shrines of female saints because of the roles of saints and their votive objects as intercessors. Such female votive objects express their messages of intervention upon a pilgrim's behalf through their gazes. See Susan Signe Morrison, *Women Pilgrims in Late Medieval England: Private Piety as Public Performance* (London: Routledge, 2000), p. 27.
8. Sarah Stanbury, "Regimes of the Visual in Premodern England: Gaze, Body, and Chaucer's *Clerk's Tale*," *New Literary History* 28 (1997): 264–65.
9. Morrison, *Women Pilgrims*, pp. 16–42, and nn. 41–43. The shrine attracted many famous women. See p. 17, and Carol F. Heffernan, "Praying Before the Image of Mary: Chaucer's *Prioress's Tale*, VII 502–12," *Chaucer Review* 39 (2004): 106.
10. Stanbury, "Regimes of the Visual," pp. 267, 269. Inside the basilica at Loreto, the shrine appears to consist of three walls made out of local bricks together with stone purportedly from the house of the holy family in Nazareth. The holy house, by tradition, was miraculously brought to Loreto by angels in 1294 (representations of this miracle appear in many churches). Entry to the shrine is gained by two side openings in its nine and one half by four meters structure. So, entering the large space of the basilica, one must make one's way to the smaller, confined space—associated with the domestic skill of Mary—in order to get into the shrine.

A pilgrim entering from one of the side doors walks into the gaze of a fresco of Mary, which dates from about the fourteenth century and is now situated about three feet above eye-level.

11. For changes in art starting in the twelfth century, see Kristeva, *Desire in Language*, p. 251.
12. The contrast is especially clear in the Saint Cecilia in Trastevere church where, inside the lower part of the altar, is a modern depiction of how Cecilia was found positioned in her grave when she was dug up. Her eyes and face are averted from the viewer. See Laura Mulvey, "Visual Pleasure and Narrative Cinema," in *Contemporary Literary Criticism: Literary and Cultural Studies*, ed. Robert Con Davis and Ronald Schleifer, 3rd ed. (New York: Longman, 1994), p. 429.
13. Stanbury, "Regimes of the Visual," p. 279.
14. This poem contains one explicit shrine (670–80) and several pseudoshrines (F 203–07, 785, 1225, etc.).
15. Morrison, *Women Pilgrims*, pp. 27–29, 84. Carol Heffernan notes that Chaucer could have been familiar with Eastern icons. See "Praying Before the Image of Mary," p. 105.
16. See Sarah Stanbury, *The Visual Object of Desire in Late Medieval England* (Philadelphia: University of Pennsylvania Press, 2008), p. 125.
17. See J. Burke Severs, *Literary Relationships of Chaucer's "Clerkes Tale"* (New Haven: Yale University Press, 1942), pp. 262–63, and Gail Ashton, "Patient Mimesis: Griselda and the *Clerk's Tale*," *Chaucer Review* 32 (1998): 234.
18. See Stanbury, "Regimes of the Visual," p. 280. Cf. *Wife of Bath's Prologue*, lines 596–602, 723.
19. See Virginia Cieffo Raguin, "Real and Imagined Bodies in Architectural Space: The Setting for Margery Kempe's *Book*," in Raguin and Stanbury, eds., *Women's Space*, pp. 116, 119; and Morrison, *Women Pilgrims*, pp. 4, 28, 112.
20. Cf. the spaces associated with Perpetua in her passion. She is able to establish a space of her own wherever she is, even highly politicized spaces such as the arena and forum in Carthage. In the martyrs' prison, she says, *ut ibi mallem esse quam alicubi* (Musurillo, ed., *Passio Sanctorum Perpetuae et Felicitatis*, 110), [I wanted to be there rather than anywhere else] (p. 111). One might note also in *The Book of Margery Kempe* an instance of Margery's expectation of being led off to prison, only to find that she ends up in a private bedchamber (p. 130).
21. Chaucer's lists of his works suggest that *The Second Nun's Tale* existed in some discrete form before its appearance in *The Canterbury Tales*. See Larry D. Benson, ed., *The Riverside Chaucer*, 3rd ed. (Boston: Houghton Mifflin, 1987), p. 942.
22. See Kristina Sessa, "Christianity and the *cubiculum*: Spiritual Politics and Domestic Space in Late Ancient Rome," *Journal of Early Christian Studies* 15 (2007): 171–204.
23. See Sanok, *Her Life Historical*, pp. 7, 168; and Miller, "The Blazing Body," pp. 27–28.

24. See Deborah S. Ellis, "Domestic Treachery in the *Clerk's Tale*," in *Ambiguous Realities: Women in the Middle Ages and Renaissance*, ed. Carole Levin and Jeanie Watson (Detroit: Wayne State University Press, 1987), pp. 106–07; and Stanbury, *Visual Object of Desire*, p. 139. Krueger notes that the various versions of the Griselda story vary greatly in their emphasis upon the heroine's domestic activities. See Roberta L. Krueger, "Uncovering Griselda—Christine de Pizan, 'une seule chemise,' and the Clerical Tradition: Boccaccio, Petrarch, Philippe de Mézières and the Ménagier de Paris," in *Medieval Fabrications: Dress, Textiles, Clothwork, and Other Cultural Imaginings*, ed. E. Jane Burns (New York: Palgrave Macmillan, 2004), p. 79.
25. Stanbury, "Regimes of the Visual," p. 282.
26. See Robin Waugh, "Word, Breath, and Vomit: Oral Composition in Old English and Old Norse Literature," *Oral Tradition* 10 (1995): 359–86.
27. Also a motif of martyrdoms. See Andrea Rossi-Reder, "Embodying Christ, Embodying Nation: Ælfric's Accounts of Saints Agatha and Lucy," in *Sex and Sexuality in Anglo-Saxon England: Essays in Memory of Daniel Gillmore Calder*, ed. Carol Braun Pasternack and Lisa M. C. Weston (Tempe: Arizona Center for Medieval and Renaissance Studies, 2004), p. 188.
28. Wolfgang E. H. Rudat, *Earnest Exuberance in Chaucer's Poetic's: Textual Games in the Canterbury Tales* (Lewiston: Mellen, 1993), pp. 187–88.
29. Patricia Cramer, "Lordship, Bondage, and the Erotic: The Psychological Bases of Chaucer's 'Clerk's Tale,'" *Journal of English and Germanic Philology* 89 (1990): 497.
30. Allyson Newton, "The Occlusion of Maternity in Chaucer's *Clerk's Tale*," in *Medieval Mothering*, ed. John Carmi Parsons and Bonnie Wheeler (New York: Garland, 1996), pp. 67, 63–65.
31. Newton, "Occlusion of Maternity," p. 69.
32. Carolyn Dinshaw, *Chaucer's Sexual Poetics* (Madison: University of Wisconsin Press, 1989), p. 146; Alcuin Blamires, *The Case for Women in Medieval Culture* (Oxford: Clarendon Press, 1997), pp. 164–71.
33. Cramer, "Lordship, Bondage, and the Erotic," p. 497; Kristeva, *Desire in Language*, pp. 247; 281–86; *Tales of Love*, trans. Leon S. Roudiez (New York: Columbia University Press, 1987), pp. 246–59. Walter tries to reproduce Grisilde with his new bride, who is her inheritor through being Grisilde's daughter. In other words, Walter wants the most refined kind of male-centered reduplication of himself together with his love-object (counterfeit consciousness) by the elimination of any possibility of female, maternal education. The daughter (in his eyes) is a duplication of the satisfaction of his sexual desire and nothing more. Counterfeit consciousness also figures in the supposed sacrificing of Grisilde's children. See Kathy Lavezzo, "Chaucer and Everyday Death: *The Clerk's Tale*, Burial, and the Subject of Poverty," *Studies in the Age of Chaucer* 23 (2001): 269, 271.

NOTES 213

34. For the gazes of the lovers in *Troilus and Criseyde* more generally, see Stanbury, *Visual Object of Desire*, pp. 106–07.
35. See, for examples, Xavier F. Baron, "Chaucer's Troilus and Self-Renunciation in Love," *Papers on Literature and Language* 10 (1974): 5–14; and Michael Masi, "Troilus: A Medieval Psychoanalysis," *Annuale Medievale* 11 (1970): 81–88.
36. Lisa Manter, "The Savior of Her Desire: Margery Kempe's Passionate Gaze," *Exemplaria* 13 (2001):39–66. See also Robert Mills, "Seeing Face to Face: Troubled Looks in the Katherine Group," in *Troubled Vision: Gender, Sexuality and Sight in Medieval Text and Image*, ed. Emma Campbell and Robert Mills (New York: Palgrave Macmillan, 2004), pp. 117–36.
37. See Carolyn Dinshaw, *Getting Medieval: Sexualities and Communities, Pre- and Postmodern* (Durham, NC: Duke University Press, 1999), pp. 144–46.
38. See Sue Ellen Holbrook, "'About Her': Margery Kempe's Book of Feeling and Writing," in *The Idea of Medieval Literature: New Essays on Chaucer and Medieval Culture in Honor of Donald R. Howard*, ed. James M. Dean and Christian K. Zacher (Newark, NJ: University of Delaware Press, 1992), pp. 265–84.
39. Even the negative reactions to Margery tend to stress the idea of space. Upon witnessing her actions people often literally want to put distance between themselves and her (69). To go about one's business as if Margery were not present would be another way of reacting to her: presumably a difficult task, and of course a highly problematic and paradoxical task for any reader of her *Book*.
40. For a late thirteenth-century or early fourteenth-century devotional object that depicts the Virgin as a container of the Holy Trinity, see Caroline Walker Bynum, *Holy Feast and Holy Fast: The Religious Significance of Food to Medieval Women* (Berkeley: University of California Press, 1988), plate 13.
41. See Sarah Beckwith, *Christ's Body: Identity, Culture and Society in Late Medieval Writings* (New York: Routledge, 1993), p. 91.
42. Ruth Summar McIntyre, "Margery's 'Mixed Life': Place, Pilgrimage, and the Problem of Genre in *The Book of Margery Kempe*," *English Studies* 89 (2008): 650. Morrison describes Gilles Deleuze's and Félix Guattari's idea of "nomad space," "open-ended, enterable at any point, acentered, anti-hierarchical, multiple, open, without borders and in marginalized areas," as the kind of space Margery wants, but I see Margery as *embodying* this idea of nomad space, a leap Morrison does not make. See *Women Pilgrims*, p. 122, n. 65.
43. McIntyre, "Margery's 'Mixed Life,'" p. 656; Raguin, "Real and Imagined Bodies," pp. 122, 125. Margery also breaks down barriers between performer and audience in these spaces. See Morrison, *Women Pilgrims*, pp. 89–90.
44. See Herbert Thurston, "Margery the Astonishing," *The Month* 168 (1936): 446–56.

45. McIntyre, "Margery's 'Mixed Life,'" p. 656.
46. Raguin, "Real and Imagined Bodies," p. 123.
47. *Burial*, in *The Late Medieval Religious Plays of Bodleain MSS Digby 133 and E Museo 160*, ed. Donald C. Baker, John L. Murphy, and Louis B. Hall, Jr. (Oxford: Oxford University Press, 1982), line 637. See also pp. lxxxviii–xcv, n. 2, and *English Lyrics of the XIIIth Century*, ed. Carleton Brown (Oxford: Clarendon Press, 1932), Number 47, lines 8–9, and Number 49, lines 40–42, 46–48, 54.
48. See Dhira B. Mahoney, "Margery Kempe's Tears and the Power over Language," in *Margery Kempe: A Book of Essays*, ed. S. J. McEntire (New York: Garland, 1992), pp. 37–50.
49. See, for example, Sarah Beckwith, "A Very Material Mysticism: The Medieval Mysticism of Margery Kempe," in *Medieval Literature: Criticism, Ideology and History*, ed. David Aers (Sussex: Harvester, 1988), pp. 34–57.
50. The content of the monk's reaction demonstrates that, significantly, Margery's main problems for him are that she is movable and speaks.

INDEX

Note: Principal discussions are noted in bold.

Abraham (Bible)
  bargaining, 102
  gaze at Loth's wife, 97, 196n56
  inheritance, 93, 105, **107-8**
abstraction, 26, 32
Achilles Tatius, 17
Acta Sanctorum, 183n120
Acts of Literature (Derrida), 75
The Acts of Martyrs, 10, 15
Adam (Bible), 104, 106
The Adventures of Leucippe and Clitophon (Achilles Tatius), 17, 26
Aeneas, 15
Aesop, 195-6n50
Agatha (saint), 26, 27, 32, 115
Agnes (saint), 26, 27, 113-14
Alceste, 132
Alcuin, 92, 101-2, 105-6, 198n70, 207n51
Alfred (king), 194n35
Ælfric, 92, 100-1, 102, 103, 107, 194n34, 196-7n59, 198n72
Amaltheias-Keras (Job's daughter), 23
Ambrose (church father)
  Agnes, 113-14
  female line of knowledge, 46
  patience and clothing, 192n5
  pornographic aspects, 117, 201n10
  Saint Cecila, 164
  space in writing, 190n70
  see also *De Virginibus* (Ambrose)
Ammon (Lot's grandchild), 106
Andreas Capellanus, 121

Anistrude (nun), 73
Annals (Tacitus), 11
Antiochus (Roman authority figure), 19, 20
Antiquities (Josephus), 98
Apollonius of Tyre, 111
Apologeticum (Tertullian), 21, 24, 178n41
Arcadia (Pausanias), **21-3**
Artaxius (martyr), 57
artificiality
  cyborgs, 137, 139-40, 150, 205nn23, 49
  element of narratives, 26
"The Assumption of the Virgin" (Jacobus de Voragine), 118
athletic allegory, 190n74
  about, **13-14**
  Legenda Aurea, 114-15
  Perpetua, 49, 52-5, 55-6, 186nn21-22
  Roman space, 27-8
  Virgin of Antioch, 68
  women, 49
Augustine (saint), 4, 24, 93, 102, 196n51
authority. see break with authority
averted eyes. see gaze(s)

Bailey, Harry, 134, 154
Bakhtin, M. M., 3, 13, 15, 16, 157
Barthes, Roland, 22, 128, 182n107
Bede, 95, 101, 194nn30, 38, 195n45, 197n66, 198n73

belief identification
  Blandina, 13, 14, 34
  defined, **26**
  Griselda legend, 135
  martyrs, 9
  Passio Sanctarum Perpetuae et Felicitatis, **39–43**, 48, 181n94
  patience literature, 9
  suffering, 9
Beowulf, 110, 200n89
Bernabo (character), 139
Bhabha, Homi K., 33
Biggs, Frederick M., 194n34
Blandina (martyr), 4, **11–13**
  Dialogue Portion, 12
  egalitarian ideas, 153
  fame of, 24
  heroic values, **14**, **15**, 20–1
  Legenda Aurea, 115, 119
  martyrdom of, 28, 60, 68, 140
  motherhood, **18–21**
  space, 28
  undercutting of, 19
  within literary tradition, 23
blood
  blood as milk, 46, 197n61
  Lot's wife, 99, 197n60
Bloom, Harold, 142
Boccaccio, Giovanni, 133, 139, 143
Book of Margery Kempe (Kempe)
  analysis of, 1, 36
  patience literature, **157–9**, **172–3**
  prison, 211n20
  suffering, 157–9, 210n5
  visionary paralysis, 35, 163, 168, 171–2, 173
  women and the Shrine, 162, 163, **168–73**
  see also Kempe, Margery
Book of Revelation, 45
The Book of the City of Ladies (Christine de Pizan), 133–4, **138–9**, 144
  see also Gliselidis (Christine's character)
The Book of the Duchess (Chaucer), 131

Boyarin, Daniel, 190n68
Braswell, Laurel, 3
break with authority
  defined, **25–6**
  Loth's wife, 81, 87, 100, 107–8, 195nn41, 45
  patience literature, 24
  Perpetua, 37–8, 43–4, **56–8**
  romance genre, 37
  Sarra, 107–9
  Vitae Columbani, 72
  compare egalitarian ideas; power structures
breast-feeding, 40, 45–6, 54
Brody, Saul Nathaniel, 3
brothels
  as By Way, 63
  introduction of, **27**
  Irenê, 31
  Virgin of Antioch, 63–6
  compare By Ways; sexuality; space
Brown, Peter, 200n88
Burgundofara (royal abbess), **71–4**
Burrus, Virginia, 13–14, 57, 60, 64–5, 68, 70
Butler, Judith, 1
Butler, Rex, 55
By Ways
  defined, **27**
  female protagonists, 44
  Griselda legend, 145
  Loth's wife, 82
  Margery Kempe, 168–9
  Perpetua, 43, 44, 181n94
  prisons, 181n93, 211n20
  Second Nun's Tale, 163–4
  compare brothels; space

The Canterbury Tales (Chaucer), 134, 165–6
  order of, 141
  retraction, 204n17
  see also Chaucer, Geoffrey; *The Clerk's Tale* (Chaucer)
Cassia (Job's daughter), 23
Castelli, Elizabeth A., 29, 38, 55, 57, 156

castration, 117
Cazelles, Brigitte, 126
Cecilia (saint)
    abstraction, 26
    chastity, 27
    churches, 160, 196n57, 211n12
    gender inequality, 32
    inheritance, 153, 164
    musical language, 32, 119
    Second Nun's Tale, **163–5**
Cecilie (character), **163–5**
Cecilie, inheritance, 164
Chaucer, Geoffrey
    The Book of the Duchess, 131
    Eastern icons, 211n15
    Griselda legend, 155
    hagiography, 208n56
    impatience, 133
    The Legend of Good Women, 3, 33, **131–3**, 142, 162
    The Man of Law's Tale, 7, 131, 134, 139, 141
    The Merchant's Tale, 37
    patience literature, 131–2, 132, 142
    The Physician's Tale, 131
    Prioress's Tale, **119–20**, 201n18
    satire, 120, 132–3, 137, 140–2, 145, 146, 152–3, 156, 201n20, 204n14
    Second Nun's Tale, 131, 139, **163–5**, 211n21
    Tale of Melibee, 5–6, 131, 139, 141
    Troilus and Criseyde, 131, **167–8**
    women and the Shrine, 159, **162–7**
    see also *The Canterbury Tales* (Chaucer); *The Clerk's Tale* (Chaucer)
cheese, 45, 186nn25, 27
childbirth comparison, martyrs, 15–16
Childress, Diana T., 3
chora, 185n10
Chrétien de Troyes
    satire, 124, 202n10
    see also *Cligés* (Chrétien de Troyes)
Christ
    cyborg nature, 205n23
    Lot's wife, 101, 103, 196n58
    Perpetua, 59, 188n46
    sexuality, 168
    as virgin, 46
Christianity
    birth imagery, 15–16, 50, 187n41
    Christian language, 48
    egalitarian ideas, 10–11
    heritage of, 46, 50–1
    oral modes of thought, 8
    public space, 28
    saints and civic authority, 200n88
    use of "Christian," **41–2**
    visions, 44
Christina (martyr), 21, 46
Christine de Pizan, 1, 133–4, 204n17, 205n33
    Griselda legend, 155
    on patience, 138
    satire, 142, 145, 146
    source for, 206–7n44
churches, **160–1**, 164, 196n57, 211n12
Cicero, 22, 194n35
Cixous, Hélène, 22, 29–30, 31
class. *see* egalitarian ideas
Cleanness, 87, 95
Clement of Alexandria, 45, 46
Clement of Rome, 10, 12, 92, 95
The Clerk's Tale (Chaucer), 149–51
    definition of patience, 5
    fame, 2–4
    Griselda legend, **133–7**, 155–6
    iconography of, 36
    patience figures, 23
    patience literature, 9, 131, 133–4, 138
    satire, 36
    the Shrine, 162
    songs, 141, 205n27
    source for, 206–7n44
    see also Chaucer, Geoffrey; Grisilde (Chaucer's character); Walter (Chaucer's character)
Cligés (Chrétien de Troyes)
    intervention, **126–9**
    as profeminine work, 36
    see also Chrétien de Troyes; Fénice (empress)

218 INDEX

Cligés (titular character), 121–2, 123, 129
clothing
  Griselda legend, 136, 145–6
  Margery Kempe, 168
  patience as, 192n4, 192n5
  Perpetua, 52–4, 186n21
  sexual conquest, 190n75
  transvestite saints, 62
  Virgin of Antioch, 64–6, 68–70, 190–1n83
Colgrave, Bertram, 183n114
complexity (growth of), **26**
conquered demon story, 5
Corinthians, 52
counterfeit consciousness
  egalitarian ideas, **31–3**, **35**, 133
  Fénice, 124
  Griselde, 134, 152, 212n33
  Legenda Aurea, 117, 132–3
  Prioress's Tale, **119–20**, 201n18
  compare mimicry; repetition syndrome
courtly love, 8, 66, 121–2, 124–6
court records. *see* Dialogue Portion
Cramer, Patricia, 165
Criseyde (character), 9, 167–8
Crispina (martyr), 10
Custance (character), 7, 134, 139, 141, 205n30
cyborgs, 137, 139–40, 150, 205nn23, 49
Cynewulf, 110
Cyprian (church father), 6, 24, 194n32

Daly, Emily Joseph, 180n79, 191n3
Dame Prudence (character), 5
de bono patientiae (Cyprian), 24
Decameron (Boccaccio), 139
Delany, Sheila, 29, 204n14
Delehaye, Hippolyte, 183n115
Deleuze, Gilles, 213n42
de Nie, Giselle, 45, 54, 187n28, 188n44
de patientia (Augustine), 24
de patientia (Tertullian), 24, 75, **76–80**
Derrida, Jacques
  history of patience, 4–5
  power relationships, 18

  theories of language, 75, 182n104
  theory of desire, 8, 30
desire
  Derrida's theories, 8, 30
  Griselda, 135–7
  Grisilde (Chaucer's character), 135–7, 162–3, 206n36
  Loth's wife, 98, **100–4**, 196n58, 197n66
  Walter (Chaucer's character), 135–6, 154, **165–7**, 203n11, 206–7n44, 208n53, 212n33
  compare sexuality
Desire in Language (Kristeva), 167
Dialogia (Gregory), 24
Dialogic Imagination (Bakhtin), 3
Dialogue Portion
  Blandina, 12
  defined, **25**, 26
  Felicitas (martyr), 38
  judicial hearings, 181n94
  marriage disputes, 25
  Passio Sanctarum Perpetuae et Felicitatis, 38
  see also judicial hearings
Dinocrates (Perpetua's brother), 48–9, 50, 57, 59, 185n8, 189n58
Dinshaw, Carolyn, 148, 149
divine language, 73
Doane, A. N., 80
Dodds, E. R., 186n27
Domna (nun), 73
doubling. *see* mimicry

The Earliest Life of Gregory the Great (Colgrave), 183n114
Easton, Martha, 116–17
ecstatic languages, 32
Edden, Valerie, 3
egalitarian ideas
  Blandina, 12, 153
  Christianity, 10–11, 18, 30
  Christine de Pizan, 138–9
  counterfeit consciousness, **31–3**, **35**, 133
  de Patientia, 78

gender order, 62
glimpses in literature, 182n104
Griselda legend, 139–40
martyrologies, 11, 178n43
saints' lives, **30**
statis motif, 34
Tertullian, 10, 178n41, 192n8
Virgin of Antioch, 69–71
Vitae Columbani, 72–3
compare break with authority; power structures
the Egyptian, 52–4, 56, 59
Eleazar (martyr), 16, 19–20
Elene (Cynewulf), 110
endurance. see *hypomonê*
Epistola I (Jerome), 18
Ercantrude (nun), 71–2
Eugenia (martyr), 115, 188n44
Eulalia (saint), 114, 118
Eusebius of Caesarea, 11, 12, 14, 24
expressive power
automatic speech, 48
biting out tongue, **21–3**, 180n81
Grisilde, 135
Lot/Loth story, 91–7, 96, 106
Margery Kempe, 168–71, 213n39, 214n50
Marian sorrow, 171
Perpetua, **45–7, 48–9, 51**, 96
Prioress's Tale, 119–20
Sarrah, **107–9**
subversivenss of, 110
Virgin of Antioch, 191n87
writing with the body, **21–3**
compare language

fame
de Patientia, 76
evolution of attitudes, 24
Griselda legend, 2–4, 147
Lot's daughters, 106
patience literature, 1
Perpetua, 55
reputation, 2–3, 14–15
sources of, 1
women, 1

family
authority in Roman Empire, 181n94
impact on, 47
Perpetua, 41–2
Farrell, Thomas J., 145, 182n109
Felicitas (martyr)
Dialogue Portion, 38
martyrdom, 53–4, 59–60, 68
motherhood and inheritance, 50–1, **60–1**, 115
Felicity (saint), 118, 153
Felix, Minucius, 10
female protagonists
By Ways, 44
hagiography, 7, 201nn11, 13
Legenda Aurea, **116–19**
martyrologies, **9–11**
Passio Sanctarum Perpetuae et Felicitatis, 37
secular hagiography, 7
Tertullian, 192n4
feminism
feminist methodology, **28–30**
l'écriture féminine, **28–30**, 31
temporal context, 29, 182n104, 188n51
Tertullian, 190n2
feminist methodology
Passio Sanctarum Perpetuae et Felicitatis, criticism of masculinist traditions in, **55–6**
readings of Chaucer, 205n26
Fénice (empress)
counterfeit consciousness, 124
courtly love, 121–2, 124–6
desire, 121–2, 123
Griselda legend, 121
martrydom, 122–6
passivity, 140
patience figures, 128
stasis motif, 124–5, 126, 136, 159, 173
see also *Cligés* (Chrétien de Troyes)
fertility. *see* inheritance
film screening, 36, 168

Foucault, Michel, 17–18, 22
Frantzen, Allen J., 87, 198n74, 199n80
Frese, Dolores Warwick, 198n73
Friedman, Susan Stanford, 12

Galatians, 62
gaze(s)
    Abraham, 97, 196n56
    averted eyes imagery, 160–2, 211n12
    the daisy, 162
    female saints, 160, 210n7
    Griselda legend, 136, 143–4, 147–51, 153–4, 156, 162–3, 206nn35–36, 207n47
    language, 28
    Lot/Loth's wife, 81–2, 86–7, 91–2, 98–102, 108–9, 195nn41, 45
    Margery Kempe, 168–9
    Perpetua, 53–4, 59
    power of, 167
    screen theory, 36, 168
    Stanbury on, 162, 167, 207n46
    Troilus, 167
    Virgin Mary, 160, 210n10
    Virgin of Antioch, 63, 190–1n84
    compare imagery
gendering
    class issues, 12
    de Patientia, 76–9
    development of, **26–7**
    heroic values, **14–15**
    hypomonê, 17
    Legenda Aurea, 117–18
    Lot's wife, 36
    patience, 134, 134–5
    reputations, **2–3**
    saints' lives, 24
    statis motif, **34–5**
    suffering, **17–18**, 173
    compare women
gender order
    Cligés, **126–9**
    egalitarian ideas, 62
    inequality, Cecilia (saint), 32
    Lot's daughters, 106
    saints' lives, 39, 61
    sex-distinguishing punishments, **31–2**, 59–60, 68
    transvestite saints, 62
    Virgin of Antioch, 63–4
gender roles
    de Patientia, 79
    Legenda Aurea, 117
    masculine identity, 181n91
    Passio Sanctarum Perpetuae et Felicitatis, 52–5
    passivity as role, 9, 134
    patience (virtue), 167
    saints' lives, 61
Genesis (Old Testament), 80
Genesis A
    dating of, 80
    expansions of Vulgate-Genesis, 80
    patience figures, 76
    punishments, 102, 103
    see also Loth's wife (*Genesis A*)
Gliselidis (Christine's character), 139, **143–7**, 154, 163
    see also Book of the City of Ladies (Christine de Pizan)
glory. *see* fame
God
    de Patientia, patience figures, 78–9
    Griselda legend, 155
    language, 81, 91–2
    patience figures, 78–9
    plans of, 176n17
    source of all knowledge, 45–6
Godden, Malcolm R., 101, 102, 106, 107, 199n80
Gregory the Great, 9, 24, 33
Grimbert, Joan Tasker, 129, 202n14
Griselda legend, 1–2
    belief identification, 135
    The Book of the City of Ladies, 133–4
    The Clerk's Tale, **133–7**
    counterfeit consciousness, 134, 152, 212n33
    desire, 135–7
    domestic space, 139–40, 212n24

Fénice (empress), 121
heroic virtues, 145
patience as female, 134–5
patience figures, 152, 152–3
Petrarch, 133, 141, 143–5, 147, 155, 203n10, 206–7n44
popularity of, 152, 158
repetition syndrome, 152
the Shrine, 163
stasis motif, 135–7, 159, 173
suffering, 135
Griseldis (Petrarch's character), 143, 144, 150
Grisilde (Chaucer's character), 1
artificiality/cyborg nature, 139–40, 150, 204n13
as art object, **153–6**
casting out of, 3, 151, 155, 166
Clerk's sympathy for, 149
connection with saints, 7
counterfeit consciousness, 134, 212n33
death of, **141–2**
desire, 135–7, 162–3, 206n36
exemplarity of, **152–3**, 208n60
objectification of women, 29, 144–5, 150, 156
patience figure, 4, 5, 6–7, 134, 208n53
pseudo-saints, 3–4
the Shrine, **165–7**, 170, 206n41
virtue of, 147, 148
vow to Walter, 144, 146
see also *Clerk's Tale* (Chaucer)
Gualtier (Christine's character), 139, 143, 144–5, 146, 147
Guattari, Félix, 213n42

hagiography, 3
belief identification, **26**
Book of Margery Kempe, 157–8
Chaucer, 3–4, 5–7, 131–2, 208n56
endurance, 16
female protagonists, 7, 201nn11, 13
heroic vitures, **13–16**

Miracles of the Virgin, 118–19
other genres, 2, 17
compare patience literature
Hahn, Cynthia, 159
Hanna, Ralph, III, 9, 177n35
Haraway, Donna, 137, 140
Harries, Martin, 87, 94, 103, 196n58
heaven
By Ways, 164
gender, 68
Perpetua, 45, 57, 188n46, 189n61
Heffernan, Carol, 211n15
Helena (saint), 164
Hemera (Job's daughter), 23
Heptateuch, 92, 196n56
heroic values
Blandina, 14, 15, 20–1
fame, 1
gendering, 17
Griselda legend, 145
hagiography, **13–16**
martyrs, 15, 22
patience literature, 23–4
Perpetua, 55–6
Hilarianus (governor), 47
Historia Ecclesia (Eusebius of Caesarea), 11, 12
History of Sexuality, 17–18
Holy House of Nazareth, 163, 210–11n10
honey, 45, 186n26
Huppé, Bernard, 101
Hurley, Margaret, 3
hypomonê
first appearance of noun, 16
gendering, **17–18**
patience literature, 7–8, 23–4
shift towards, **16–17**
see also suffering

identity
masculine identity, 59, 181n91
Perpetua (Vibia Perpetua) (martyr), 42
Ignatius of Antioch, 16, 179n67

imagery
  athletic imagery, 50
  averted eyes, 160–2, 211n12
  blood as milk, 46
  breast-feeding, 40, **45–6**, 54
  Christ-like, 188n46
  Eastern icons, 211n15
  executions, 117
  Father-with-breasts, **45–6**
  of the feminine, 42
  Griselda legend, 149
  inheritance, 199n79
  Lot text, **83–4**, **84–92**, 98–9, 100, 193nn21, 25-28, 197n62, 197n67, 199n80
  Margery Kempe, 172
  vases and waterpots, 42, 145, 154, 165, 185–6nn15, 17, 186n19
  compare gaze(s)
impatience
  Chaucer, 133
  2 Maccabees, 20
  sin of, 176n17
  compare patience
inheritance
  Cecilia, 153, 164
  Felicitas, 50–1, 115
  Felicity [mentioned in passing], 153
  female line of knowledge, 46, 49–50, 116, 153, 188n44, 212n33
  female saints, 153
  imagery, 199n79
  Job's daughters, 23, **104–5**
  Lucy [mentioned in passing], 153
  Paula [mentioned in passing], 153
  phantom inheritance, 35
Interrogationes Sigewulf Presbyteri (Alcuin/Ælfric), 92, 101, 102
Irenaeus (c. 180), 95–6
Irenê (saint), 27, 31

Jacobo (saint), 115
Jacobus de Voragine
  etymologies of saint's names, 200n5
  Roman authorities, 124
  Saint Lucy source, 183n120
  see also *Legenda Aurea* (Jacobus de Voragine)
"James the Dismembered," 115–16
Jerome (saint), 18, 117, 185n17, 185–6n17, 191n87, 194n35
Job (Bible)
  de Patientia, 76, 77
  family legacy, 23, 104
  Job's daughters, 23, 32, 35
  proverbial patience figure of, 6, 23
  Vitae Columbani, 71
  women as inheritors of, 23
  see also *The Testament of Job*
John (Margery's husband), 171, 172
Jonas of Bobbio, 71–3
Josephus, 98
Jucundus (martyr), 57
judicial hearings
  Dialogue Portion, 181n94
  Passio Sanctarum Perpetuae et Felicitatis, 181n94
  see also Dialogue Portion
Julian of Norwich, 35

Karkov, Catherine E., 199n79
Katherine of Alexandria, 26
Kempe, Margery
  expressive power, 168–71, 213n39, 214n50
  the Shrine, 159
  space, 213nn39, 42-43
  see also *Book of Margery Kempe* (Kempe)
Kidd, Peter, 193n25
Kirk, Elizabeth D., 28
knowledge
  female line of, 46, 49–50, 116, 153, 188n44, 212n33
  Prioress's Tale, 119–20
  source of, 45–6
  women's tradition, 181–2n104
Kraemer, Ross Shepard, 38
Kristeva, Julia
  on language, 39–41, 43, 48, 50, 72, 167, 185n10
  sacrifice for family, 47

space, time and separation, 82, 97, 159
Krueger, Roberta L., 212n24
Kuefler, Mathew, 62

Lacan, Jacques, 28, 96–7
Langland, William, 191n1
language
  Christian language, 48
  Derrida's theories of, 75, 182n104
  divine language, 73
  ecstatic languages, 32
  feminine language, 39–40, 43–4, 46, 47, 73–4, 208–9n63, 210n5
  forms of address, 56
  gaze, 28
  God, 81, 91–2
  language acquisition, 39–40, 49, 50, 165–7
  oral vs. written language, 8, 97, 99, 196n55
  paternal function of, 41
  poetic language, 43
  semen and speech, 45, 95, 186n27
  symbolic language, 40–1
  transformational language, 39–43, 97, 185n15
  compare expressive power
Laurence (saint), 114–15
Leaena (martyr), **21–3**
Legenda Aurea (Jacobus de Voragine), 200n6
  abstraction, 26
  apex of patience literature, 8, 30, **113–14**
  contest between saints, 134
  counterfeit consciousness, 117, 132–3
  female patience figures, **116–19**
  gender roles, 117
  James the Dismembered, 115–16
  patience attributes, **114–16**
  stasis motif, **33–4**
  suffering, 135
  Virgin Mary, 118
  Virgin of Antioch, 62
  see also Jacobus de Voragine

The Legend of Good Women (Chaucer), 3, 33, **131–3**, 142, 162
Lerer, Seth, 148, 207n47
lesbian relationships, 60
Levinas, Emmanuel, 30
Le Livre de la cité des dames. see *Book of the City of Ladies*
Lot (Old Testament), 101, 102, 105–6, 194n36, 199n80
  see also Loth (*Genesis A*)
Loth (*Genesis A*), 80, 85, 86, 96, 97
  see also Lot (Old Testament)
Loth's daughters, 84–5, 97, 102, **104–7**, 109, 111, 198n68, 199n80
Loth's wife (*Genesis A*)
  Abraham, 97, 196n56
  break with authority, 81, 87, 100, 107–8, 195nn41, 45
  By Ways, 82
  desire, 98, 196n58, 197n66
  frozen speaker, 96, 170
  Genesis A story, 80–2
  imagery of, **84–92**, 98–9, 100, 193nn21, 25-28, 197nn62, 67
  interpretations of, **83–4**
  Old English tradition, **80–2**
  paralysis, 81–2, 94–7
  patience figures, 76, 80, 104, 111–12
  place, 96–7, **98–100**, **109–11**, 196–7n59
  poet's work on, 199n77
  punishment of, 102
  symbolic role, **91–4**, 103
  transformation, 81–2, 91, 94–100, 103, 109, 195nn41, 43, 50
  see also Genesis A; Lot's wife (Old Testament)
Lot's wife (Old Testament)
  desire, **100–4**
  first appearance of, 80
  gendering, 36
  landscape, 98, **98–100**, 196n51
  Margery Kempe, 173
  passion figures, 36, 171, 198n68
  the Shrine, 159, 163

224 INDEX

Lot's wife (Old Testament)—*Continued*
   transformation, 84, 93, 95–6, 99,
      173, 193n20, 195–6n50, 197n60,
      198n68
   De Virginibus, 92
   see also Loth's wife (*Genesis A*)
Lucy (saint)
   chastity, 27
   inheritance, 153
   Jacobus's source for, 183n120
   mimicry, 34, 135, 137, 183n122
   stasis motif, **33–4**, **35**, 124,
      125–6, 159
   visionary paralysis, 173

2 and 4 Maccabees, 14, **18–21**, 22–3,
   117–18, 180n77
mægða sið, 104–7, 111
Mann, Jill, 209n68
The Man of Law's Tale (Chaucer), 7,
   131, 134, 139, 141
Manter, Lisa, 168
marriage disputes
   Dialogue Portion, 25
   *Passio Sanctarum Perpetuae et
      Felicitatis*, 181n94
martyrdom
   Blandina, 28
   crown of, 114
   de Patientia, 78
   Fénice, 122–6
   Irenê, 31
   narrative mechanic of, **26**
   *Passio Sanctarum Perpetuae et
      Felicitatis*, 49–52, 53–4, 57,
      189nn59, 60
   Saint Cecilia, 164
   Virgin of Antioch, 69–70
martyrologies
   Blandina, **11–13**
   egalitarian ideas, 11, 178n43
   fact and fiction, 25
   female protagonists, **9–11**
   patience (virtue), 18
   prisons, 181n93
   study of, 3
   virgin martyrs, 34–5
   see also saints' lives
martyrs
   belief identification, 9
   bodies of martyrs, 113–14, 182n107
   childbirth comparison, 15–16
   Christian historical traditions, 18
   classical comparisons, 14
   Griselda, 137
   growth of cults, 24
   heroic values, 15, 22
   Leaena and, 21
   martyrs of love, 131–2
   virtue of patience, 4
"The Martyrs of Lyon and Vienne,"
   12–13, 15, 28
Mary (Virgin), 121, 213n40
   gaze of, 160
   Holy House of Nazareth, 160, 163,
      210–11n10
   Legenda Aurea, 118
   Margery Kempe, 163, 171, 172
   Miracles of the Virgin, 118–19
   Prioress's Tale, 119–20
Mary Magdalene, 103
masculinity
   de Patientia, 79–80
   Loth's wife, 100
   masculine identity, 59, 181n91
   Psychomachia, 79–80
   Virgin of Antioch, 64–5, 70
   compare men
masculinization
   Perpetua, 53–5, 69
   Virgin of Antioch, 68–71
Matthew (apostle), 157
Maurus, Rabanus, 98
McClellan, William, 142
McInerney, Maud, 34, 63, 117, 118,
   188n47, 191nn85, 87
McIntyre, Ruth Summar, 170
McKinley, Kathryn, 3, 204n13
medieval romance genre. *see* romance
   genre

Melibee (character), 5, 6
men
    domination of, **56–60**
    fame, 1
    language, 40–1
    male discourse, *Passio Sanctarum Perpetuae et Felicitatis*, 48–9
    passivity as choice, 9
    search element, **26**
    compare masculinity
The Merchant's Tale (Chaucer), 37
milk, 45, 186n25
mimicry
    character repetition, 61
    Lucy (saint), 34, 135, 137, 183n122
    Passio Sanctarum Perpetuae et Felicitatis, 51, 61
    Perpetua, 38
    saints' lives, **33**
    compare counterfeit consciousness; repetition syndrome
Moab (Lot's grandchild), 106
moral amnesia, 30, 31, 117
Morrison, Signe, 213n42
Morse, Charlotte C., 208n57
Moses (Bible), 103
motherhood
    Blandina and 2/4 Maccabees, **18–21**
    heritage of the mother, 50–1
    language, 39–40
    Perpetua (martyr), 39, **60–1**
    pregnancy and martyrdom, 50
    semiotic language, 39–40, 49, 50
    compare women
Mulvey, Laura, 36, 162, 168
musical language, Cecilia (saint), 32
Musonius Rufus, 17
Musurillo, Herbert, 176n16

naming
    Loth's daughters, 106
    Perpetua, 40–2, 43–4, 53, 186n22
narcissism, 47, 66
Naturalis historia (Pliny the Elder), **21–3**

Newton, Allyson, 166
Niobe, 96, 195n50

Old Testament
    Book of Job, 23
    Lot's wife, 84
    patience figures, 76
    suffering, 80
    sweetness in the mouth, 45
    written texts, 196n55
oral modes of thought, 8
Orth, William, 119

paralysis
    about, **35**
    Legenda Aurea, 117
    Loth's wife, 81–2, 94–7
    Passio Sanctarum Perpetuae et Felicitatis, 47
    compare stasis motif
Paschasius, 33–4
passion figures, Lot's wife (Old Testament), 36, 171
Passion of Lucy, 35
passios
    academic neglect of, 184n2
    description of martyrs, 4
    heroic rhetoric, **13–16**
Passio Sanctarum Perpetuae et Felicitatis, 37
    about, 37
    art, 42
    athletic imagery, 49
    belief identification, 39–43, 48, 181n94
    break with authority, 37–8, 43–4, **56–8**
    By Ways and space, 43, 43–4, 44, 181n94, 185n14, 211n20
    dating of, 37
    Dialogue Portion, 38
    feminine language, 39–40
    gender, 52–5, **55–6**, **56–60**
    judicial hearings, 181n94
    male discourse, 48–9
    marriage disputes, 181n94

Passio Sanctarum Perpetuae et Felicitatis—Continued
  martyrdom portion, 49–52, 53–4, 57, 189nn59, 60
  mimicry, 51, 61
  naming, 40–2, 43–4, 53, 186n22
  prayer, 48–9
  protofeminism of, 36, 38–9
  vase debate, 39–43, 185nn15, 17
  visions, **45–7**, **48–9**, **51**, 53–4, 55, 57–8, 186n20, 188n46, 189nn55, 59, 60, 62
  compare Roman Empire; *see also* Perpetua (Vibia Perpetua) (martyr)
patience (virtue)
  Chaucer, 138
  Christine de Pizan, 138
  Clerk's Tale, 2–4
  conquered demon story, 5
  definition of, 4–5
  difficulty of establishing, 15, 20
  gendering, 134, 134–5
  gender roles, 167
  Legenda Aurea, **114–16**
  martyrologies, 18
  medieval tradition of, **4–7**
  miraculous nature of, 6–7
  negative establishment of, 4
  patientia corporis, Leaena, 22
  proof of, 4
  righteous patience, about, **5–6**
  compare impatience
patience figures
  de patientia (Tertullian), 75, **76–80**
  Fénice, 128
  Genesis A, 76
  God, 78–9
  Griselda legend, 4–7, 134, 152–3, 208n53
  Job, 6, 23
  Legenda Aurea, **116–19**
  Lot/Loth's wife, 36, 76, 80, 104, 111–12
  as male, 191n1
  medieval tradition, **4–7**, 75–6

  popularity of, 32
  pseudo-saints, 3–4
  Psychomachia, 75–6, 79–80
  representations of the virtue, 3
  Vitae Columbani, 71–3
patience literature
  ability to endure, **7–8**
  birth of genre, **23–4**
  Book of Margery Kempe, **157–9**, **172–3**
  Chaucer, 132, 142
  Christine de Pizan, 138
  The Clerk's Tale (Chaucer), 131, 133–4, 138
  counterfeit consciousness, **31–3**
  functioning of genre, 8
  gendering, **8–9**
  as genre, **1–2**, 80
  mechanics of, **24–7**
  compare hagiography; satire
Patientia (character), 75–6, 79
patriarchy, 29
  Grisilde, 137, 165–6
  inheritance, 104–5
Patterson, Lee, 119
Paul (apostle), 34
Paula (saint), 116, 153
Pausanias, 21, 22, 180n82
Peristephanon (Prudentius), 114, 118
Perkins, Judith
  Christian community, 28
  Perpetua, 37–8, 54, 55, 56
  self as sufferer, 7, 8, 16–17
  significance of martyrs, 18
Perpetua (Vibia Perpetua) (martyr)
  emotions of, 47–8
  expressive power of, 96
  fame, 55
  identity, 42
  later influences of, 62
  leadership role of, 47, 52–3, 54
  Legenda Aurea, 115–16
  mimicry, 38
  motherhood, 39, **60–1**
  sex change of, **52–5**, 186nn21-22, 188nn45-47
  space, 211n20

see also *Passio Sanctarum Perpetuae et Felicitatis*
Petrarch, Francis
   Griselda legend, 133, 141, 143–5, 147–50, 155, 203n10, 206–7n44, 47
   rule of God and man, 138
The Physician's Tale (Chaucer), 131
Piers Plowman (Langland), 191n1
place. *see* space
Plato, 185n10
Pliny the Elder, 21
Pliny the Younger, 10, 11
Pluto (character), 37
Polycarp (martyr), 26, 28
Pomponia Graecina, 11, 15
Pomponius (deacon), 52–3, 58, 59, 189n62
Ponticus (martyr), 20
Potamiaena (martyr), 15
power structures
   counterfeit consciousness, **31–3**
   and Leaena, **21–3**
   patience literature, 24
   patriarchy, 29
   sexuality, **22–3**
   compare break with authority; egalitarian ideas
prayer
   ecstatic language, 73
   Passio Sanctarum Perpetuae et Felicitatis, 48–9, 186n20
   pregnancy and martyrdom, 50
   Virgin of Antioch, 63
Prioress's Tale (Chaucer), **119–20**, 201n18
prisons
   By Ways, 181n93
   Margery Kempe, 211n20
   martyrologies, 181n93
   Perpetua, 211n20
profeminine work, *Cligés* (Chrétien de Troyes), 36
Proserpine (character), 37
prostitutes
   brothels, 27, 31, 63–6
   Leaena, 21–3, 180nn81-82

protofeminism
   de Patientia, 79
   The Passion of Perpetua and Felicitas, 36
   Passio Sanctarum Perpetuae et Felicitatis, 36, 38–9
pseudo-saints, 3–4
Psychomachia (Prudentius), patience figures, 75–6, 79–80

Quilligan, Maureen, 139

Raguin, Virginia Chieffo, 170
Ramsey, Boniface, 190n70
Reames, Sherry L., 183n115
Rebecca, 185–6n17
reductio ad absurdum. *see* satire
Regulae Pastoralis (Gregory), 24
Remley, Paul G., 80
repetition syndrome
   bodies of martyrs, 182n107
   Griselda legend, 152
   repeating events, 61
   saints' lives, **30**, 35, 183nn114, 116
   compare counterfeit consciousness; mimicry
reputation. *see* fame
Richards, Earl Jeffrey, 204n16
Riedinger, Anita R., 111
romance genre
   break with authority, 37
   Chrisine de Pizan, 146–7
   relationship to hagiography, 17
   saints' lives, 3
Roman Empire
   egalitarian ideas, 10–11, 178n41
   family authority, 181n94
   gender and politics, 37
   gendering of virtues, 17
   self-understanding, 7–8
   space, 27–8
   compare Passio Sanctarum Perpetuae et Felicitatis
Ronsse, Erin, 38, 42, 49, 50, 51, 184n2
Rousselle, Robert, 189n55
Rudat, Wolfgang, 165

Sainted Women of the Dark Ages
(McNamara, Halborg, and
Whatley, eds.), 74
saints
  civic authority, 200n88
  patience attributes, **114–16**
  pseudo-saints, 3–4
saints' lives
  difficulty of patience, 15
  gendering, 24
  gender order, 39
  gender roles, 61
  medieval romance genre, 3
  mimicry, **33**
  repetition syndrome, **30**, 35,
    183nn114, 116
  statis motif, **33–4**, 135
  see also martyrologies
Sanctus (martyr), 11, 34
Sanok, Catherine, 210n5
Sarra (Abraham's wife), 81, 105,
  107–9, 111
satire
  Chaucer, 120, 132–3, 137, 140–2,
    145, 146, 152–3, 156, 201n20,
    204n14
  Chrétien de Troyes, 124,
    202n10
  Christine de Pizan, 142, 145, 146
  Margery Kempe, 210n5
  patience literature, 1
  compare patience literature
Saturninus (martyr), 57, 115
Saturus (martyr), 38, 56, 57, 58, 115,
  189nn59-61
search, **26**
Second Nun's Tale (Chaucer), 131, 139,
  163–5, 211n21
secular hagiography.
  see hagiography
self-consciousness, 26
semen, 45, 93, 186n27
semiotic language, 39–40, 49, 50
Seneca, 17
Severs, J. Burke, 144
sex change

Perpetua, **52–5**, 186nn21-22,
  188nn45-47
Virgin of Antioch, 66–8
sexuality
  Christ, 168
  clothing, 190n75
  erotic fantasy/assault, 186n19
  erotic stasis, 117
  Foucault on, 17–18
  Genesis A, 81
  lesbian relationships, 60
  Loth, 97, 98, 102, 198n68, 199n80
  Margery Kempe, 171–2
  phallic symbols, 189n55
  pornographic aspects, 117, 201n10
  power structures, **22–3**
  self-castration, 180n81
  Sodomites, 198nn72, 74,
    199nn80, 86
  statis motif, **33–4**
  taste in the mouth, 45
  Virgin of Antioch, 63–9
  visions, 45
  compare desire
Shaw, Brent D.
  ability to endure, 7, 8, 16, 17, 18, 20
  Blandina, 12
  egalitarian ideas, 10
  Foucault's ideas, 17–18
  on gender, 9, 11, 14, 17
  heroic values, 14, 22
  patience as clothing, 192n4
  Perpetua, 39, 59–60
  public shaming, 28
  relationships between works, 23
  the Shrine
    Book of Margery Kempe, 162, 163,
      168–73
    Chaucer's works, **162–7**, **165–7**,
      167–8
    context of, 36
    feminine language, 210n7
    Griselda legend, 163, **165–7**
    innovation and, 36
    Shrine to the Virgin, 160
    space and, 27

women, **159–62**, 210n9
compare space
Sodoma (anon), 95, 194n32, 195nn40, 47, 197n60
Sodom and Gomorrah, 80, 87, 94–8, 101–9, 193n28, 196n59, 198nn68, 72, 74, 199nn80, 86
Song of Songs, 45
space
   brothels, **27**, 31, 63–6
   domestic space, 44, 117, **162–3**, 185n14, 210–11n10, 212n24
   language as space, 41
   Lot/Loth's wife, 96–7, **98–100**, **109–11**, 196–7n59
   Margery Kempe, 213nn39, 42
   patience figures, 75
   patience literature, **27–8**
   Perpetua, 43–4, 211n20
   writings of Ambrose, 190n70
   compare brothels; By Ways; the Shrine
Stanbury, Sarah, 159–60, 162, 165, 167, 206n43, 207n46
stasis motif, **34–5**
   erotic stasis, 117
   Fénice, 124–5, 126, 136, 159
   Griselda, 135–7
   Lucy, **33–4**, **35**, 124, 125–6, 159
   saints' lives, **33–4**, 135
   compare paralysis
suffering
   belief identification, 9
   Book of Margery Kempe, 157–9, 172, 210n5
   castration, 117
   focus on motif, 24
   gendering, **17–18**, 173, 181n91
   Griselda, 135
   Legenda Aurea, 135
   2 and 4 Maccabees, 20
   multiplication of suffering, **26**
   mutilation, 21–3, 117
   Old Testament, 80
   prisons, 181n93
   self as sufferer, **7–8**
   Suffering Portion (defined), **25**, 26

Vitae Columbani, 71–2
see also *hypomonê*

Tacitus, 11, 15
The Tale of Melibee (Chaucer), 5–6, 131, 139
Tertullian (early church father)
   Apologeticum, 21, 24, 178n41
   athletic allegory, 49, 190n74
   egalitarian rhetoric, 10, 178n41, 192n8
   feminism/protofeminism, 79, 190n2
   heroic virtues, 14
   Leaena (martyr), **21–3**, 180n82
   Lot's wife, 194n32
   martyrdom metaphor of, 46
   patience as woman, 192n4
   de patientia, 24, 75, **76–80**
   stasis motif, 34
The Testament of Job
   dating of, 181n88
   ecstatic languages, 32, 73
   female patience figures, 23
   societal benefits, 35
   see also Job (Bible)
Thessala (Fénice's servant), 121, 128
Trajan (emperor), 10
transformation
   Lot/Loth's wife, 81–2, 84, 91, 93–100, 103, 109, 173, 193n20, 195–6nn41, 43, 50, 197n60, 198n68
   Sarra, 109
   transformational language, 39–43, 97, 185n15
transubstantiation, 73
transvestism
   Jewish virgin story, 190n68
   Psychomachia, 79–80
   Virgin of Antioch, **61–71**, 190–1nn79, 83
Travels of John Mandeville, 98, 110
Troilus (character), 167
Troilus and Criseyde (Chaucer), 131, **167–8**

undercutting of women
    Blandina, 19
    Grisilde, 165–6
    mother in 2 Maccabees, 19, 180n77
    status of motherhood, 61
    compare women
Urban (pope), 164

Valerian (saint), 160, 163–4
Valterius (Petrarch's character), 143, 150, 206n35
vases. *see* waterpots
Vettius Epagathus (martyr), 7, 13, 176n24
Vincent (saint), 115, 125
virgin(s)
    Chaucer, 133
    Christ as, 46
    Margery Kempe, 169
    martyrologies, 34–5
    Shrine to the Virgin, 160
    virgin martyrs, 46
    Virgin of Antioch, **61–71**, 190–1nn79, 83, 87
De Virginibus (Ambrose), **61–71**
    Ambrose's writing style, 190nn72, 80, 191n85
    athletic allegory, 190n74
    Christ as virgin, 46
    Lot's wife, 92
    related works, 79–80
    significance of, 62
    see also Ambrose (church father)
visions
    female leadership, 47
    Margery Kempe, 163, 168, 171–2
    Perpetua's visions, 38, 39, **45–7, 48–9, 51**, 53–4, 55, 57–8, 115, 186n20, 188n46, 189nn55, 59, 62

Saturninus' visions, 115
Saturus' vision, 57, 189n60
Vitae Columbani (Jonas of Bobbio), **71–4**
Vitz, Birge, 46

Walter (Chaucer's character)
    casting out of Grisilde, 3, 155, 166
    desire, 135–6, 154, 165–7, 203n11, 206–7n44, 208n53, 212n33
    gaze of, 147–8, 150, 151, 206–7nn41, 44
    mirror to Grisilde, 153
    reconciliation with Grisilde, 6, 209n67
    space, **165–7**
    testing of Grisilde, 134, 148, 207n45
    vow to, 144, 146, 209n67
    see also The Clerk's Tale (Chaucer)
waterpots, 39–43, 145, 154, 165, 185–6nn15, 17, 19
weapons, 55–6, 189n55
wic (word), **110–11**, 200n89
Wife of Bath (character), 23, 128, 134, 153, 156
Wilcox, Jonathan, 107, 199n84
Wogan-Brown, Jocelyn, 3
women
    commodification of, 42, 81
    emotions of, 47–8
    feminine language, 39–40, 43–4, 47, 73–4
    monumental quality, 80, 82
    objectification of, 80, 136, 139–40, 165
    patience literature, 24
    compare gendering; motherhood; undercutting of women
Woolf, Virginia, 140, 141

Printed in the United States of America